Gospel Light's

BIG REALLY BOOK

OF COOL CRAFTS FOR KIDS

Over 200 Craft Projects for Ages 4 to 12

CD-ROM included!

- 11 Kid-Appealing Themes, including Around the World, Bible Verse, God's Kingdom and MORE!
- Age and Time Guidelines provided
- Conversation ideas provided to enrich craft times

Reproducible!

8"

24"

Gospel Light

HOW TO MAKE CLEAN COPIES FROM THIS BOOK

Editorial Staff

Founder, Dr. Henrietta Mears • **Publisher Emeritus,** William T. Greig • **Publisher, Children's Curriculum and Resources,** Bill Greig III • **Senior Consulting Publisher,** Dr. Elmer L. Towns • **Product Line Manager,** Cary Maxon • **Senior Managing Editor,** Sheryl Haystead • **Senior Consulting Editor,** Wesley Haystead, M.S.Ed. • **Senior Editor, Biblical and Theological Issues,** Bayard Taylor, M.Div. • **Editor,** Mary Gross Davis • **Contributing Editors,** Linda Crisp, Kim Sullivan Fiano • **Art Directors,** Lenndy McCullough, Christina Renée Sharp, Samantha A. Hsu • **Designer,** Zelle Olson • **Illustrator,** Chizuko Yasuda

Originally Published as *Celebrating Our Families Crafts for Kids* (Ventura, CA: Gospel Light, 1995), *High Adventure Crafts for Kids* (Ventura, CA: Gospel Light, 1997), *Kingdom Crafts for Kids* (Ventura, CA: Gospel Light, 1999) and *Gold Mine of Crafts for Kids* (Ventura, CA: Gospel Light, 2001).

Scripture quotations are taken from the *Holy Bible, New International Version®*. Copyright © 1973, 1978, 1984 by International Bible Society. Used by permission of Zondervan Publishing House. All rights reserved.

© 2005 Gospel Light, Ventura, CA 93006. All rights reserved. Printed in the U.S.A.

The Really Big Book of Cool Crafts for Kids

CONTENTS

CRAFTS

introduction

Crafts are an excellent way for children to express their creativity while they build relationships with others. When children are focused on using their hands to create a project, they are often more relaxed, willing to talk and eager to listen than they might be in formal classroom settings. As children create their crafts, look for times when you can talk about the ways God shows His love to us. Ask open-ended ("What do you think?") kinds of questions. Listen with interest to the answers and give them opportunities to ask questions of their own. We hope that you and your students will enjoy not only your creativity but also the relationships you build as you complete projects together.

PERSONALIZE IT!

Feel free to alter the craft materials and instructions in this book to suit your children's needs. Consider what materials you have on hand, what materials are available in your area and what materials you can afford to purchase. In some cases, you may be able to substitute materials you already have for the suggested craft supplies.

In addition, don't feel confined to the crafts marked for a particular age. You may want to

adapt a craft for younger or older children by using the simplification or enrichment ideas where provided.

THREE KEYS TO SUCCESS

How can you make craft time successful and joyful? First, encourage creativity in each child! Always remember that for a child, the process of creating is more important than what the final product may look like to an adult! Provide a variety of materials with which children may work so they may make creative choices on their own. Don't insist that children "stay inside the lines" or make their projects "look just like the sample."

Second, choose projects that are appropriate for the skill level of your children. Children may become discouraged when a project is too difficult for them. Finding the right projects for your children increases the likelihood that they will be successful and satisfied with their finished products.

Finally, show an interest in the unique way each child approaches a project. Avoid the temptation to say, "That's cute." Instead, affirm the choices he or she has made during the process ("I see you like to paint with blue, Lily." "You really used lots of circles, Jed.") Treat each child's work as a masterpiece! The comments you give a child today can affect the way he or she views art in the future, so be positive! Being creative is part of being made in the image of God, the ultimate creator!

CRAFT AGE LEVELS

Many of the craft projects are appropriate for more than one age level. Under the titles, you'll find the age-level designations shown. As you select projects, consider the particular children you are working with. Feel free to use your own ideas to make projects simpler or more challenging depending on the needs of your children.

BE PREPARED

If you are planning to use crafts with a child at home, here are some helpful tips:

• Focus on crafts designed for your child's age, but don't ignore projects for older or younger ages. Elementary-age children enjoy many of the projects geared for preschool and kindergarten children. And younger children are always interested in doing "big kid" things. Just plan on working along with your child, helping with tasks he or she can't handle alone.

• Start with projects that call for materials you have around the house. Make a list of items you do not have so you can gather them.

• If certain materials seem too difficult to obtain, a little thought can usually lead to appropriate substitutions. Often your creative twist ends up being an improvement over the original plan.

If you are planning to lead a group of children in doing craft projects, keep these hints in mind:

• Choose projects that allow children to work with a variety of materials.

• Make your project selections far enough in advance to allow time to gather all needed supplies.

• Make a sample of each project to be sure you understand the directions so you can avoid potential problems. You may want to adapt some projects by simplifying procedures or varying the materials.

• Items can often be acquired as donations from people or businesses if you plan ahead and make your needs known. Some items might be brought in by the children themselves. Many churches distribute lists of needed materials to their congregations for fulfillment, as well.

• In making your supply list, distinguish between items needed for each individual child and those that will be shared among a group.

• Keep in mind that some materials may be shared among more than one age level. To avoid frustration, coordinate with other groups who might be using the same supplies you need so that children can complete their craft projects. Basic supplies that are used in many projects, such as glue, scissors, markers, etc., should be available at all times.

CRAFTS WITH A MESSAGE

Many projects can easily become crafts with a message. Invite older children to create slogans or poetry that they may write on their projects. Write out the words younger children dictate to you; make photocopies or invite them to copy words as they are interested. You may also wish to provide photocopies of an appropriate poem, thought or Bible verse for children to attach to their crafts.

CONVERSATION

Each craft in this book provides sample conversation that is designed to help you enhance craft times with thought-provoking, age-appropriate conversation. The conversation for a project may relate to a biblical principle, to a Scripture verse or to a Bible story. It may include interesting facts related to the craft. If your craft program includes large groups of children, share these conversation suggestions with each helper so he or she can use them with individuals or small groups. Because children are absorbed in their work and their ears and minds are uncluttered, use this time to its greatest potential—keep the conversation going!

USING A CRAFT CENTER AND COORDINATOR

The projects in this book can be done in individual classrooms or in a Craft Center.

Making a Craft Center Work

★ Select projects that will appeal to several age levels. (Sometimes you'll find one project that all children will enjoy making. Other times you'll need to select one project for the younger children and one for the older children.)

★ Recruit adults and/or youths to prepare for and lead the Craft Center.

★ Decorate your center with samples of crafts your kids will be making.

★ As groups visit the Craft Center, lead them in making projects, tailoring instructions and conversation to the children's age level.

The Craft Coordinator— A Very Important Person

As Craft Coordinator, you play a key role in determining the quality of your craft program. Here are four crucial steps in achieving success at your task:

1. Plan ahead. Familiarize yourself with each day's craft project and plan any necessary changes.

2. Be well organized.

3. Secure your supplies in advance. Prepare a bulletin notice listing items you need donated from members of your congregation. Also, people are often happy to help if you personally ask them to donate or purchase specific items.

4. Communicate with everyone involved. People who do not know what to do may not ask for help.

HELPFUL HINTS

Using Glue with Young Children

Since preschoolers have difficulty using glue bottles effectively, try one of the following procedures. Purchase glue in large containers (up to one gallon size).

a. Pour small amounts of glue into margarine tubs.

b. Dilute glue by mixing a little water into each container.

c. Children use paintbrushes to spread glue on their projects.

d. When project is completed, place lids on margarine tubs to save glue for future projects.

OR

a. Pour small amounts of glue into several margarine tubs.

b. Give each child a cotton swab.

c. Children dip cotton swabs into the glue and rub glue on projects.

d. When project is completed, place lids on margarine tubs to save glue for future projects.

Cutting with Scissors

When cutting with scissors is required for crafts, remember that some children in your class may be left-handed. It is very difficult for a left-handed person to cut with right-handed scissors. Have available two or three pairs of left-handed scissors. These can be obtained from a school supply center.

If your craft involves cutting fabric, felt or ribbon, have available several pairs of fabric scissors for older children.

Using Paints

Paints are required for some projects. Our suggestions:

★ Provide smocks or old shirts for your children to wear, as paints may stain clothes.

★ Some paints like acrylics can be expensive for a large group of children. To make paint go further, dilute it with a small amount of water. Or use house paints thinned with water.

★ Fill shallow containers with soapy water. Clean paintbrushes before switching colors and immediately after finishing project.

LEADING A CHILD TO CHRIST

One of the greatest privileges of serving in children's ministry is to help children become members of God's family. Pray for the children you know. Ask God to prepare them to understand and receive the good news about Jesus and to give you the sensitivity and wisdom to communicate effectively and to be aware as opportunities occur.

Because children are easily influenced to follow the group, be cautious about asking for group decisions. Instead, offer opportunities to talk and pray individually with any child who expresses interest in becoming a member of God's family—but without pressure. A good way to guard against coercing a child to respond is to simply ask, "Would you like to hear more about this now or at another time?"

When talking about salvation with children, use words and phrases they understand; never assume they understand a concept just because they can repeat certain words. Avoid symbolic terms that will confuse these literal-minded thinkers. (You may also use the evangelism booklet *God Loves You!*) Here is a simple guideline:

1. God wants you to become His child. Why do you think He wants you in His family? (See 1 John 3:1.)

2. Every person in the world has done wrong things. The Bible word for doing wrong is "sin." What do you think should happen to us when we sin? (See Romans 6:23.)

3. God loves you so much that He sent His Son to die on the cross to take the punishment for your sin. Because Jesus never sinned, He is the only One who can take the punishment for your sin. (See 1 Corinthians 15:3; 1 John 4:14.)

4. Are you sorry for your sin? Tell God that you are. Do you believe Jesus died for your sin and then rose again? Tell Him that, too. If you tell God you are sorry for your sin and believe that Jesus died to take your sin away, God forgives you. (See 1 John 1:9.)

5. The Bible says that when you believe Jesus is God's Son and is alive today, you receive God's gift of eternal life. This gift makes you a child of God. (See John 3:16.) This means God is with you now and forever.

There is great value in encouraging a child to think and pray about what you have said before responding. Encourage the child who makes a decision to become a Christian to tell his or her parents. Give your pastor and the child's Sunday School teacher(s) his or her name. A child's initial response to Jesus is just the beginning of a lifelong process of growing in the faith, so children who make decisions need to be followed up to help them grow. The discipling booklet *Growing as God's Child* (available from Gospel Light) is an effective tool to use.

Around The World

Here are crafts with an international flavor that can help you experience other cultures and traditions!

Around the World

Materials: Yarn or leather lacing, crayons, hole punch, transparent tape, scissors, measuring stick. For each child—one 6x9-inch (15x22.5-cm) manila envelope, four wooden beads.

Preparation: Cut off 2 inches (5 cm) from the top of each manila envelope (sketch a). Punch six evenly spaced holes along both sides of envelope (sketch b). Cut yarn or leather lacing into 4-yard (1.2-m) lengths—one for each child. Wrap a piece of tape around one end of each yarn or leather lacing piece and tie a knot at other end.

Instruct each child in the following procedures:

★ Use crayons to draw designs or nature scenes on both sides of envelope.

★ Slide two beads onto yarn or leather lacing piece just above knot (sketch c). Thread yarn through holes on both sides of envelope, leaving a large loop at the top (sketch d). Slide two beads onto remaining end of yarn and, with teacher's help, tie a knot to secure.

★ Wear Message Pocket on shoulder or attach to belt loops.

Enrichment Idea: Older children can punch own holes in envelopes.

Conversation:

Optional: Show Africa on a map. **In some parts of Africa people wear traditional clothing that consists of a piece of cloth wrapped around the body. The cloth has no buttons, zippers or pockets. Since they don't have built-in pockets, like our shirts or pants do, they carry pockets. What will you put in your Message Pocket? Write a kind note to a family member and place it in your Message Pocket. Deliver the message to him or her today!**

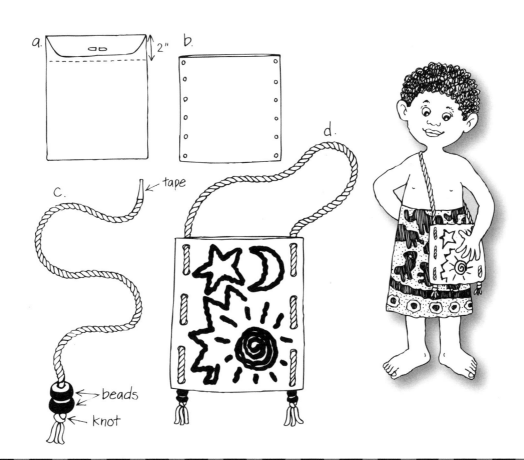

Around the World

Materials: Red, white and blue construction paper; red, white and blue crepe paper streamers; string; hole punches; craft knife; glue; scissors; measuring stick. For each child—one half-gallon round ice cream container without lid.

Preparation: Use craft knife to cut bottom off of each container. Cut red and blue construction paper into 6x9-inch (15x22.5-cm) rectangles—one of each color for each child. Cut white construction paper into 2-inch (5-cm) star shapes—five for each child. Cut additional white construction paper into 1x6-inch (2.5x15-cm) strips—two for each child. Cut remainder of white construction paper into 1x16-inch (2.5x40-cm) strips—one for each child. Cut streamers into 2-foot (.6-m) lengths—six for each child. Cut string into 2-foot (.6-m) lengths—four for each child.

Instruct each child in the following procedures:

★ Glue red construction paper onto half of container. Glue blue construction paper onto other half of container (sketch a). Overlap edges.

★ Glue short white strips onto container to cover overlapping edges (sketch b).

★ Glue one end of each streamer onto bottom edge of wind tube (sketch c).

★ Glue long white strip onto wind tube to cover bottom edge (sketch d).

★ Glue stars randomly onto wind tube to decorate.

★ Punch four evenly spaced holes directly under top rim of container (sketch e).

★ Tie one length of string through each hole (sketch e).

★ Gather loose ends of string together and tie ends in a knot. Tie a knot halfway down length of strings (sketch f).

★ Tie wind tube to pole or porch railing for decoration. When wind blows, wind tube will float in the air.

Simplification Ideas: Cover container with one large piece of construction paper or use acrylic paint. Use silver or gold self-adhesive stars instead of cutting from construction paper.

Enrichment Idea: Older children may measure and cut their own paper, streamers and string. Provide construction paper in a variety of colors and allow children to decorate container. Tube can be decorated to commemorate any flag.

Conversation:

What popular holiday do Americans celebrate in July? The Fourth of July celebrates freedom in America. Does your family celebrate the Fourth of July? What do you do to celebrate? Many people hang the American flag in front of their houses to show respect for their country. What do people in other countries do to celebrate their country's history? (Mexican Independence Day, Queen's Birthday, etc.)

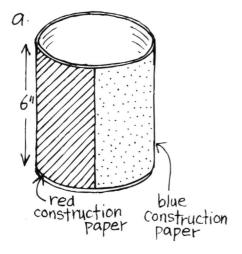

a. 6"

red construction paper

blue construction paper

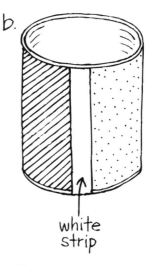

b. white strip

(Sketches continued on page 15.)

ALL-AMERICAN WIND TUBE

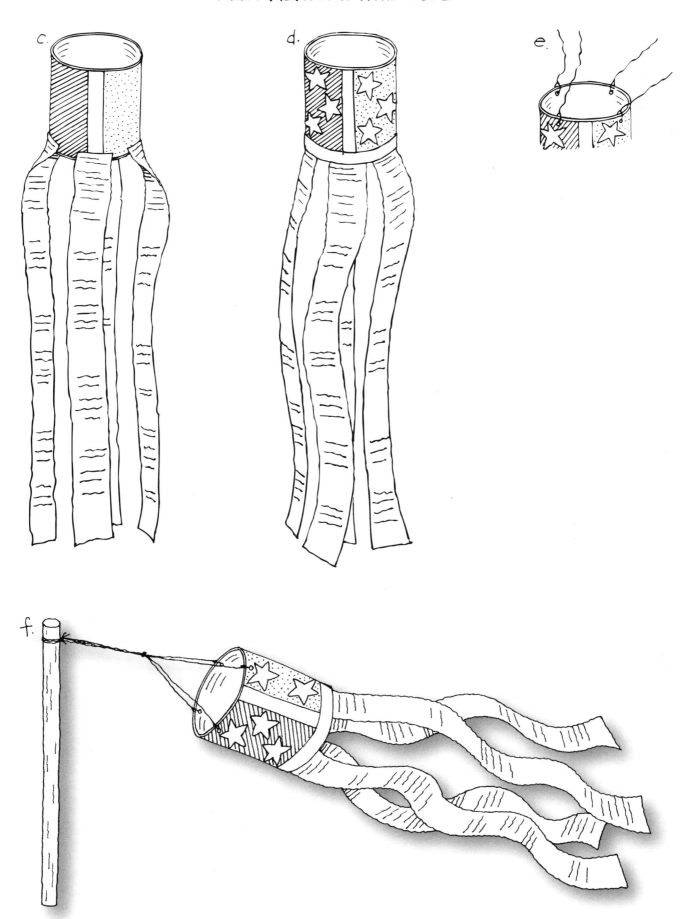

c.

d.

e.

f.

Around the World

Materials: Pencils, glue, craft knives or scissors with pointed tips. For each student—four sheets of 9x12-inch (22.5x30-cm) construction paper in four different colors.

Instruct each child in the following procedures:

★ Choose four different colors of construction paper.

★ Draw a simple outline of your house on first sheet of paper (sketch a).

★ Carefully cut out shape of outline (shaded area on sketch).

★ Lay first sheet of paper on top of second sheet of paper. Draw another outline about ¼ inch (.625 cm) in from the first (sketch b).

★ Carefully cut out shape of outline from second sheet of paper.

★ Lay second sheet on top of third sheet. Use pencil to draw a few simple details of your house (sketch c).

★ Carefully cut out details from third sheet of paper.

★ Glue the three cut sheets of paper together, and then glue them onto the fourth sheet of paper (sketch d).

Enrichment Idea: Mount completed picture onto a 12x18-inch (30x45-cm) sheet of black construction paper. Letter a Bible verse on a small sheet of construction paper and glue to black paper as well (see sketch).

Conversation:

In Panama, these pictures are called molas. The Cuna Indians there make their molas out of brightly colored fabric. Panama is a small country in Central America. Optional: Show Panama on map. **Do any of your relatives come from or live in Central America? In South America? Has any family member ever visited any countries in South America?**

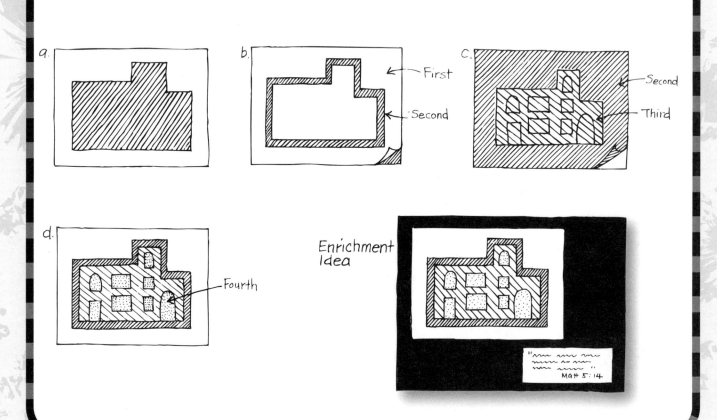

Around the World

Materials: Crepe paper streamers in a variety of bright colors, string, foil star stickers, transparent tape, scissors, measuring stick. For each child—one large plastic or wooden thread spool.

Preparation: Remove labels from spools. Cut crepe paper into 1-yard (.9-m) lengths—three different colors for each child. Cut string into 18-inch (45-cm) lengths—one for each child.

Instruct each child in the following procedures:

★ Fold one end of streamer into a point (sketch a). Repeat for other two streamers.

★ Tape points of streamers onto spool (sketch b).

★ Decorate streamers with star stickers.

★ Thread string through center of spool. With teacher's help, tie a knot to secure string (sketch b).

★ Hold spool by string and wave in the air. Wind streamers around spool when not in use.

Enrichment Idea: Instead of holding spool by string, make a long handle by inserting and gluing a dowel into center of spool (sketch c).

Conversation:

Optional: Show China on a map. **In a country called China, children wave streamers like these during parades. Tell about a time when your family went to a parade. What did you see in the parade? What shapes can you make by waving your streamers in the air? Can you make a circle?**

Around the World

EAST INDIAN RING-AND-STICK GAME
(20-30 MINUTES)

Materials: Toilet paper or paper towel tubes, tempera paint, paintbrushes, shallow containers, cotton string, self-adhesive paper in colorful patterns, hole punch, masking tape, scissors, measuring stick, newspaper. For each child—one unsharpened pencil.

Preparation: Cut cardboard tubes into 1-inch (2.5-cm) lengths—two for each child. Cut string into 30-inch (75-cm) lengths—one for each child. Cut self-adhesive paper into ½x20-inch (1.25x50-cm) strips—one for each child. Cover work area with newspaper. Pour paint into shallow containers.

Instruct each child in the following procedures:

★ Cut open two cardboard tube pieces (sketch a).

★ Use masking tape to join the two pieces together to make a larger ring (sketch b).

★ Punch a hole in ring.

★ Paint the outside of ring and allow to dry.

★ Peel backing from self-adhesive paper strip. Hold one end of string on pencil while spiraling paper strip tightly around length of pencil (sketch c).

★ Tie loose end of string through hole in ring.

★ Hold pencil with one hand and toss ring in the air, trying to catch it on the stick.

Simplification Idea: Use a wooden ring (available at most craft stores) instead of making one from cardboard tube.

Enrichment Ideas: Spray cardboard ring with acrylic spray paint. Or, cover ring with self-adhesive paper or wrapping paper.

Conversation:

Ring-and-Stick is a game played by children who live in the country of India. Optional: Show India on a map. **Do you know anybody from India? People play games all over the world. Some games you can play by yourself, some you can play with a partner and some games you can play with many people. What games do you play with your family? At school?**

a. cut open

b.

c. string backing self-adhesive tape

ESkimo Snow SHADES
(10-15 MINUTES)

Materials: Poster board, cotton string, felt pens in a variety of colors, hole punch, paper hole reinforcements, ruler, pointed scissors.

Preparation: Cut poster board into 2x6-inch (5x15-cm) rectangles—one for each child. Cut string into 18-inch (45-cm) lengths—two for each child.

Instruct each child in the following procedures:

★ Fold poster board in half (sketch a).

★ Use scissors to cut off all four corners (sketch b).

★ Starting at folded edge, cut a ⅛-inch (.3125-cm) slit in the middle of poster board. Stop 1 inch (2.5 cm) before the opposite edge (sketch c).

★ Open poster board.

★ Punch holes in opposite sides of rectangle. Place paper hole reinforcements over holes (sketch d).

★ Use felt pens to decorate shades.

★ Tie a piece of string through each hole.

★ Tie the string around your head to wear your Snow Shades.

Conversation:

Eskimos wear goggles like these to protect their eyes from the cold Arctic wind. A thin slit is cut to see through. The small opening also helps to dim the bright glare from the snow and sun. Eskimos used to carve their goggles out of whale bone or wood. They carved interesting shapes and designs on the goggles. How do you want to decorate your Snow Shades?

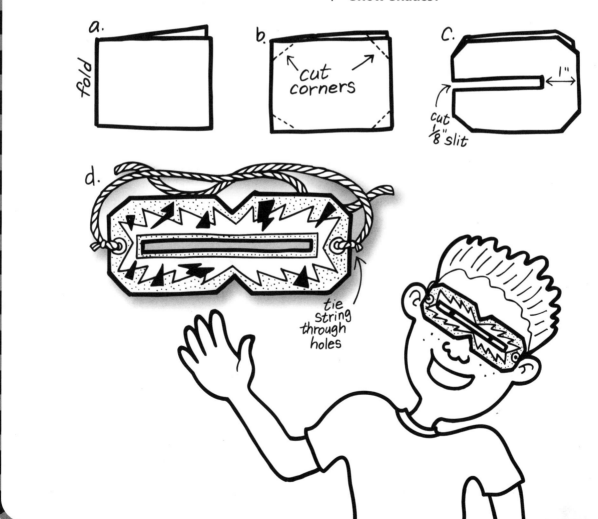

a. fold

b. cut corners

c. cut ⅛" slit 1"

d. tie string through holes

Materials: Body Pattern, white poster board, drill, ⅛-inch (.31-cm) drill bit, cotton string, felt pens in a variety of colors, pencils, transparent tape, scissors, ruler. For each child—four tongue depressors.

Preparation: Trace Body Pattern onto poster board and cut out—one for each child. Use drill to make five holes in poster board as shown on pattern. Drill a hole about ¾ inch (1.9-cm) from one end of each tongue depressor (sketch a). Cut string into 5-inch (12.5-cm) lengths—three for each child. Cut additional string into 10-inch (25-cm) lengths—one for each child.

Instruct each child in the following procedures:

★ Use felt pens to draw a head and body on poster board cutout.

★ Color two tongue depressors to look like arms and two to look like legs (sketch a). Draw hands and feet at opposite ends of drilled holes.

★ Wrap a piece of tape around one end of each length of string. Thread shorter length of string through body and arms as shown in sketch b. Tie knots on both ends of string at front of body. Repeat process to attach legs to body.

★ Thread other short length of string through hole at top of head and make a loop for holding (sketch c).

★ Tie longer length of string to the other strings as shown in sketch c.

★ In one hand, hold figure by loop. With other hand, pull on string below to make figure jump into action!

Conversation:

In England, Germany and other European countries, these toys are called "Jumping Jacks." What were your favorite toys when you were younger? Is there a family member you would like to give your Jumping Jack to?

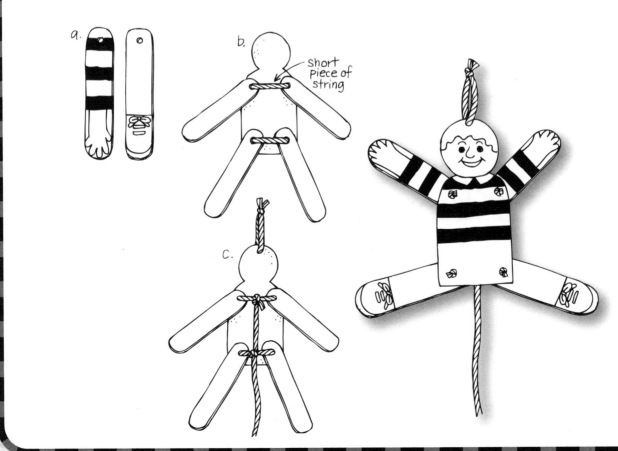

a.

b. short piece of string

c.

EUROPEAN JUMPING JACK BODY PATTERN

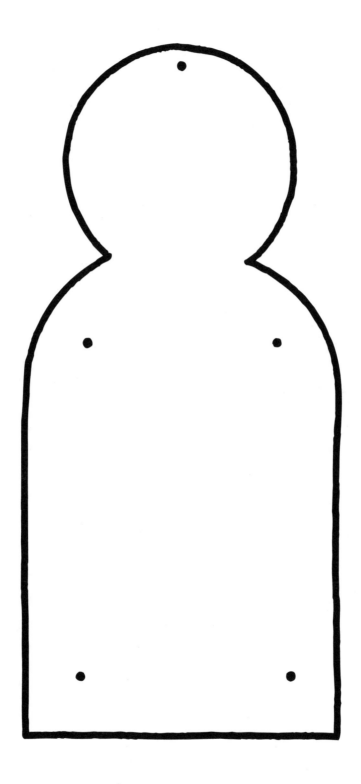

Around the World

Materials: Acrylic paint in a variety of colors including yellow, red, brown, black and beige; small paintbrushes; shallow containers; fishing line; craft glue; scissors; ruler; newspaper. For each child—four large flat wooden clothespins (non-spring type), four ¾-inch (1.9-cm) wooden balls, five chenille wires in a variety of colors.

Preparation: Cut some of the chenille wires into 6-inch (15-cm) lengths—four for each child. Cut fishing line into 10-inch (25-cm) lengths—five for each child. Cover work area with newspaper. Pour paint into shallow containers.

Instruct each child in the following procedures:

DAY ONE:

★ Paint each clothespin a different color. Let dry.

★ Paint each wooden ball a different flesh-tone color. Let dry.

★ Glue painted ball onto top of each painted clothespin to form a head (sketch a). Allow glue to dry.

DAY TWO:

★ Twist piece of chenille wire around top notch of each clothespin to make arms (sketch a). Pull ends tightly.

★ Form a circle with an uncut piece of chenille wire. Twist ends together to secure.

★ Twist "arms" of each clothespin around the circle (sketch b).

★ Tie ends of four lengths of fishing line onto circle at places where arms intersect (sketch c).

★ Gather loose ends of fishing line and tie together. Make a loop with additional fishing line and tie at intersecting points of other fishing lines.

★ Hang from window or ceiling.

Simplification Idea: Use round-headed clothespins and paint top of clothespin for head.

Enrichment Idea: Glue fabric scraps on clothespins to make clothes.

Conversation:

What does this mobile represent to you? Why did God create people to be different? What would the world be like if everyone looked the same? When God looks at us, He looks beyond the color of our skin or the clothes we wear. He sees us and loves us for who we are on the inside!

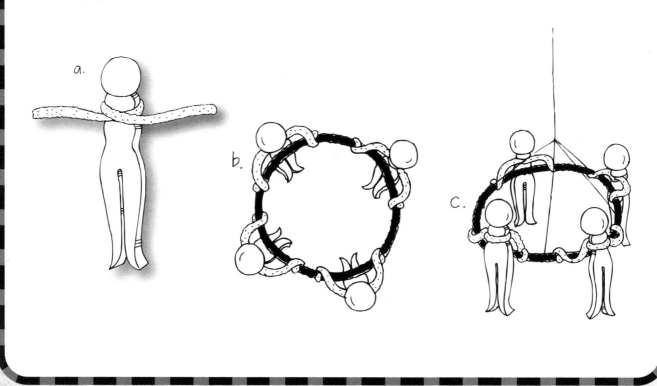

Around the World

Materials: Permanent felt pens in a variety of colors, ³⁄₁₆-inch (⅕-cm) dowels, saw, kite string, transparent or masking tape, scissors, measuring stick. For each child—one white plastic 13-gallon (49.4-L) garbage bag, one toilet paper tube or small wood scrap.

Preparation: Cut bottom seam off plastic bag. Draw kite outline on each plastic bag as shown in sketch a. Saw dowels into 29-inch (72.5-cm) lengths—two for each child. Cut string into 5-foot (15-m) lengths—one for each child. Cut additional string into 30-foot (9-m) lengths—one for each child.

Instruct each child in the following procedures:

★ Cut along lines on plastic bag.

★ Unfold kite. Use permanent felt pens to decorate kite.

★ Turn kite over, decorated side down. Tape a dowel to each side of kite as shown in sketch b.

★ Reinforce corners of kite with tape (sketch b).

★ Use tip of scissors to poke a tiny hole in top two corners. Tie ends of shorter length of string through holes to make a bridle (sketch c).

★ Tie a loop at midpoint of bridle. Tie end of longer length of string to loop. Wrap remaining string or "flying line" around toilet paper tube or wood scrap to make a kite reel.

★ To fly kite: Take kite outside and hold it up. As wind begins to carry kite, slowly release string so kite rises with the wind.

Simplification Idea: For younger children, teacher cuts out kite ahead of time.

Enrichment Idea: Decorate kite reel.

Conversation:

Kites are very popular in Japan. Optional: Show Japan on a map. **What makes kites fly? Wind! Can you see wind? We can't see God either, but we know He's there. You can talk to God at home, in the car, in your backyard—anywhere and He will be there. Sometimes your friends and family are too busy to listen—but God will always listen to your prayers!**

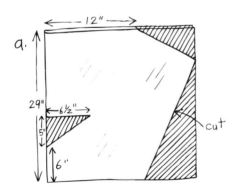

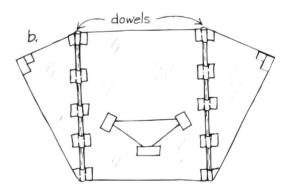

Around the World

Materials: Tempera paint in a variety of bright colors, paintbrushes, shallow containers, white butcher paper, pencils, black permanent felt pens, fishing line, craft knife, transparent tape, glue, scissors, rulers, measuring stick, newspaper. For each child—one plastic lid (from small coffee can or small margarine tub).

Preparation: Cut butcher paper into 16x24-inch (40x60-cm) rectangles—one for each child. Cut out center of each plastic lid to make a rim (sketch a). Cut fishing line into 15-inch (37.5-cm) lengths and 30-inch (75-cm) lengths—one of each length for each child. Fold butcher paper in half lengthwise and draw a fish shape as shown in sketch b—one for each child. Cover work area with newspaper. Pour paint into shallow containers.

Instruct each child in the following procedures:

★ Cut out fish shape from folded paper.

★ Unfold paper. Use pencil to sketch details on fish such as scales, eyes and fins.

★ Paint fish and allow to dry.

★ Use black felt pen to outline details on fish.

★ Turn fish over, painted side down, and fold mouth opening down 1 inch (2.5 cm). Squeeze a line of glue along folded area (sketch c).

★ Insert plastic rim inside folded area and fold paper around rim. Hold in place until glue dries.

★ Glue seams of fish together.

★ Fold a small piece of tape over each side of rim to reinforce fish's mouth (sketch d).

★ Use tip of scissors to poke a small hole through each piece of tape.

★ Tie ends of shorter length of fishing line through holes to make a bridle. Tie one end of longer length of fishing line to the midpoint of bridle (sketch d).

★ Tie wind sock to pole or porch railing for decoration. When wind blows, wind sock will fill up with air and float horizontally.

Simplification Idea: Use felt pens or crayons instead of tempera paint.

Enrichment Ideas: Children draw their own fish or other kinds of animals. To make a longer lasting wind sock, use white fabric instead of paper.

Conversation:

The Japanese often make wind socks in the shape of one of their favorite fishes—the carp. Do you know anybody from Japan? Optional: Show Japan on a map. **The Japanese display their wind socks each year during a festival called "Children's Day." The carp is a Japanese symbol of strength, courage and determination. What animal would you choose to describe yourself? Your family?**

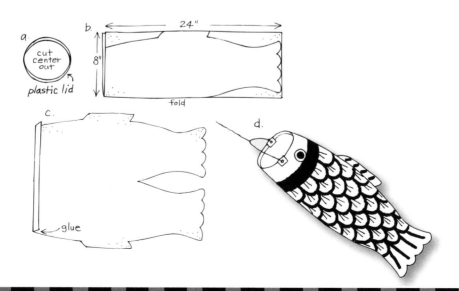

Around the World

Materials: Large brown paper grocery sacks, fluorescent poster paints, shallow containers, black felt pens, scissors, ruler, newspaper. For each child—one cotton swab.

Preparation: Cut grocery sacks into 10x12-inch (25x30-cm) rectangles—one for each child. Turn paper printed side down. Use felt pen to draw a double border along edge of paper (sketch a). Cover work area with newspaper. Pour paint into shallow containers.

Instruct each child in the following procedures:

★ Use felt pen to draw a family scene inside the border on brown paper.

★ Crumple picture into a ball as tight as possible. Then open and smooth paper. This makes the paper look like bark.

★ Dip cotton swab into paint and dab dots inside the border (sketch b). Add touches of paint to color in the picture.

Enrichment Idea: For a more authentic look, dip crumpled paper into a mixture of water and brown tempera paint. Open and smooth paper. Hang to dry before using felt pens or paint. Glue small pieces of bark around edge of paper to create a border. To hang picture: Fold top edge of picture back, place a length of string or yarn inside fold and staple fold shut (sketch c).

Conversation:

What is paper made from? Trees! In Mexico, people paint pictures on the bark of trees. Optional: Show Mexico on a map. **Do you know anybody from Mexico? Has anyone in your family ever visited Mexico? Mexican artists paint colorful pictures of celebrations and people working and playing in the village. You can make a picture of your family working and playing together!**

a.

draw two borders

b.

cotton swab

Enrichment Idea

staples

Around the World

Materials: Construction paper in a variety of colors, string, hole punches, felt pens, transparent tape, craft knife, scissors, ruler. For each child—one large orange juice can, one ¾-inch (1.9-cm) wooden bead.

Preparation: Cut off 2 ¾ inches (6.9 cm) from top of each orange juice can and discard (sketch a). Cut construction paper into 2x9-inch (5x22.5-cm) rectangles—one for each child. Cut string into 12-inch (30-cm) lengths—one for each child. Wrap a piece of tape around one end of each string and tie a knot at other end.

Instruct each child in the following procedures:

★ Use felt pens to decorate paper.

★ Wrap paper around can and tape in place.

★ With teacher's help, punch hole near top edge of can.

★ Thread bead onto string and slide just above knot. With teacher's help, tie bead to string (sketch b).

★ Tie opposite end of string through hole (sketch c).

★ Hold cup and try to toss the bead into the cup.

Enrichment Ideas: Use self-adhesive paper instead of construction paper to cover cup. To make a handle: Glue one end of a 6-inch (15-cm) length of dowel to bottom of cup (sketch d).

Conversation:

This cup catch game is played by children in Mexico. What kinds of games does your family like to play? Do your games have rules? It's fun to play games when everybody obeys the rules of the game. What happens when we don't follow the rules?

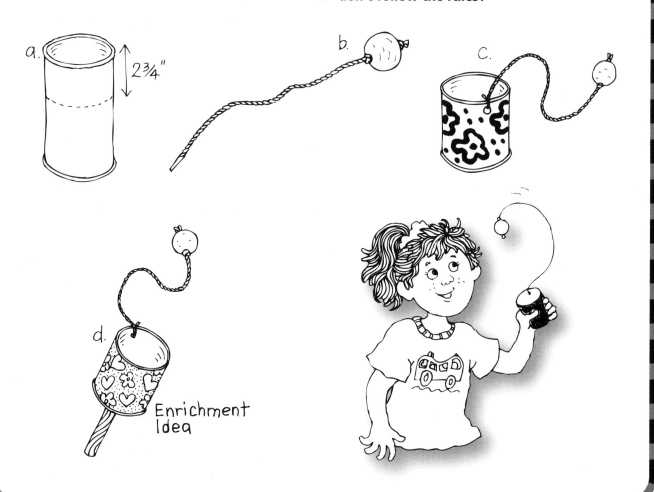

a. 2¾"

b.

c.

d. Enrichment Idea

Around the World

Materials: Rug yarn in a variety of colors, cardboard, self-adhesive paper, glue, scissors, measuring stick.

Preparation: Cut the cardboard into 9-inch (22.5-cm) squares—one for each child. Cut adhesive paper into 9-inch (22.5-cm) squares—one for each child. Glue nonsticky side of adhesive paper directly on top of cardboard square (sketch a). Cut yarn into 2-foot (.6-m) lengths—three different colors for each child.

Instruct each child in the following procedures:

★ Remove backing from adhesive paper. Arrange one length of yarn into outline of a large enclosed shape. Press yarn onto adhesive paper so it sticks. Cut off excess yarn (sketch b).

★ Choose a different color of yarn and lay it directly next to previous piece of yarn (sketch c). Continue to fill in shape with yarn, working from the outside in. Cut yarn as needed. Fill all blank spaces with yarn.

★ With teacher's help, cut cardboard around the shape (sketch d).

★ Use Yarn Art at home as a coaster, mat or hang as a picture.

Simplification Idea: Stick yarn onto adhesive paper in simple spiral design, starting in the center and working out.

Enrichment Idea: For older children, use glue instead of adhesive paper.

Conversation:

What did we use to make our designs today? In Mexico, people make bold, beautiful designs and pictures with yarn. What else can we use yarn for? We use yarn to make blankets, sweaters and other kinds of clothes. God gave each of you someone to take care of you by providing food, clothing and a place to live. Let's thank God for parents and other people who take care of us!

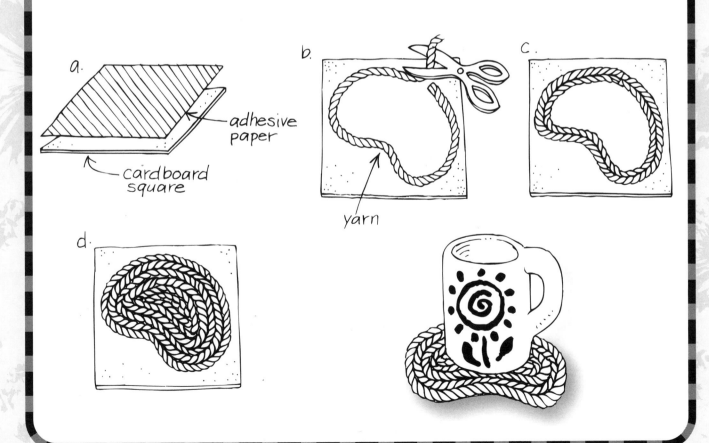

a. adhesive paper / cardboard square

b. yarn

c.

d.

Around the World

PEG RACK
(TWO-DAY CRAFT/30 MINUTES EACH DAY)

Materials: Peg Rack Patterns, 1x6-inch (2.5x15-cm) pine boards, ½-inch (1.25-cm) wood dowels, drill with ½-inch (1.25-cm) bit, fine-tooth saw, sandpaper, hammer, wood glue, white latex paint, acrylic paints in various colors, disposable plastic plates, self-adhesive paper, old sponges, pencil, photocopier, card stock, pencils, scissors, narrow and wide paintbrushes, measuring stick, shallow containers, damp paper towels, newspaper. For each child—two picture hangers with nails.

DAY ONE Preparation: Do craft in well-ventilated area. Saw pine boards into 16-inch (40-cm) lengths—one for each child. Saw dowels into 2½-inch (6.25-cm) pegs—four for each child. Referring to sketch a and using pencil, on each board mark position of peg holes. Drill peg holes ½ inch (1.25 cm) deep in each board. Cover work surface with newspaper. Pour white paint into shallow containers.

Instruct each child in the following procedures:

★ Use sandpaper to sand pegs and board until smooth. Use a damp paper towel to wipe off sawdust.

★ Squeeze several drops of glue into each peg hole. Insert pegs. Use damp paper towel to wipe off excess glue around peg.

★ Paint entire peg board with white paint. Allow to dry overnight.

DAY TWO Preparation: Photocopy several copies of patterns onto card stock and cut out. Cut self-adhesive paper into 3½-inch (8.75-cm) squares—four for each child. Pour acrylic paints onto plastic plates. Cut old sponges into 2-inch squares.

Instruct each child in the following procedures:

★ Choose patterns to decorate drilled, painted board. Trace patterns onto self-adhesive squares and cut out shapes.

★ Peel backing off cutout shapes and arrange them as desired along front of pegboard. Press down firmly.

★ Dip sponge into paint and blot excess paint on side of plate. Then lightly sponge-paint board, making sure to sponge-paint along edges of patterns (sketch b).

★ If desired, sponge-paint another color on top of first color.

★ Allow paint to dry before removing patterns to reveal designs (sketch c).

★ With teacher's help, nail picture hangers to back of peg rack.

Simplification Idea: Use store-bought shaker pegs or unfinished peg racks (available at craft stores).

Enrichment Idea: Use paint pens to letter a short memory verse along top or bottom of rack. Spray finished peg rack with clear acrylic spray. Allow to dry.

Conversation:

People in many parts of the world don't have dressers or closets. They hang their clothes and hats on pegs much like the peg rack you've made. It's fun to use something that you make. Where will you hang your peg rack? What will you use it for?

a.
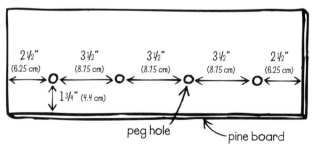

2½" (6.25 cm) 3½" (8.75 cm) 3½" (8.75 cm) 3½" (8.75 cm) 2½" (6.25 cm)

1¾" (4.4 cm)

peg hole   pine board

b.

Sponge-paint over patterns.

pattern

Materials: Neck Pattern, poster board, white muslin, colorful fabric in a variety of patterns, ¼-inch (.625-cm) dowels, saw, fabric markers or permanent felt pens, yarn, pencils, transparent tape, fabric glue, scissors, ruler. For each child—one toilet paper tube, one 1½-inch (3.75-cm) Styrofoam ball.

Preparation: Trace Neck Pattern onto poster board and cut out several patterns. Draw a 4½x6-inch (11.25x15-cm) rectangle onto poster board and cut out several rectangle patterns. Cut muslin into 5½-inch (13.75-cm) circles—one for each child. Saw dowels into 12-inch (.3-m) lengths—one for each child.

Instruct each child in the following procedures:

★ Trace Neck Pattern and rectangle pattern onto fabric and cut out.

★ Insert end of dowel into Styrofoam ball.

★ Cover ball with muslin circle to make puppet head. Twist edges around dowel and secure in place with tape (sketch a).

★ Glue neck piece into a cone shape, with a ½-inch (1.25-cm) overlap (sketch b).

★ Insert end of dowel through cone so head rests on top of cone. Tape around top of the cone to secure head onto neck (sketch c).

★ Glue bottom of neck piece to outside edge of tube (sketch d).

★ Glue rectangle fabric piece around tube (sketch d). Fold and glue bottom edge of fabric inside tube.

★ Use fabric markers or felt pens to draw a face on muslin.

★ Cut yarn for hair or fabric scraps for scarf. Glue onto puppet head.

★ Use dowel to move puppet head up and down or hide inside tube.

Simplification Idea: For younger children, cut out all fabric pieces ahead of time.

Conversation:

This puppet is a popular handmade toy in the country of Poland and some other European countries. Optional: Show Europe on a map. **Europe is a continent. There are many countries in Europe—Poland is one of them. Are any of your relatives from Poland? England? Germany? Who else do you know from Europe?**

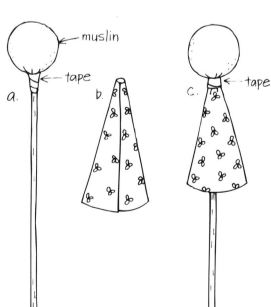

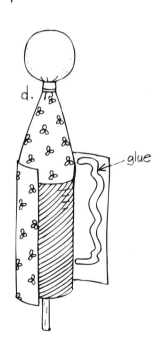

POLISH STICK PUPPET
NECK PATTERN

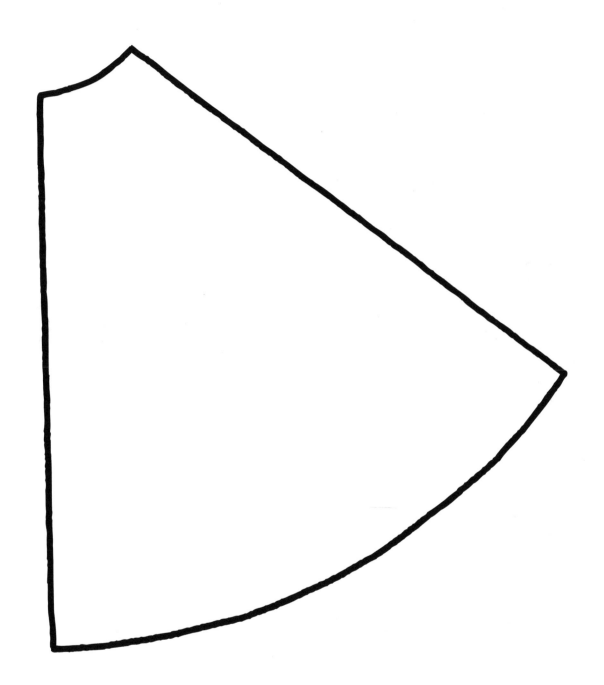

Around the World

Materials: Tissue paper in a variety of bright colors, yarn, hole punch, glue, scissors, measuring stick. For each child—one large paper grocery sack.

Preparation: Cut tissue paper into 3-inch (7.5-cm) wide strips. Cut yarn into 6-foot (1.8-m) lengths—one for each child.

Instruct each child in the following procedures:

★ Fold down top edge of bag (sketch a).

★ Cut slits along bottom edge of each tissue paper strip to make fringe (sketch b).

★ Glue top edge of strip around bottom of sack (sketch c).

★ Overlap and glue fringe of next strip to cover glued area of previous strip. Glue additional rows onto sack until entire sack is covered (sketch d).

★ Punch holes about 2 inches (5 cm) apart along top edge of bag.

★ Weave length of yarn through holes (sketch d).

★ Take piñata home and fill with individually wrapped candies and small toys. Pull ends of yarn to gather top of piñata. To use piñata: Tie yarn to the branch of a tree. Blindfold a friend and allow him or her to swing at piñata with a stick or rolled up newspaper. When bag breaks everyone scrambles to pick up goodies.

Conversation:

Piñatas were first used in the country of Italy. Clay pots were filled with goodies and then broken. Italians brought their custom to Spain, and the Spanish brought the custom to Mexico. It was the Mexicans who began making piñatas from papier-mâché and decorating them with colored tissue paper. Now piñatas are used to celebrate birthdays and other special days. How do you celebrate birthdays in your family? Do you know how your family's birthday tradition was started?

Materials: Very fine sandpaper, 8½x11-inch (21.5x27.5-cm) white paper, crayons, iron(s), ironing board, scissors, ruler, newspaper.

Preparation: Cut sandpaper into 2x5-inch (5x12.5-cm) rectangles—one for each child. Cut white paper in half—several sheets for each child. Cover ironing board with newspaper.

Instruct each child in the following procedures:

★ Use crayons to draw a design on sandpaper (sketch a). Color heavily.

★ Lay white paper on ironing board. Place colored sandpaper facedown on top edge of paper (sketch b). With teacher's help, iron until design is transferred to paper.

★ Make additional sheets of stationery by applying more color to original design and ironing onto another sheet of paper.

★ Use stationery at home to write letters.

Enrichment Idea: Children create complementary designs to decorate back flap of envelopes.

Conversation:

Native Americans are known for the beautiful sand paintings they create. Do you know any Native Americans? Who will you write to on your sand-painted stationery? How do you feel when you get a letter in the mail? How do you think (your grandmother) will feel when she gets your letter?

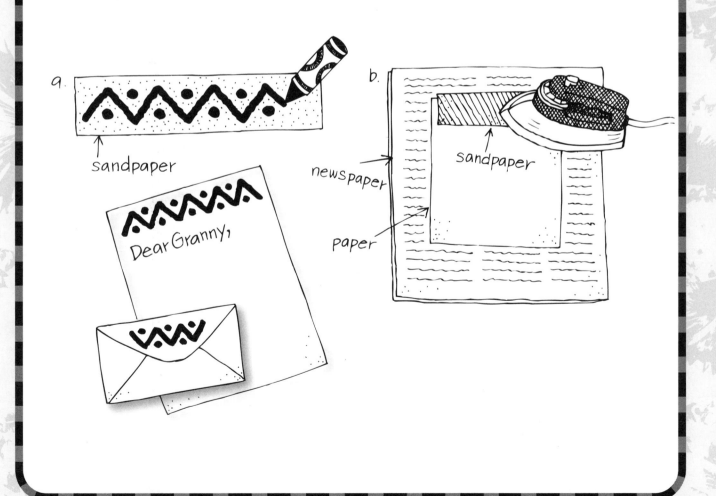

a. sandpaper

Dear Granny,

b. newspaper

sandpaper

paper

Around the World

Materials: Wood-grained Con-Tact paper, nails with large-diameter flat head, glue, masking tape, scissors, ruler. For each child—half-gallon cardboard milk carton, two small margarine tub lids, two ¾-inch (1.9-cm) paper fasteners, one tongue depressor.

Preparation: Cut each milk carton to 3-inch (7.5-cm) height (sketch a). Use nail to make holes on opposite sides of each milk carton, about ⅜ inch (.9 cm) from bottom (sketch a). Use nail to make hole in center of each margarine lid. Cut Con-Tact paper into 3x12-inch (7.5x30-cm) strips—one for each child. Cut additional Con-Tact paper into 2x4-inch (5x10-cm) rectangles—one for each child.

Instruct each child in the following procedures:

★ Pull backing off long Con-Tact strip and wrap around milk carton. Smooth paper to fit snugly around corners.

★ Cut six 4-inch (10-cm) strips from other piece of Con-Tact paper. Pull backing off strips. Place three strips on the inside of each margarine lid to make wheel spokes (sketch b).

★ With teacher's help, poke nail through lid and milk carton to reestablish holes.

★ On each side of cart, push paper fastener through lid and milk carton. Spread ends of fastener apart to secure in place (sketch c).

★ Glue end of tongue depressor to bottom of wagon. Tape in place to reinforce (sketch c).

Conversation:

In many parts of the world, people do not have cars. They live far from grocery stores. So they hitch an animal to a cart like this and go to a town for supplies like food and tools. It may take days to go to town, buy supplies and return home!

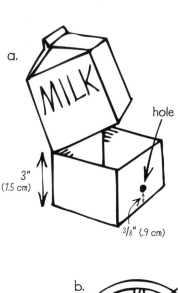

a.

MILK

hole

3"
(7.5 cm)

⅜" (.9 cm)

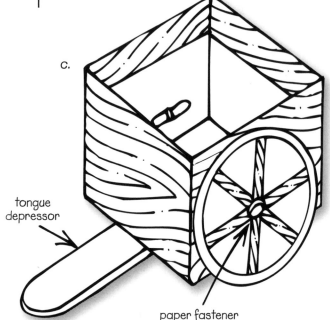

c.

tongue depressor

paper fastener

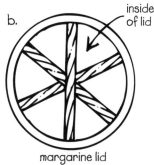

b.

inside of lid

margarine lid

Bible Story

Bible Story crafts related to your lesson's Bible story can help to reinforce the facts—and the biblical principles you want kids to remember!

Bible Story

Materials: Bible, peach-colored felt, black permanent felt pens, fiberfill stuffing, yellow or tan construction paper, raffia or straw, scissors, measuring stick, glue. For each child—one toilet paper tube, one white baby sock, one small rubber band.

Preparation: Cut felt into 1½-inch (3.75-cm) circles—one for each child. Cut a ½-inch (1.25-cm) strip out of toilet paper tubes as shown in sketch a. Cut construction paper into 1x13-inch (2.5x32.5-cm) strips—one for each child.

Instruct each child in the following procedures:

★ Use felt pen to draw a baby face on felt circle.
★ Fill baby sock with stuffing almost to the top.
★ With teacher's help, secure rubber band around top of sock as shown in sketch b.
★ Glue face on sock directly under rubber band (sketch c).
★ Fold top of sock over to make hat (sketch d).
★ Spread glue on the construction paper strip.
★ Wrap construction paper around toilet paper tube to make basket (sketch e).
★ Glue pieces of straw or raffia on basket.
★ Place "Baby Moses" in his basket after glue dries.

Conversation:

Open your Bible to Exodus 2. **In the Bible, there is a story about a girl named Miriam who did something very special. Miriam had a baby brother named Moses. Miriam's mother had to hide Moses in a basket because the mean Pharaoh wanted to kill all the baby boys in Egypt. Miriam's mother put Moses in a little basket boat and hid it in the river. Miriam stayed to watch over her baby brother. God made Miriam special. God made you special, too. What is a special way you help your mom?**

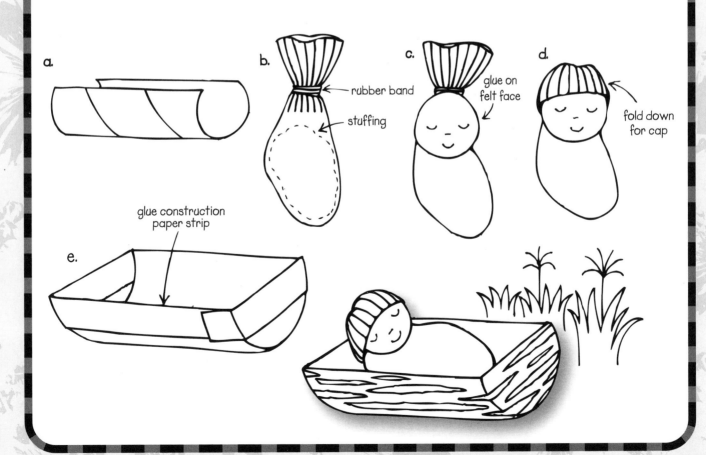

a.

b.
rubber band
stuffing

c.
glue on felt face

d.
fold down for cap

e.
glue construction paper strip

Bible Story

Materials: Bible, air-drying clay, pennies, nickels, quarters, embossed buttons, waxed paper.

Preparation: Tear waxed paper into squares for children to work on—one for each child. Give each child a piece of clay.

Instruct each child in the following procedures:

★ Make several small balls of clay.

★ Flatten each ball with your fingers (sketch a).

★ Press coin or button onto top of clay circles to make a design (sketch b).

★ Let clay dry on waxed paper overnight until hard.

Enrichment Idea: Teacher paints coins with gold or silver spray paint after clay has dried.

Conversation:

Open your Bible to Luke 19:11. **In Luke, Jesus told a story about a master who asked his servants to help take care of his money while he was gone. Two of the servants used the money to make even more money for their master. They were good helpers! The master was very happy with them. But the third servant didn't help his master at all. He buried his money in the ground. The master was very unhappy with the lazy servant. Jesus wants us to be good helpers. How can you help at home?**

a.

b.

Bible Story

Materials: Bible, table salt, candle wicks, scissors, ruler, black, red, orange and yellow dry tempera paint, paraffin wax, measuring utensils, spoons, bamboo skewers, four shallow containers, empty coffee can, stove, saucepan, water. For each child—one clean baby food jar.

Preparation: Cut candle wick into 3-inch (7.5-cm) lengths. Pour 1 cup (.24 liter) of salt into each container. Mix 1 tsp. dry tempera into each container of salt to make four colors. (Add more tempera for greater color intensity.) Melt wax in a can set into a saucepan of water. Heat on low. (Watch closely as wax will melt quickly.)

Instruct each child in the following procedures:

★ Spoon defined layers of red, orange and yellow salt into the jar.

★ Add a final layer of black salt, stopping 1 inch (2.5 cm) from top of jar (sketch a).

★ Press a skewer against the inside of the jar and push skewer down through all salt layers.

★ Carefully pull skewer out and repeat procedure around the sides of the jar to make "flames" (sketch b).

★ Push the wick down through the middle of the salt (sketch c).

★ With adult supervision, carefully pour the hot wax into the jar, filling it to the top (sketch c).

★ Trim wick if necessary.

★ Allow wax to harden.

Conversation:

Open your Bible to Daniel 3. **This chapter tells about the fiery furnace that Shadrach, Meshach and Abednego were thrown into. This furnace was probably used as a huge kiln to fire pottery. Even though they faced death in the fire, Shadrach, Meshach and Abednego showed their faith in God by obeying Him.**

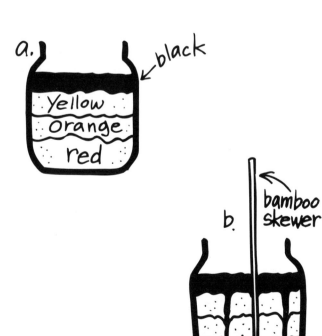

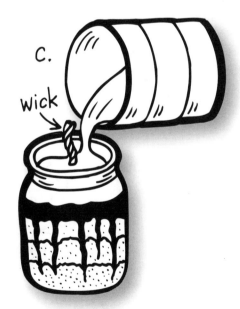

Materials: Bible, yellow card stock, red and orange food coloring, scrap fabric and felt, fine-tip felt pens, ruler, glue, transparent tape, pinking shears, newspaper, scissors. For each child—three tongue depressors, one plastic straw, six small wiggle eyes and three mini pom-poms.

Preparation: Cut scrap fabric and felt into 2-inch (5-cm) squares—three for each child. Cut card stock into 7-inch (17.5-cm) squares—one for every two children. Fold squares in half diagonally. Use pinking shears to cut square into two equal triangles (sketch a). Cover work area with newspaper.

Instruct each child in the following procedures:

★ Teacher puts a drop of red and orange food coloring on bottom corner of card stock triangle. Child quickly blows through straw to spread the color (sketch b). Repeat if desired. Allow to dry.

★ To make Shadrach, Meshach and Abednego, glue wiggle eyes onto each of the three tongue depressors (sketch c). Glue on pom-poms for noses.

★ Wrap and glue fabric and felt squares around puppets to make clothes.

★ Use felt pens to draw hair and other features on figures.

★ With teacher's help, fold paper into a cone shape (sketch d). Tape edges closed.

★ Place puppets in cone pocket to show Shadrach, Meshach and Abednego in the fiery furnace.

Simplification Idea: Draw eyes and nose instead of using wiggle eyes and pom-poms.

Enrichment Idea: Children cut tiny pieces of yarn and glue them onto puppets for hair and beards.

Conversation:

Open your Bible to Daniel 3. **In Daniel, we meet Shadrach, Meshach and Abednego. They loved God. They wanted to obey Him. How did they obey God?** (They only worshiped God. They wouldn't bow down to the king's statue.) **How did God save them from the fiery furnace?** (He sent an angel in the fire to protect them.) **How can we show our love to God?** (Praying to Him, singing, going to Sunday School to learn about Him, being kind and loving to other people.)

a.

7"

7"

b.

straw

d.

front

back

tape

c.

pom-pom

wiggle eyes

Bible Story

EARLY CHILDHOOD • YOUNGER ELEMENTARY • OLDER ELEMENTARY

Materials: Bible, metallic gold spray paint, fringed fabric trim, yarn, acrylic jewels, leather-like cording, paper, masking tape, measuring stick, hole punch, newspaper, crayons, scissors, glue. For each child—one paper towel tube.

Preparation: Cover an outdoor area with newspaper and paint each paper towel tube with gold spray paint. Cut yarn into 6-inch (15-cm) lengths—several for each child. Cut cording into 2-foot (60-cm) lengths—one for each child. Cut fringe into 6-inch (15-cm) lengths—one for each child.

Instruct each child in the following procedures:

★ Place two pieces of masking tape criss-cross at one end of tube (sketch a).

★ Glue fringe around taped end of tube, hiding tape ends (sketch b).

★ With teacher's help, punch two holes at top of message carrier (sketch c).

★ With teacher's help, tie one end of leather cording through each hole.

★ Glue yarn pieces and jewels onto tube to decorate (sketch d).

★ With paper and crayons, draw a picture to give to someone. Roll it up and carry it in your message carrier!

Conversation:

In Bible times, people often carried important papers by rolling them up. Open your Bible to Acts 8. **In this Bible story, a man named Philip traveled around the country, bringing a message of good news to the people. He told them that God loved them and sent Jesus to be their friend. This message is true for us, too: God loves us and sent Jesus to be our friend. What good news can you carry in your message carrier?**

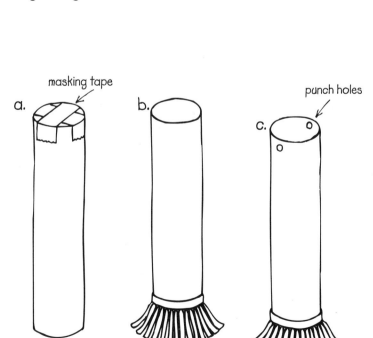

masking tape

a.

b.

c.

punch holes

glue fringe over taped end

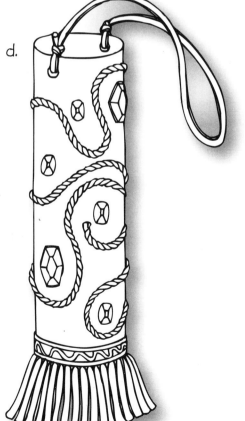

d.

41

Bible Story

"HE IS RISEN" SHADOW BOX

(ONE- OR TWO-DAY CRAFT/ 30-35 MINUTES TOTAL TIME)

Materials: Bible, Angel Picture, photocopier, copier paper, ruler, lightweight cardboard, grey, brown and green tempera paint, fine aquarium gravel, course sand or bird grit, white glue, measuring cups and spoons, mixing bowl, paintbrushes, shallow containers, hole punch, yarn, ruler, paper clips, scissors, crayons, newspaper. For each child—two sturdy, large paper plates, one paper fastener.

DAY ONE Preparation: With photocopier set at 300% enlargement, make one photocopy of Angel Picture for each child. Cut out center of plate slightly smaller than the size of Angel Picture (sketch a)— one plate for each child. Cut cardboard into circles or "stone" shapes the same size as Angel Picture— one for each child. With hole punch, punch one hole close to the edge of each cardboard shape. Make textured paint by mixing in bowl: 2 cups of grey paint, ½ cup of grit, sand or gravel and 4 tablespoons of white glue. Pour textured paint into shallow containers. Pour brown and green paint into shallow containers. Cover work area with newspaper.

Instruct each child in the following procedures:

★ Paint the underside of cut plate brown for a cave and green for grass (sketch b).

★ Paint one side of cardboard circle with grey textured paint. Let dry.

DAY TWO Preparation: Cut yarn into 6-inch (15-cm) lengths—one for each child.

Instruct each child in the following procedures:

★ Use crayons to color Angel Picture.

★ Cut out picture and glue to front center of uncut plate.

★ With teacher's help, punch two holes in the cut-out paper plate as indicated in sketch c. Punch a hole at the top of uncut plate.

★ Line up the holes at the top of paper plates and glue the rims of plates together. The Angel Picture will show through the cut-out paper plate. Have teacher paper clip edges until glue has dried (sketch c).

★ With teacher's help, attach the painted "stone" to the top paper plate with a paper fastener (sketch d).

★ Thread yarn through hole at top of plates and tie for a hanger.

★ Cover the opening with the stone; then roll it away to see the angel tell the happy news that Jesus is risen!

Enrichment Idea: Children may glue dried flowers and greenery onto grass portion of paper plate.

Conversation:

Read Matthew 28:5. **What did the angel tell Jesus' friends when they saw the empty tomb?** (Jesus is alive. He is risen.) **Jesus' friends were very happy. We can be happy that Jesus is alive, too. We can pray to Jesus anytime. We can talk to Him when we are afraid, sad or happy. Jesus loves and cares for us.**

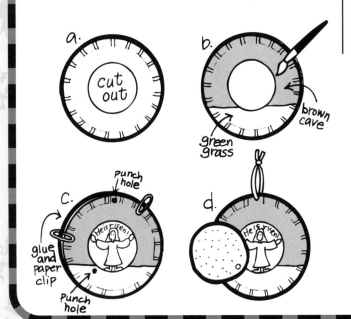

Angel Picture

Bible Story

Materials: Bible, Jonah and Fish Patterns, white or blue plastic disposable plates, permanent felt pens, plastic fish-shaped confetti (found at craft or party supply stores), water, pitcher, blue and green food coloring, blue electrical tape, small fish or seashell stickers, scissors, shallow containers. For each child—one small, clear plastic beverage bottle with cap.

Preparation: Trace patterns onto plastic plates and cut out—one Jonah and one fish figure for each child. Fill pitcher with water. Put confetti in shallow containers.

Instruct each child in the following procedures:

★ Use permanent felt pens to decorate plastic fish and Jonah.

★ Gently bend fish to fit through bottle opening and push fish into bottle. Put Jonah into bottle.

★ Drop several confetti fish into bottle.

★ With teacher's help, fill bottle with water until 1 inch (2.5 cm) from the top.

★ Put a few drops of food coloring into water to make ocean. Use blue or green food coloring, or mix blue and green together.

★ Put cap on bottle and twist tightly to close.

★ With teacher's help, wrap tape around bottle cap to secure (sketch a).

★ Shake bottle to mix food coloring with water.

★ Put a few stickers on outside of bottle.

★ Tip bottle back and forth to see Jonah and the fish swim under the sea.

Conversation:

Open your Bible to Jonah 2. **What did God send to swallow Jonah and keep him safe in the ocean?** (A big fish.) **God loved Jonah and took care of him, even though Jonah ran away and didn't obey God. God loves you, too. He takes care of you by giving you mommies and daddies who love you.**

Fish Pattern

Jonah Pattern

a. wrap tape

Bible Story

Materials: Bible, Tool Patterns, muslin fabric, ¼-inch (.625-cm) bias tape, sewing machine and thread, felt pens or squeeze bottles of fabric paints in a variety of colors, tongue depressors, safety pin, photocopier, colored card stock, glue, fabric scissors, scissors, measuring stick.

Preparation: Photocopy Tool Patterns onto card stock—one set for each child. Make a tool apron for each child according to the following directions: Cut a 10x12-inch (25x30-cm) rectangle out of muslin. Sew a ½-inch (1.25-cm) hem on both short sides and one long side of fabric (sketch a). Fold up the hemmed long side of fabric to make a 4-inch (10-cm) pocket as shown in sketch b. Sew pocket along sides; then stitch down the middle of pocket to make two smaller pockets. Fold down the top edge of apron ½ inch (1.25 cm) and sew along edge to make casing. Pin safety pin to one end of a 3-foot (.9-m) length of bias tape and thread through casing (sketch c).

Instruct each child in the following procedures:

★ Cut out card stock tools.

★ Glue a tongue depressor to the back of each tool to make sturdy (sketch d).

★ Decorate apron using felt pens or squeeze bottles of fabric paint (sketch e). Allow to dry.

★ Put tools in your apron and with teacher's help, tie around waist.

Simplification Idea: For younger children, teacher cuts out card stock tools.

Conversation:

Open your Bible to 2 Chronicles 3. **In Bible times, it took lots of people to help build God's Temple. There were workers who cut the stones for the steps. There were woodcutters who cut the trees for the walls. There were metalworkers who made beautiful things out of gold and bronze. Everyone worked together. If you were helping to build the Temple, what work would you like to do, (Eric)? What jobs do you like to do at home? You can wear your apron when you work at home with your family.**

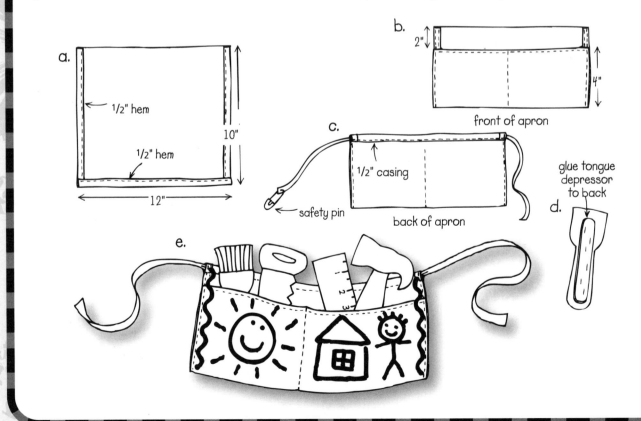

a. ½" hem ½" hem 10" 12"

b. 2" 4" front of apron

c. ½" casing safety pin back of apron

d. glue tongue depressor to back

e.

LITTLE WORKER'S APRON TOOL PATTERNS

1   2   3   4   5   6

Bible Story

Materials: Bible, muslin fabric, a variety of coins, 1-mm leather-like cording, an awl or hole punch, crayons in a variety of colors, fabric scissors, transparent tape, measuring stick, pencil. Optional—chocolate or play coins.

Preparation: Cut muslin into 9-inch (22.5-cm) circles—one for each child. Cut cording into 24-inch (60-cm) lengths—one for each child. Wrap tape around one end of each cord. Use awl or hole punch to make 20 evenly spaced holes about 1 inch (2.5 cm) from edge of circle (sketch a). Make sure holes are large enough for children to thread cording through.

Instruct each child in the following procedures:

* Choose a coin and crayon. Wrap muslin cloth tightly around coin and rub crayon across top of covered coin to make an imprint (sketch b).
* Continue crayon rubbing process all over muslin circle, using different-sized coins and different-colored crayons.
* Tie a knot in untaped end of cord.
* Beginning on the colored side of fabric, weave taped end of cord in and out of holes (sketch c).
* Pull ends of cording together to gather opening into a pouch (sketch d).
* Optional: Place chocolate or play coins in pouch. Wrap and tie ends together.

Conversation:

Open your Bible to Luke 19. **Here in Luke, Jesus told a story about a master who was going on a trip. He called his three servants and gave them his money to take care of while he was gone. Two of the servants were helpful. They used the money to make even more money for their master. The other servant was lazy. What do you think he did with the money?** (Children respond.) **He buried it in the ground and didn't do anything. When the master came back, who do you think he rewarded? Who do you think got fired?** (Children respond.) **Jesus told this story to teach us that He wants us to use the abilities and talents He has given to us to do good things. So don't hide your talents! (Terence), what is something you like to do with your talents?**

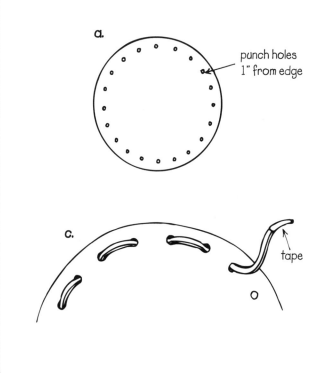

a. punch holes 1" from edge

c. tape

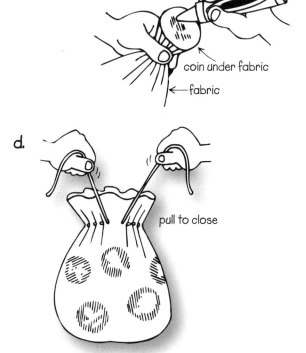

b. coin under fabric / fabric

d. pull to close

Bible Story

Materials: Bible, acrylic paints in peach, brown, blue and grey, small paintbrushes, black fine-tip permanent felt pen, drill, ⅛-inch (.3125-cm) drill bit, shallow containers, newspaper. For each child—one large wooden, flat doll clothespin, one eye hook, one split key ring.

Preparation: Drill starter hole in top of each clothespin. Cover work area with newspaper. Pour acrylic paint into shallow containers.

Instruct each child in the following procedures:

★ Paint lower portion of clothespin brown for body. Paint peach skin-tone face, grey hair and beard and blue headdress. (See sketch.) Let dry.

★ Add facial features and headband with felt pen.

★ Screw eye hook into top of head.

★ Attach key ring.

Enrichment Idea: Children make other Bible people of faith (Elisha, Jonah, Shadrach, Meshach, Abednego, etc.). Hang several Bible characters together to make a mobile.

Conversation:

Open your Bible to Exodus 14. **When Moses and the Israelites came to the Red Sea, what did God tell Moses to do?** (Hold up his staff.) **Moses had faith that God would help them escape from the Egyptians. But he also did his part by listening to God. We can have faith that God is with us, too. God also wants us to listen to Him and follow His instructions every day. How can we listen to God?** (Read the Bible, learn about Him at church, pray, etc.)

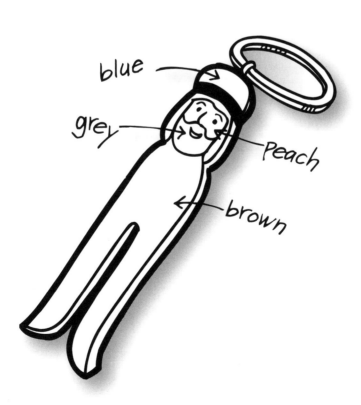

blue

grey

Peach

brown

Bible Story

Materials: Bible, Peter's Picture Patterns, letter-sized manila file folders, sandpaper, string, photocopier and paper, pencil, crayons, glue sticks, glue, scissors, hole punch, ruler. For each child—five craft sticks, paper fastener, hole reinforcement, one old key.

Preparation: Cut 1 inch (2.5 cm) off of tabbed edge of file folders and discard. Then cut folders in half to make small books—one half for each child (sketch a). Punch a hole through back page of book, near edge of right side. Photocopy Peter's Storybook Picture Patterns onto white paper—one for each child. Cut sandpaper into 1x2-inch (2.5x5-cm) rectangles—fourteen for each child. Cut string into 8-inch (20-cm) lengths—one for each child.

Instruct each child in the following procedures:

* Color pictures and cut out along dotted line.
* Apply glue stick to backs of pictures. Glue picture of Peter on front center of folder (sketch b). Glue picture of Peter and Rhoda inside folder on right-hand side (sketch c). Glue verse on left-hand side.
* Glue sandpaper rectangles around picture on front of book (sketch d).
* Glue craft sticks across front picture to make prison bars (sketch d).
* With teacher's help, push paper fastener through front page of book, near right edge.
* Place hole reinforcement over punched hole in back page. With teacher's help, tie one end of string to the hole and other end of string to key.
* To keep storybook closed, coil string around paper fastener (sketch e).

Simplification Idea: Instead of gluing on sandpaper, children color front of book.

Conversation:

Open your Bible to Acts 12. **Our storybook shows a story from the Bible about a man named Peter. Peter was in prison. How do you think Peter felt in prison?** (Lonely, sad, afraid.) **What can you do when you're lonely, sad or afraid?** (Pray.) **In this story, Peter's friends prayed, too. God heard Peter's friends' prayers and set Peter free. You can use your storybooks to tell the story about Peter.**

a.

cut

cut

b.

Punch hole in back page.

front of book

c.

inside book

d. craft sticks

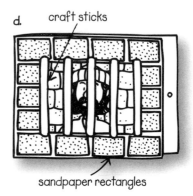

sandpaper rectangles

e. paper fastener

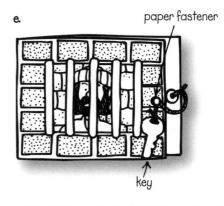

key

"The Lord will hear when I call to him."
Psalm 4:3

Bible Story

Materials: Bible, raffia, pink Fun Foam, red construction paper, crayons, felt pen, glue sticks, scissors, stapler and staples, measuring stick, newspaper. For each child—large white paper plate, tongue depressor, two 14-mm wiggle eyes, two paper fasteners.

Preparation: Fold paper plate in half and staple around edges. Make a 2-inch (5-cm) slit on the folded edge near the center (sketch a). Cut a 3½-inch (8.75-cm) heart shape from red construction paper—one for each child. Use felt pen to letter on each heart "Love each other." Cut pink Fun Foam into 1½-inch (3.75-cm) and 3½-inch (8.75-cm) circles—one of each size for each child. Cut additional Fun Foam into 1-inch (2.5-cm) squares—two for each child. Cut raffia into 18-inch (45-cm) lengths—one strand for each child. Cover work area with newspaper.

Instruct each child in the following procedures:

★ Use crayons to color one side of paper plate to look like a quilt.

★ With teacher's help, attach small pink circle to large pink circle by inserting paper fasteners for pig's nostrils (sketch b).

★ Glue large pink circle to end of tongue depressor.

★ Glue wiggle eyes just above pig's snout.

★ Cut one pink foam square diagonally to make two triangles. Glue triangles to top of circle to make pig's ears (sketch c).

★ Glue heart onto center of paper plate.

★ Insert end of tongue depressor through slit in plate.

★ Cut one pink foam square in half. Glue one half to each side of slit to make pig's hooves.

★ With teacher's help, staple each end of raffia to corner of paper plate to make a hanger (sketch d).

Conversation:

Our Bible says, "Love each other as I have loved you" (John 15:12). **One of Jesus' friends named Peter had a strange dream. He dreamed that lots of different animals were on a blanket together. God gave Peter this dream to tell him to love others who are different from him. What are some ways we can show love to others?**

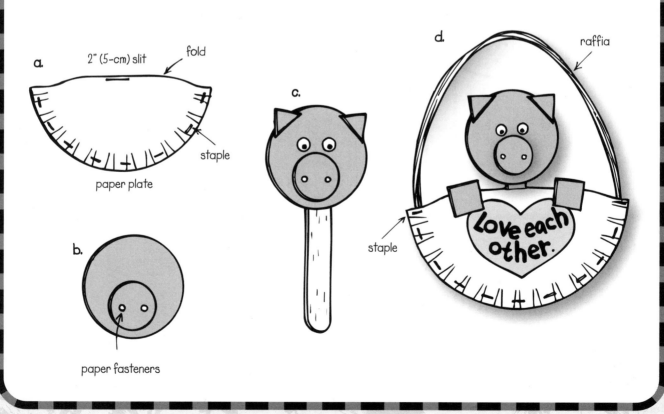

Bible Story

Materials: Bible, tan and blue acrylic paint, sponges, spring-type clothespins, brown and orange construction paper, colored dot label stickers, yarn, hole punch, glue sticks, pencil, ruler, scissors, shallow containers, newspaper. For each child—one 8½x11-inch (21.5x27.5-cm) sheet of white card stock, one overhead transparency.

Preparation: Draw a pencil line horizontally across the center of each sheet of card stock and transparency (sketch a). Cut brown construction paper into wavy mountain range shape approximately 2x11 inches (5x27.5 cm)—one for each child (sketch b). Cut orange construction paper into 1½-inch (3.75-cm) circles—one for each child. Cut damp sponges into small squares—one for each child. Clip a clothespin to each sponge. Cover work area with newspaper. Pour paint into shallow containers.

Instruct each child in the following procedures:

★ Use tan paint to sponge paint bottom half of white card stock (sketch c).

★ Use blue paint to sponge paint bottom half of transparency. Allow paint to dry.

★ Use glue stick to glue mountain range above tan section on card stock (sketch d).

★ Use glue stick to glue orange sun above mountains.

★ Stick dot labels in the middle of tan section to represent the Israelites crossing the dry ground.

★ Lay transparency on top of paper so that the blue paint is covering the tan paint. With teacher's help, use hole punch to punch four evenly-spaced holes along both sides of card stock and transparency (sketch e).

★ With teacher's help, insert yarn through first hole and tie a knot. Thread yarn through remaining holes as shown in sketch e and tie another knot to secure. Repeat process for opposite edge of picture.

★ Teacher uses scissors to cut transparency in half vertically (sketch f).

★ Open and close top sheet to show how God parted the Red Sea and allowed the Israelites to cross on dry ground.

Simplification Idea: Use Bible character stickers for Moses and the Israelites.

Enrichment Idea: Older children may draw happy faces on dots with fine-tip felt pens.

Conversation:

Open your Bible to Exodus 14. **God took care of the Israelites when they escaped from Egypt. He wanted them to travel safely to a new home. How did God help them escape when they reached the Red Sea?** (God sent a big wind that blew the sea back. Then the people could walk across to the other side.) **What do you think the Israelites said after God helped them escape?**

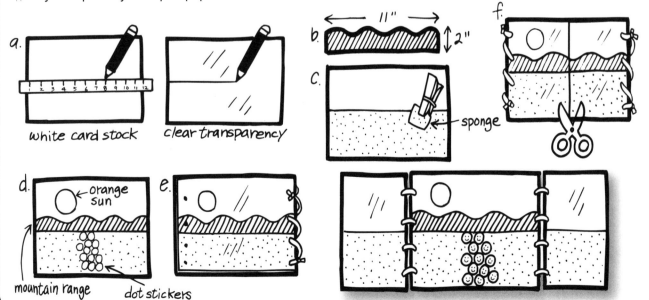

a. white card stock   clear transparency

b. 11" 2"

c. sponge

d. orange sun / mountain range / dot stickers

e.

f.

Bible Story

Materials: Bible, poster board, ribbon, fabric scraps, buttons in various shapes and sizes, pinking shears, pencil, craft glue, scissors, masking tape, stapler and staples, measuring stick.

Preparation: Cut poster board into 4x5-inch (10x12.5-cm) rectangles—two for each child. Cut a 2x3-inch (5x7.5-cm) opening from center of rectangles to make frames—one for each child (sketch a). Leave remaining rectangles uncut. Use pinking shears to cut fabric scraps into 1x36-inch (2.5x90-cm) strips—two strips for each child. Cut ribbon into 12-inch (30-cm) lengths—one for each child.

Instruct each child in the following procedures:

★ Staple one end of ribbon onto corner of uncut poster-board piece. Staple other end of ribbon onto opposite corner to make hanger (sketch b).

★ Tape one end of fabric strip to border of frame and then tightly wrap fabric around frame, leaving a few inches of fabric unwrapped (sketch c). Tie end of strip to second fabric strip and continue wrapping around frame. Tuck end under wrapping.

★ Spread glue around bottom and side edges of frame border on the back side. Place uncut poster-board piece on back of frame with staples facing in (sketch d).

★ Glue buttons on fabric frame to decorate (sketch e).

★ At home, slide a photograph through top of the frame.

Simplification Idea: Instead of making a backing for frame, tape photograph to back of the frame.

Conversation:

In the Old West, instead of throwing away their old clothes, folks cut them up and used the scraps to make quilts, rag rugs and even other clothes. They made something new out of something old. Open your Bible to Acts 9. **When Saul met Jesus on the road to Damascus, something new happened to the old Saul. He believed Jesus was God's Son and started a new life as part of God's family. What was the old Saul like?** (He was mean. He wanted to kill Jesus' followers.) **What was the new Saul (Paul) like?** (He traveled to tell everyone about Jesus and God's love.)

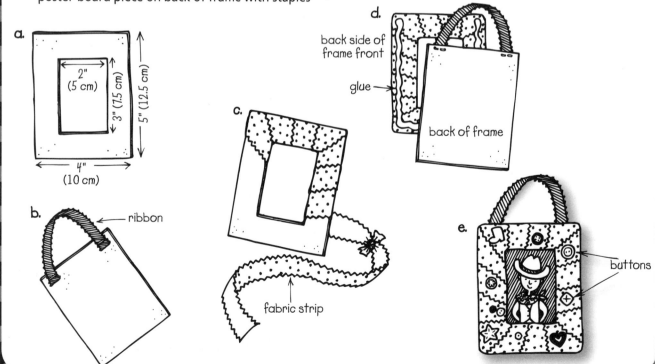

a.
2" (5 cm)
3" (7.5 cm)
5" (12.5 cm)
4" (10 cm)

b. ribbon

c. fabric strip

d. back side of frame front — glue — back of frame

e. buttons

Bible Story

Materials: Bible, weaving material (yarn, twine, strips of cloth), saw, ¼-inch (.625-cm) dowels, measuring stick, scissors. For each child—one loom (see Wooden Loom, p. 54), one large blunt craft needle.

Preparation: Cut the dowels into 18-inch (45-cm) lengths—one for each child.

Instruct each child in the following procedures:

★ Thread the loom with yarn to make the warp of loom as follows: Tie and knot yarn to the first nail on either side of loom. Bring yarn across loom and wrap around the corresponding nail on the opposite side. Then bring yarn back across loom to the next nail (sketch a).

★ Continue process until you thread the entire loom. If you need to add yarn, just tie and knot yarn end to one nail, tie a new length to the same nail and continue. When done, tie the yarn to the last nail with a knot.

★ Weave the dowel over and under yarn warp. This separates threads to make weaving easier. The dowel should be a few inches above the bottom of loom (sketch b).

★ Thread needle with a long length of yarn. Start near the bottom edge of loom and weave a length of yarn over one warp thread and then under the next thread, then over, then under, pulling length of yarn through the warp and continuing through the entire row (sketch b).

★ Weave yarn back to the opposite side of loom, weaving under and over alternate threads of the previous row.

★ Slide dowel down to "beat" it against previous row of weaving.

★ Continue weaving with the same yarn or create a pattern using different colors or textures of materials. Knot ends when adding yarn.

★ When you complete your weaving, cut warp threads, one pair at a time, as close to nails as possible. Tie ends in a knot. Continue cutting and knotting threads until both ends of weaving are free from loom (sketch c).

★ You may leave knotted thread ends as fringe for your weaving or trim them, turning ends under and hemming them to finish the edges.

★ You can use your finished tapestry to decorate a wall or a table, or sew the sides together to make a wallet or purse.

(Note: Weaving time may vary from child to child. Depending on the size of tapestry, this craft could be an ongoing project at home, or an ongoing project that children can work on when other activities are completed early.)

Conversation:

In Exodus 36, God's people began to make the parts of the Tabernacle. God told them how to build it. One part was to weave curtains. Read Exodus 36:8-10 aloud. **A cubit is about the distance from a grown man's elbow to the tip of his middle finger. Were these big curtains or small curtains?**

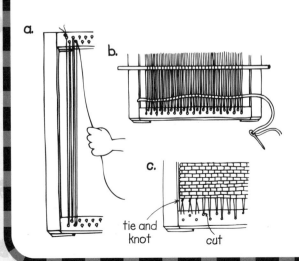

a.

b.

c.

tie and knot

cut

Bible Story

Materials: Bible, 1x2-inch (25x5-cm) pine lumber, 1¼-inch (3.125-cm) nails, saw, hammers, sandpaper, pencils, rulers, measuring stick. For each child—approximately 80 1-inch (2.5-cm) nails.

Preparation: Saw pine lumber into the following lengths for each child: two 12-inch (30-cm) pieces, two 16-inch (40-cm) pieces, and four 4-inch (10-cm) pieces.

Instruct each child in the following procedures:

★ Use sandpaper to smooth rough edges of wood pieces.

★ Lay a 12-inch (30-cm) pine board with 2-inch (5-cm) side facing up. Place ruler on top about ½ inch (1.25 cm) from the long edge (sketch a). Mark a pencil dot 1 inch (2.5 cm) from the end. Then mark every ½ inch (1.25 cm), ending 1 inch (2.5 cm) from the opposite end of board.

★ With hammer, pound a 1-inch (2.5-cm) nail into each mark. Leave about ¼-inch (.625 cm) of nail sticking above the wood.

★ Nail a second row of nails below the first row, but stagger them as shown (sketch b).

★ Repeat process for the second 12-inch board.

★ Make a frame by positioning the 16-inch (40-cm) boards for sides and the 12-inch boards for the top and bottom. Place a 4-inch (10-cm) length underneath each corner of frame. Using longer nails, hammer two nails in each corner as shown in sketch c.

★ Make a tapestry weaving on your loom by following the directions on p. 53.

Conversation:

Until looming machines were invented, people worked together to make cloth for sale. Spinsters spun the wool into thread. Then the dyer colored the wool yarn or thread with dyes made from plants. Next, weavers sat at looms to weave the thread into cloth. Fullers put the woven cloth into a trough of water and trampled it to mat the threads together. Finally, a shearer trimmed off the loose threads. It took many workers' different skills to make the cloth. Then tailors and seamstresses sewed cloth into clothing. In Acts 16, God sent Paul to preach to some women. Read Acts 16:13-15 aloud. **What job did Lydia do?**

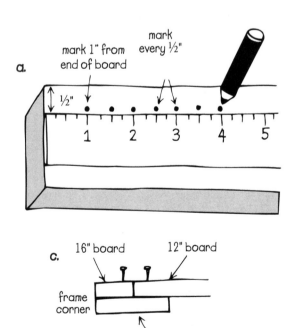

a.

mark 1" from end of board
mark every ½"
½"

c. 16" board   12" board
frame corner
4" board

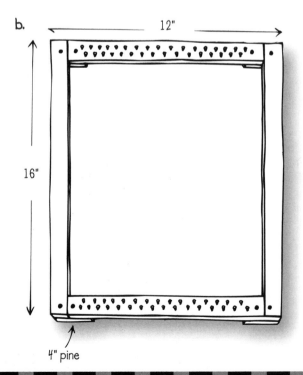

b. 12"

16"

4" pine

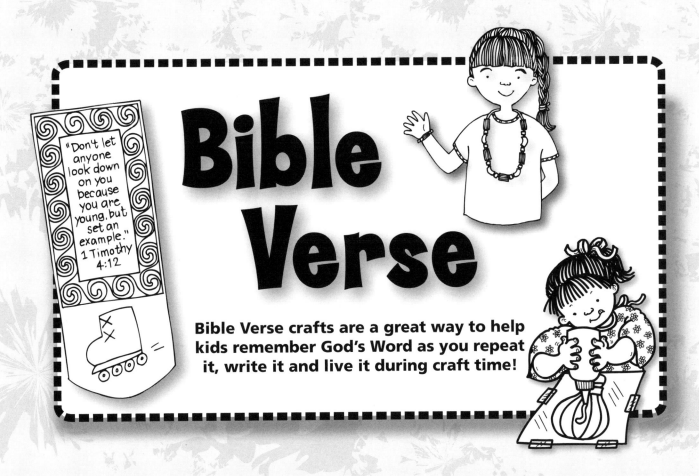

Bible Verse

Bible Verse crafts are a great way to help kids remember God's Word as you repeat it, write it and live it during craft time!

"Don't let anyone look down on you because you are young, but set an example." 1 Timothy 4:12

Bible Verse

Materials: Bible, beeswax honeycomb sheets (available at craft stores), candle wicking, aluminum foil, salt, flour, cutting board, mixing spoon, mixing bowl, measuring cups, resealable plastic bags, baking sheets, hot pads, oven, oven mitt, toothpicks, craft knife, scissors, ruler, water.

Preparation: Use craft knife to cut beeswax into 4x8-inch (10x20-cm) sheets—one for each child. Cut wicking into 11-inch (27.5-cm) lengths—one for each child. Follow directions below to make a sample candle. Crumple foil to make small cylinders with same diameter as candle—one cylinder for each child. To make enough dough for eight children: Mix 8 cups flour, 2 cups salt and 3 cups water until mixture clings together. Knead dough on floured surface until smooth. Divide dough into eight balls and place in individual plastic bags. Preheat oven to 350 degrees. Line baking sheets with foil.

Instruct each child in the following procedures:

To make candleholder:

⋆ Use a small amount of dough to make a flat circle about 2 inches (5 cm) in diameter (sketch a). Use toothpick to carve initials into dough circle.

⋆ Roll remaining dough into a rope about 16 inches (40 cm) long (sketch b).

⋆ Stand foil cylinder on top of dough circle. Coil dough rope around foil until about 5 inches (12.5 cm) of rope remains (sketch c). Lightly squeeze coils together, so they stick to one another.

⋆ Fold remaining length of dough rope in half to make thick handle piece. Press handle in place at top and bottom of candleholder (sketch d).

⋆ Crumple additional length of aluminum foil and place inside handle to retain its shape while baking (sketch e).

⋆ Place candleholder on foil-lined baking sheet. Teacher bakes candleholders for 45 minutes. Remove foil from candleholder and let cool.

To make candle:

⋆ Lay wick along longer edge of beeswax sheet (sketch f).

⋆ Place hands palms-down on beeswax sheet for several seconds. (Body heat will soften beeswax, allowing it to roll without cracking.) Roll beeswax sheet lengthwise around wick as tightly as possible (sketch g).

⋆ With teacher's help, seal candle edge by pressing briefly against a warmed baking sheet (sketch h).

⋆ Place candle in holder.

Simplification Ideas: Use air-drying clay to make candleholders. Younger children can make simple candleholder by rolling clay into a ball and then inserting thumb in center to make a hole. To cut costs, use store-bought candles wrapped in one layer of beeswax.

Enrichment Idea: Paint candleholder and seal with clear acrylic spray.

Conversation:

These candles will make a big change in a dark room! Jesus said we are like candles. He said, "Let your light shine before men, that they may see your good deeds and praise your Father in heaven." That's Matthew 5:16!

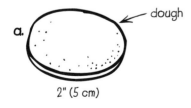

a.

dough

2" (5 cm)

b.

16" (40 cm)

(Sketches continued on page 58.)

BEESWAX CANDLE AND HOLDER

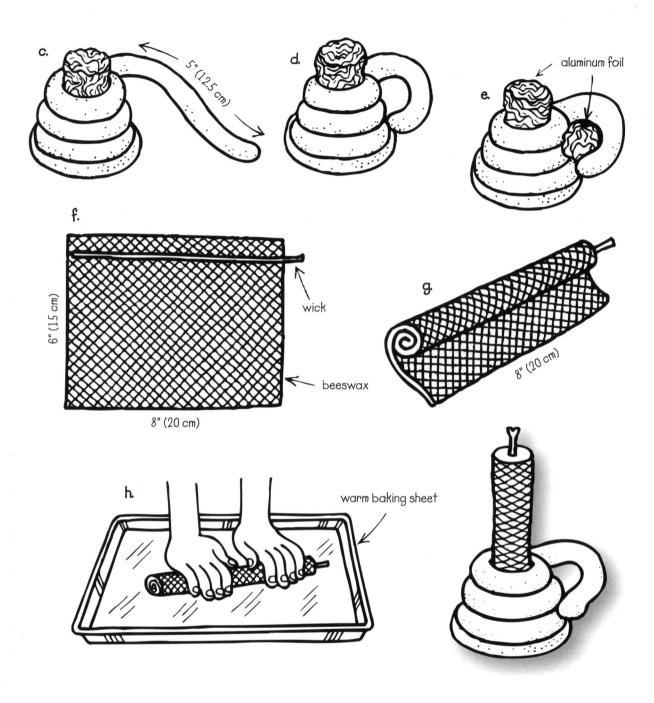

c.

5" (12.5 cm)

d.

e.

aluminum foil

f.

6" (15 cm)

8" (20 cm)

wick

beeswax

g.

8" (20 cm)

h.

warm baking sheet

Bible Verse

Materials: Bible, cloud-print or blue fabric, nylon parachute-type fabric in various bright colors, cotton or nylon cording, fusible webbing (such as Wonder Under™), burlap, sewing machine, thread, straight pins, measuring stick, small bottles of fabric paint, scratch paper, pencils, iron and ironing board, scissors, masking tape.

Preparation: Cut fabric into 14x36-inch (35x90-cm) rectangles—one for each child. Cut cording into 40-inch (1-m) lengths—one for each child. Fold a ¾-inch (1.9-cm) hem on both ends of fabric and sew with sewing machine to make casing (sketch a). Fold fabric, right sides together and hemmed edges even. Sew sides of bag, starting from stitching line of hem and ending at the bottom of the bag. Casing openings should remain unstitched (sketch b). Trim corners and turn sewn bag right-side out. Make one bag for each child. Follow directions on package of fusible webbing and iron onto parachute material and burlap. Cut prepared parachute material into 3x7-inch (7.5x17.5-cm) rectangles—three different colors for each child. Cut prepared burlap into 2-inch (5-cm) squares—one for each child.

Instruct each child in the following procedures:

★ On paper, draw an outline of a balloon. Make outline no larger than 7x8 inches (17.5x20 cm). Then draw a simple design on balloon (horizontal or vertical stripes, wavy sections, etc.) as shown in sketch c.

★ Cut out balloon and cut apart on design lines to make pattern pieces.

★ Lay pattern pieces on parachute material and pin in place. Cut out patterns (sketch d).

★ Peel paper backing from webbing on cutout shapes.

★ Arrange shapes to make balloon on front of bag, fabric side up (sketch e). Fuse to bag with iron.

★ Cut burlap piece into a basket shape and iron onto front of bag.

★ Use fabric scraps to make additional tiny hot air balloons in the distance. Cut out and iron onto bag.

★ Wrap masking tape around ends of cording to prevent fraying.

★ Work cording through top hem of bag to make a drawstring for your Balloon Gear Bag.

★ Use fabric paint to draw details such as *m* shapes for flying birds, dots or squiggles to decorate balloon, balloon ropes and your name (sketch e).

Simplification Idea: Buy inexpensive pre-made tote bags available at most craft stores.

Enrichment Idea: Embellish bags with buttons, ribbon or sequins. Glue on with fabric glue or fabric paint.

Conversation:

If you were going on a real balloon flight, what gear would you pack to be prepared? (Flight instruments, fuel, food, warm clothes, radio communication equipment.) **Being prepared often helps people have courage in new adventures.** Read 1 Peter 1:13 aloud. **What are ways we can prepare our minds to obey God?** (Pray. Read God's Word.) **God can help us obey Him and be ready for any adventure!**

a. wrong side of fabric   ←→ ¾" seam   ¾" seam

b. wrong side of fabric   ↖ leave unstitched

c.

d.

e. KIM

Bible Verse

Materials: Bible, Balloon Pattern, white glue in squeeze bottles, food coloring, small mixing bowls, spoon, funnels, copier paper, photocopier, masking tape. For each child—one clear overhead transparency.

Preparation: Make colored glue by pouring glue into bowls and adding a few drops of food coloring. Mix several different colors in bowls. Use funnel to pour glue back into squeeze bottles. Photocopy Balloon Pattern (p. 61) onto paper—one copy for each child.

Instruct each child in the following procedures:

* With teacher's help, tape hot air balloon photocopy onto table. Tape transparency directly over photocopy (sketch a).
* Squeeze colored glue over the photocopied balloon shape onto transparency. Use different colors to make designs. Completely fill in balloon shape with a thick layer of glue (sketch b).
* Allow glue to dry overnight.

* With teacher's help, gently peel balloon shape from transparency.
* Children stick their balloons on a classroom window.

Simplification Idea: Purchase premade colored glue in squeeze bottles.

Enrichment Idea: Children use Weather Patterns on p. 196 to make additional decal shapes.

Conversation:

(Jordan), what would happen if you didn't listen to the directions for making your balloon? (I wouldn't know what to do. It might not turn out right.) **Because you listen and follow directions, your balloon decal will be very bright and beautiful! God wants you to follow His directions in the Bible. He also wants you to follow your parents' directions and obey them.** (See Ephesians 6:1.) **What are some things you can do to obey your mom or dad?**

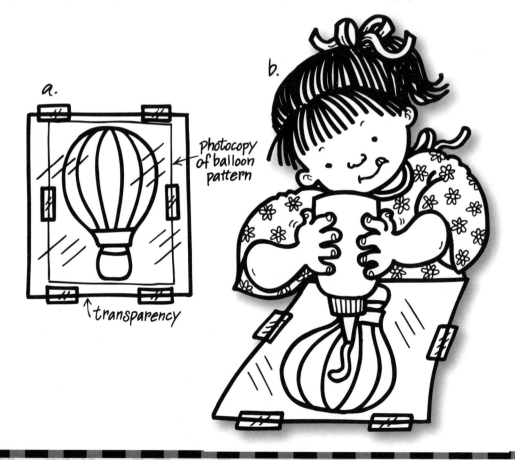

a.

photocopy of balloon pattern

↑ transparency

b.

BALLOON WINDOW DECALS PATTERN

Materials: Bible, Roof Pattern, brown paper bags or brown construction paper, brown or black felt pens, wide-tip felt pens, pencil, glue, transparent tape, scissors, ruler. For each child—half-gallon cardboard milk carton.

Preparation: Cut off bottom half of each milk carton 3½ inches (8.75 cm) from the bottom (sketch a). Cut brown paper into 3x¾-inch (7.5x9.4-cm) strips and 3x5-inch (7.5x12.5-cm) strips—eight of each length for each child. Cut additional brown paper into 5½x7-inch (13.75x17.5-cm) rectangles—one for each child. Trace Roof Pattern onto brown paper and cut out—two for each child.

Instruct each child in the following procedures:

* Use brown or black felt pen to draw horizontal wood-grain markings along length of each brown paper strip (sketch b).
* To form logs, roll each paper strip around a wide-tip felt pen, tape edges and remove felt pen (sketch c).
* Alternating shorter and longer logs as shown, glue logs to milk carton (sketch d).

* Glue roof triangles to front and back of milk carton. Allow glue to dry.
* Use felt pen to draw "wood planks" across length of large rectangular roof piece.
* Fold rectangular roof piece in half and glue over top of carton (sketch d).
* Cut scraps of brown paper to make door and windows. Glue onto cabin.

Enrichment Idea: Cut fabric scraps and glue to windows for curtains.

Conversation:

When families in pioneer times needed to build their own home, their neighbors got together and helped them build a log cabin. With everyone working together, they were able to cut down trees and build a new home in just a few days. Have you ever helped a neighbor? Luke 10:27 tells us, "Love your neighbor as yourself." That means we are kind and helpful to our neighbors.

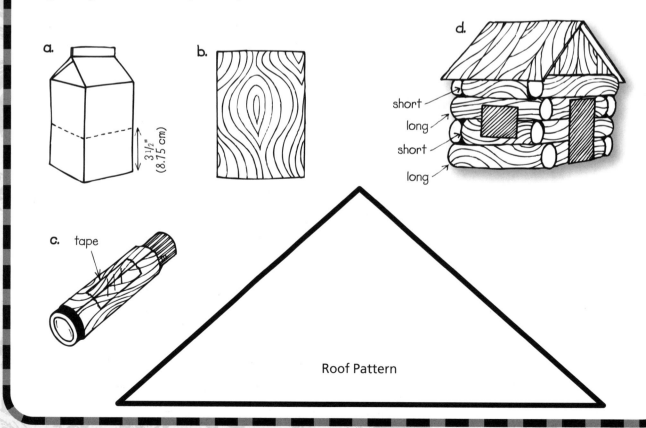

a.

3 1/2" (8.75 cm)

b.

c. tape

d.

short
long
short
long

Roof Pattern

Bible Verse

FANCY FRAME
(15-20 MINUTES)
1 John 4:10

Materials: Bible, Window Frame Patterns, mat board or poster board, heavy cardboard, metallic gold spray paint, pasta in a variety of shapes, rubbing alcohol, food coloring, cotton swabs, pencil, sharp scissors or craft knife, newspaper, white glue, paintbrushes, shallow containers.

Preparation: Trace Window Frame Front Pattern onto mat board or poster board—one for each child. Trace Window Frame Back Pattern and Stand Pattern onto cardboard—one of each for each child. Cut out all frame pieces with scissors or craft knife. Use sharp scissors or craft knife to score a line ½ inch (1.25 cm) from end of each stand piece (sketch a). Spray one side of frame fronts and some of the pasta with gold paint.

Dye the remaining pasta three bright colors as follows: Pour some alcohol into shallow containers, one container for each color. Add several drops of food coloring. Put the pasta into alcohol just long enough for color to be absorbed. Spread pasta on newspaper to dry.

Pour glue into shallow containers. Put colored pasta into separate shallow containers.

Instruct each child in the following procedures:
* Use swab to spread glue along the side and bottom edges of frame back (sketch b).
* Press unpainted side of frame front onto glued frame back.
* Use paintbrush to spread a thick coat of glue on the front of gold frame.
* Place gold and colored pasta on the glue to decorate frame.
* With teacher's help, spread glue on scored section of stand and glue onto frame back with bottom edges even (sketch c). Let dry.

Enrichment Idea: Before project, teacher photographs and develops 3x5-inch (7.5x12.5-cm) individual, vertical pictures of children. Children insert photos in completed frames.

Conversation:

(Karina), you may put a picture of someone you love in your frame. Who is someone you love? (Child responds.) **Who is someone who loves you?** (Child responds.) **God loves you, too. Our Bible says, "God loved us and sent Jesus"** (see 1 John 4:10). **Jesus came to show His love for us and to teach us how to love each other.**

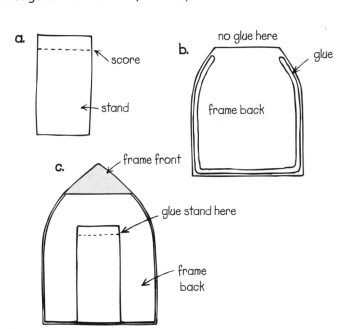

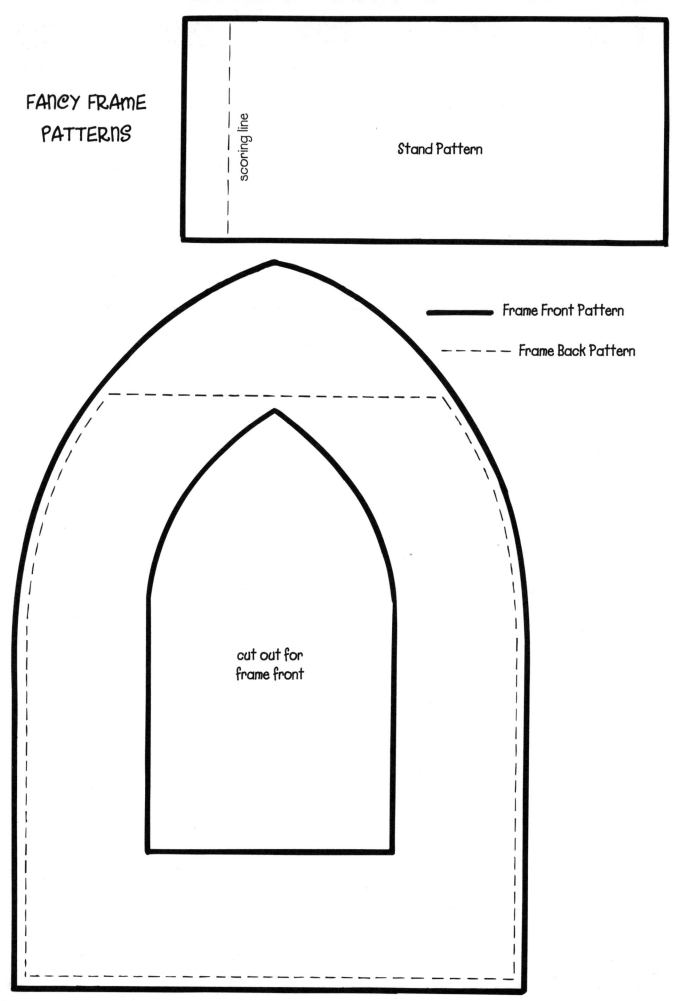

FANCY FRAME
PATTERNS

scoring line

Stand Pattern

Frame Front Pattern

Frame Back Pattern

cut out for
frame front

Bible Verse

Materials: Bible, pine board, saw, measuring stick, hammers, acrylic paints in a variety of bright colors, glow-in-the-dark star stickers or paint, paintbrushes, craft glue, shallow containers, newspaper. For each child—one toothed picture hanger with nails, 16 2½-inch (6.25-cm) flat doll clothespins. *Optional*—small wiggle eyes, colored fake fur.

Preparation: Cut pine board into 4x15-inch (10x37.5-cm) rectangles—one for each child. Count 16 clothespins—one set for each child. For each child, cut six clothespins as shown in sketch a. (Remaining 10 clothespins for each child are used whole.) Cover work area with newspaper. Pour paint into shallow containers.

Instruct each child in the following procedures:

DAY ONE:

★ Nail picture hanger to the middle of the board with hammer.

★ Paint the front and edges of the board a solid color. Let dry.

★ Arrange clothespin pieces to spell "FEAR NOT" (sketch b). Do not glue in place.

★ Paint clothespin pieces on all three sides. Use different colors so the letters are a variety of bright colors. Let dry.

DAY TWO:

★ Glue clothespins on board to spell "FEAR NOT."

★ Glue glow-in-the-dark star stickers to the board or paint stars with glow-in-the-dark paint.

Enrichment Idea: Cut tiny pieces of fake fur. Glue fur and wiggle eyes to some letters as little creatures (sketch c).

Conversation:

In many places, the Bible tells us to "fear not." What are some fears that people have? (Students respond.) **Sometimes we are afraid of new situations or things because we aren't familiar with them. Sometimes we're afraid to do what's right because of what our friends might say. Some kids might be afraid to say no to an R-rated movie or to be kind to an unpopular student. But once they learn that God will help them do what's right, they find it isn't so scary. What things have you been afraid to do in the past but are more comfortable with now?** (Volunteers respond.) **Having faith that God is with us can help us "fear not" when we feel afraid.** (See Joshua 1:9.)

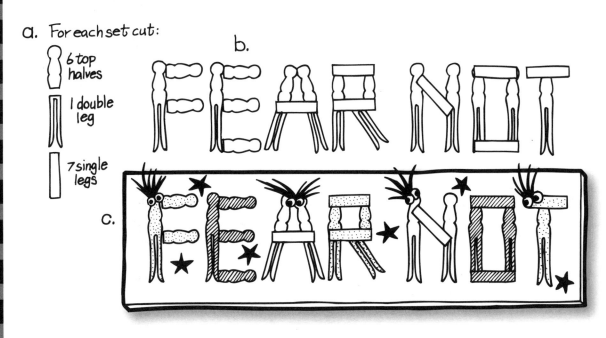

a. For each set cut:

6 top halves

1 double leg

7 single legs

b.

c.

Bible Verse

Materials: Bible, dry pasta suitable for beading (salad and elbow macaroni, rigatoni, penne, wheels, etc.), gold and/or silver metallic spray paint, clear jewel-colored pony beads, gold and silver cord, gold or silver chenille wire, transparent tape, measuring stick, scissors, shallow containers, newspaper.

Preparation: Cover work area with newspaper and spray paint pasta with gold and/or silver paint. Allow to dry. Turn pasta over and spray paint the other side. Cut cord into 3-foot (.9-m) lengths—one for each child. Wrap one end of each cord with tape. Tie the other end of each cord to a pony bead so that beads won't slide off while children are beading (sketch a). Place pasta in shallow containers.

Instruct each child in the following procedures:

★ To make necklace, string two or three pasta beads onto taped end of cord. Then add a pony bead "jewel" (sketch b).

★ Continue threading pasta and pony beads in the same manner until your necklace is finished.

★ With teacher's help, tie ends of cord together. Cut off the bead tied to cord end (sketch c).

★ To make bracelet, thread a few pasta and pony beads onto chenille wire.

★ With teacher's help, twist ends of wire together to finish bracelet (sketch d). Make bracelet large enough to slip over your hand. Teacher trims wire ends with scissors, if necessary, and bends ends to hide wire edge.

Conversation:

(Sarah), thank you for being patient while you waited for me to tie your necklace. That is a way to obey God's Word, the Bible. Our Bible says, with love help each other (see Galatians 5:13). **What are some other things you can do to help your friends?** (Share a new box of crayons. Help them learn a game, etc.)

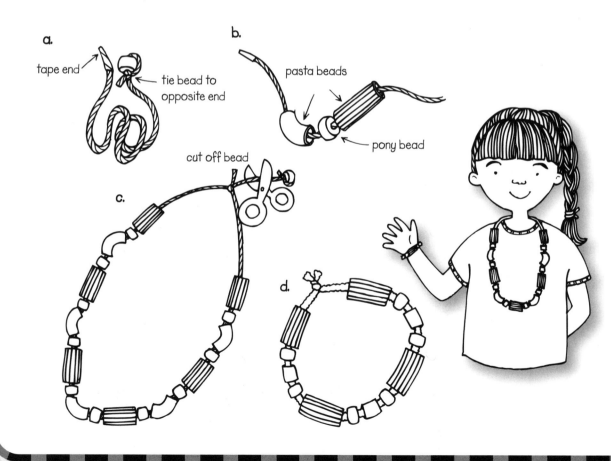

a. tape end / tie bead to opposite end

b. pasta beads / pony bead

c. cut off bead

d.

Materials: Bible, House Patterns, prepasted wallpaper scraps in a variety of small prints (include floral and foliage), pencil, scissors, ruler, craft knife, water, sponge brushes, shallow containers, damp sponges. For each child—one empty cereal box 2½ inches (6.25 cm) deep.

Preparation: Lay House Pattern on the corner of cereal box and trace outline. Repeat on opposite side of box. With craft knife or scissors, cut away box on lines to make napkin holder (sketch a). Cut out one napkin holder for each child. Trace door, roof and window patterns onto various wallpaper prints. Cut out two roof shapes, one door shape and four window shapes for each child. Cut wallpaper into 5x12½-inch (12.5x31.25-cm) rectangles—one for each child. Cut small bush shapes out of floral or foliage printed wallpaper—several for each child. Pour water into containers.

Instruct each child in the following procedures:

★ With sponge brush, brush the back of the large rectangle wallpaper piece with water to moisten wallpaper paste.

★ With teacher's help, lay piece on the front of napkin holder and wrap around the side and back of the house (sketch b). Smooth wallpaper down. Wipe excess paste, if needed, with damp sponge.

★ Brush water onto roof pieces and apply to house.

★ Apply windows, doors and bushes to house in the same manner.

★ Optional—Use felt, wrapping paper, construction paper or fabric instead of wallpaper.

Conversation:

You can use your house to hold paper napkins on your table at home. At mealtime you can tell your family that the Bible says, "God cares about you" (see 1 Peter 5:7). **God gives us food to show He cares about us!**

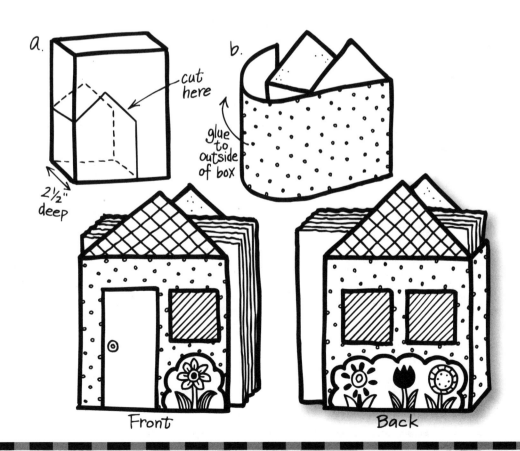

a. cut here

2½" deep

b. glue to outside of box

Front

Back

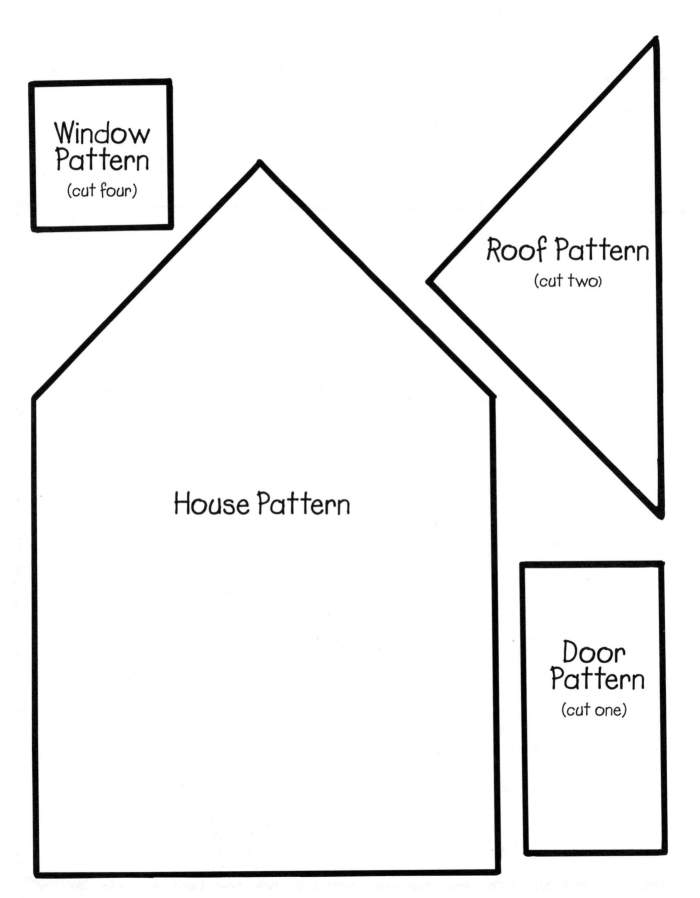

Window
Pattern
(cut four)

Roof Pattern
(cut two)

House Pattern

Door
Pattern
(cut one)

Bible Verse

Materials: Bible, pliers, wire cutters, 20-gauge wire, gravel, potting soil, large spoons, measuring stick, newspaper. For each child—one 4-inch (10-cm) flower pot, one small ivy plant.

Preparation: Cut the wire into 30-inch (75-cm) lengths—one for each child. Cover work area with newspaper.

Instruct each child in the following procedures:

- ★ Bend one end of wire into a circle shape, smaller than the bottom of flower pot (sketch a).
- ★ Bend opposite end of wire into a simple shape such as a heart, bird or star (sketch b).
- ★ Place circular end of wire into bottom of pot.
- ★ Cover bottom of pot with gravel.
- ★ Use spoons to fill pot with potting soil.
- ★ Place ivy plant in soil near wire (sketch c).
- ★ Twist ivy around wire.
- ★ Keep plant in a bright spot, away from direct sunlight. Water whenever soil feels dry, being careful not to overwater. As ivy grows it will continue to climb around wire shape (sketch d).

Simplification Idea: If pots are too expensive for a large group of children, plant ivy in milk cartons or tin cans.

Enrichment Idea: Use acrylic paints to decorate clay pots.

Conversation:

Topiary plants are plants cut or formed into familiar shapes or objects. Where will you put your Ivy Topiary? If I lay this plant on the sidewalk, will it grow? Why not? What does a plant need to be nourished and growing? What do we need to be nourished and to grow in our spiritual lives? Read Psalm 1:1-3 aloud. **What are ways we can grow in our relationship with God?** (Nourish our spiritual lives through reading the Bible, praying and worshiping God, both alone and with others.)

Bible Verse

Materials: Bible, Game Piece Patterns, construction paper in a variety of colors, photocopier, yarn, colorful fish or ocean theme stickers, glue, scissors, measuring stick, tape. For each child—one 12-inch (30-cm) stick or dowel, 12 small metal paper clips, one small round magnet, one plastic 2-liter bottle.

Preparation: Make copies of Game Piece Patterns on various colors of construction paper—four copies for each child. Cut the top off plastic bottles (sketch a)—one for each child. Cut yarn into 16-inch lengths—one for each child.

Instruct each child in the following procedures:

★ Open paper clips as shown (sketch b).
★ Cut out game pieces. Glue two identical game pieces together, placing opened paper clip between pieces (sketch c).
★ Tie yarn around one end of stick. Tape magnet to opposite end of yarn.
★ Decorate outside of plastic bottle with fish stickers.
★ Place fish, Jonah and Big Fish game pieces in bottle.
★ With one or two friends, take turns fishing. If you catch Jonah, you may use him for any part of the verse. If you catch the Big Fish, you may take a fish from any other player. The first player to place his or her fish in Bible verse order wins!

Conversation:

Who can say Galatians 5:6 in the correct order? (Volunteers respond.) **Loving others is a way we show our faith. How would you show love or kindness while playing your fishing game?** (Take turns. Don't cheat. Be a good sport whether you win or lose.) **When you love God and have faith in Him, He will help you show love to other people, too.**

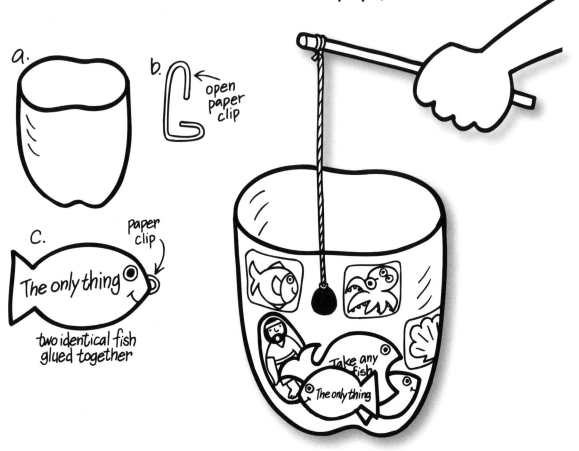

a.

b. ← open paper clip

c. paper clip

The only thing

two identical fish glued together

The only thing

Take any fish

The only thing

that counts is

The only thing

Jonah
Wild Card

faith expressing

itself through love.

Take any fish from any player.

Big Fish

Galatians 5:6

Bible Verse

Materials: Bible, Paddle Pattern, lightweight cardboard, pencils, ruler, scissors, plywood, jigsaw or scroll saw, sandpaper, acrylic paints in various bright colors, paintbrushes, shallow containers, ¼-inch (.625-cm) auto-detailing tape in a variety of colors, drill, ⅛-inch (.3125-cm) drill bit, newspaper, hammers. For each child—two toothed picture hangers with nails, four screw-in cup hooks.

DAY ONE Preparation: Trace Paddle Pattern onto cardboard, extending handle length where indicated (sketch a). Cut out. Trace pattern onto plywood. With saw, cut out paddle shape—one for each child. Drill four tiny starter holes on paddle for cup hooks (sketch c). Cover work area with newspaper. Pour paint into shallow containers.

Instruct each child in the following procedures:

★ Nail one picture hanger near each end of paddle (sketch b).

★ Sand paddle face and edges until smooth.

★ Paint paddle and allow to dry.

DAY TWO Preparation: Cut auto tape into 2-foot (60-cm) lengths—one for each child.

Instruct each child in the following procedures:

★ With pencil, sketch the words "Be Strong" on the paddle handle.

★ Cut auto-detailing tape into pieces to fit over sketched letters (sketch c).

★ Remove adhesive backing from tape and stick in place on paddle.

★ Add two bands of tape around end of handle (sketch c).

★ Screw hooks into starter holes.

★ Use your Kayak Paddle Plaque to hold your keys or camera.

Simplification Idea: Children hand letter "BE STRONG" with paint or permanent marker.

Conversation:

Who can say the rest of this verse—Deuteronomy 31:6? (Allow volunteers to quote verse.) **What are some things you do that make your body strong? Your mind strong?** (Students volunteer.) **What can we do that will make our faith strong?** (Pray, learn about God through His Word, learn from other people who know and trust Him.) **As our faith in God grows, He gives us more strength and courage, even when we feel afraid.**

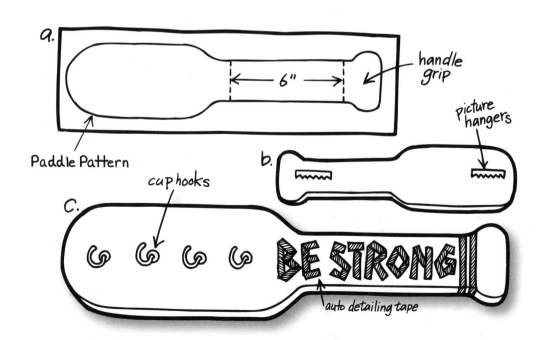

a. Paddle Pattern — handle grip — 6"

b. picture hangers

c. cup hooks — BE STRONG — auto detailing tape

KAYAK PADDLE PLAQUE PATTERNS

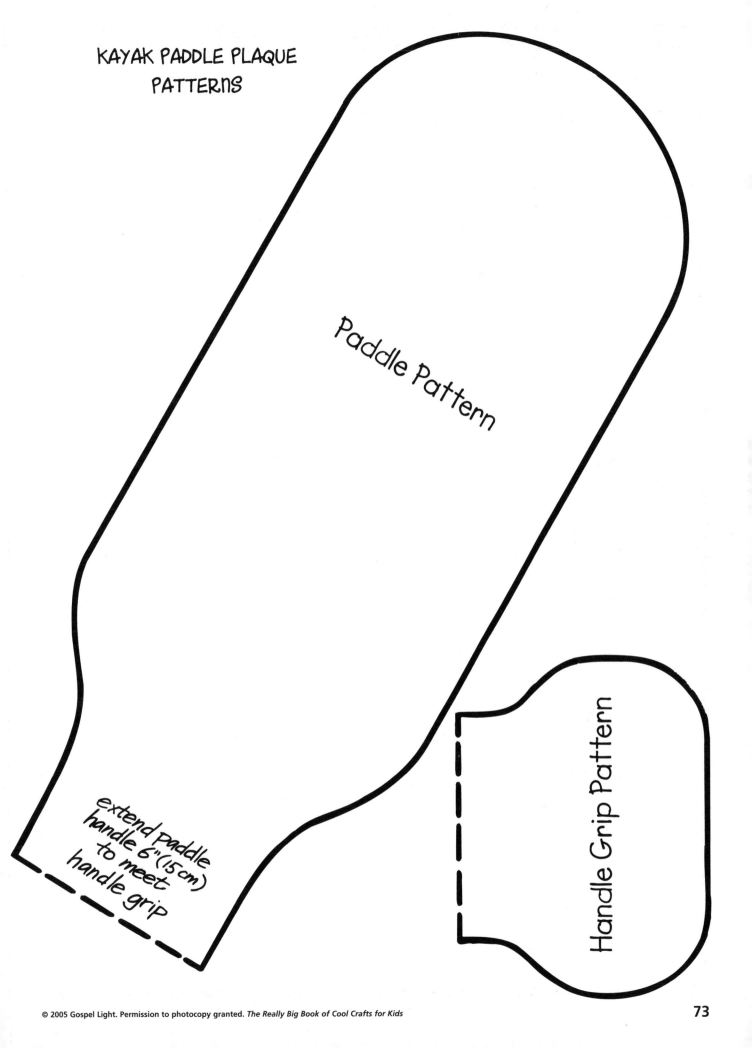

Paddle Pattern

extend paddle
handle 6" (15 cm)
to meet
handle grip

Handle Grip Pattern

Bible Verse

Materials: Bible, straight twigs or sticks, brown acrylic paint, 16-gauge wire, wire cutters, sandpaper, flathead nails, craft knife, craft glue, glue gun, glue sticks, scissors, stapler and staples, paintbrushes, shallow containers, ruler, newspaper. For each child—empty half-gallon cardboard milk carton.

Preparation: Cut off the bottom 3 inches (7.5 cm) of each milk carton and save both the top and bottom pieces. Then cut bottom pieces to a 1-inch (2.5-cm) height (sketch a). Cut sandpaper into 4x6-inch (10x15-cm) rectangles—one for each child. Cut wire into 12-inch (30-cm) lengths—one for each child. Plug in glue gun out of reach of children. Cover work area with newspaper. Pour paint into shallow containers.

Instruct each child in the following procedures:

★ Use point of scissors to poke hole in front side of top portion of milk carton, near center. Use hole to start cutting a 2-inch (5-cm) circle or square opening for birdhouse (sketch b).

★ Spread a thin layer of glue on all four exterior sides of bottom portion of milk carton. Insert bottom of carton into top of carton to make birdhouse floor (sketch c). Allow glue to dry.

★ Paint outside of milk carton. Allow paint to dry.

★ While paint is drying, break sticks so that they are approximately 4 inches (10 cm) long. Break some sticks into shorter pieces to fit around opening. (Each child should have enough sticks to cover front of birdhouse.)

★ Fold sandpaper in half and place on top of birdhouse for roof. Staple sandpaper across the top ridge (sketch d). Glue sandpaper onto roof.

★ With teacher's help, use a nail to poke two holes through top ridge. Thread ends of wire through holes to make hanger. Bend and twist ends up to secure hanger.

★ Lay birdhouse on back side so that opening faces up. Glue sticks horizontally onto front of birdhouse (sketch e). Allow glue to dry while birdhouse remains in this position. If some sticks are difficult to glue down, teacher may use glue gun to help sticks stay in place.

Simplification Idea: Instead of using sticks, decorate birdhouse with additional colors of paint, or use painted straws to cover front of birdhouse.

Enrichment Idea: Cover all sides of milk carton with sticks.

Conversation:

Some birds in your neighborhood will be happy to find the birdhouse you made! You have done a good thing for some birds. Read Galatians 6:10 aloud. **The Bible tells us to do good to everyone. What are ways we could help people in our church? What people in your neighborhood could also use your help? How could we help them?**

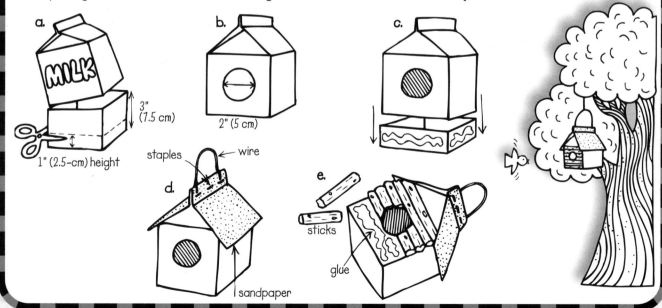

Bible Verse

Materials: Bible, Bookmark Patterns, individual photo of each child, gold and silver fine-tip metallic paint markers, sequins, photocopier, card stock in a variety of colors, glue, colored felt pens, scissors, pens or pencils.

Preparation: Photocopy Bookmark Patterns for appropriate age group onto colored card stock. Trim around outline of each child's photo.

Instruct each child in the following procedures:

✶ Cut out contrasting colors of front and back Bookmark Patterns.

✶ Write in the spaces provided on bookmark front to complete sentences and tell about self.

✶ Glue photo to the top of the unprinted side of bookmark back (sketch a).

✶ Glue bookmark front piece onto unprinted side of bookmark back (sketch b).

✶ Write name below photo and decorate bookmark front and back with felt pens, metallic paint markers and sequins (sketch c).

Conversation:

Show 1 Timothy 4:12 in Bible. **Our Bible verse says to set an example. What is a way you can set an example for others to follow at home? at school? at church?**

a.

b.

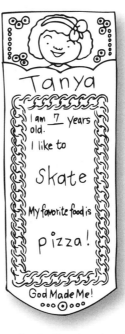

c.

glue photo

glue onto back

back bookmark piece   front bookmark piece   finished bookmark   back of bookmark

MAKING MY MARK BOOKMARK

Younger Elementary Bookmark Patterns

Bookmark Back

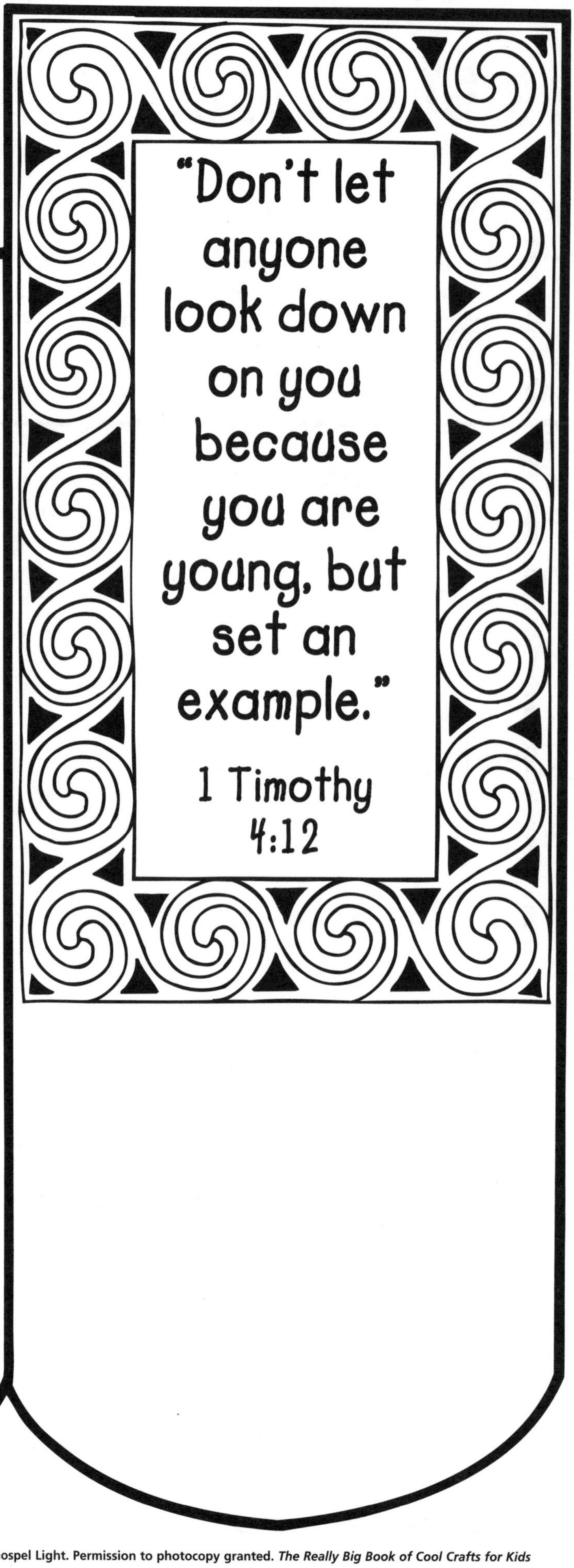
"Don't let anyone look down on you because you are young, but set an example."
1 Timothy 4:12

Bookmark Front

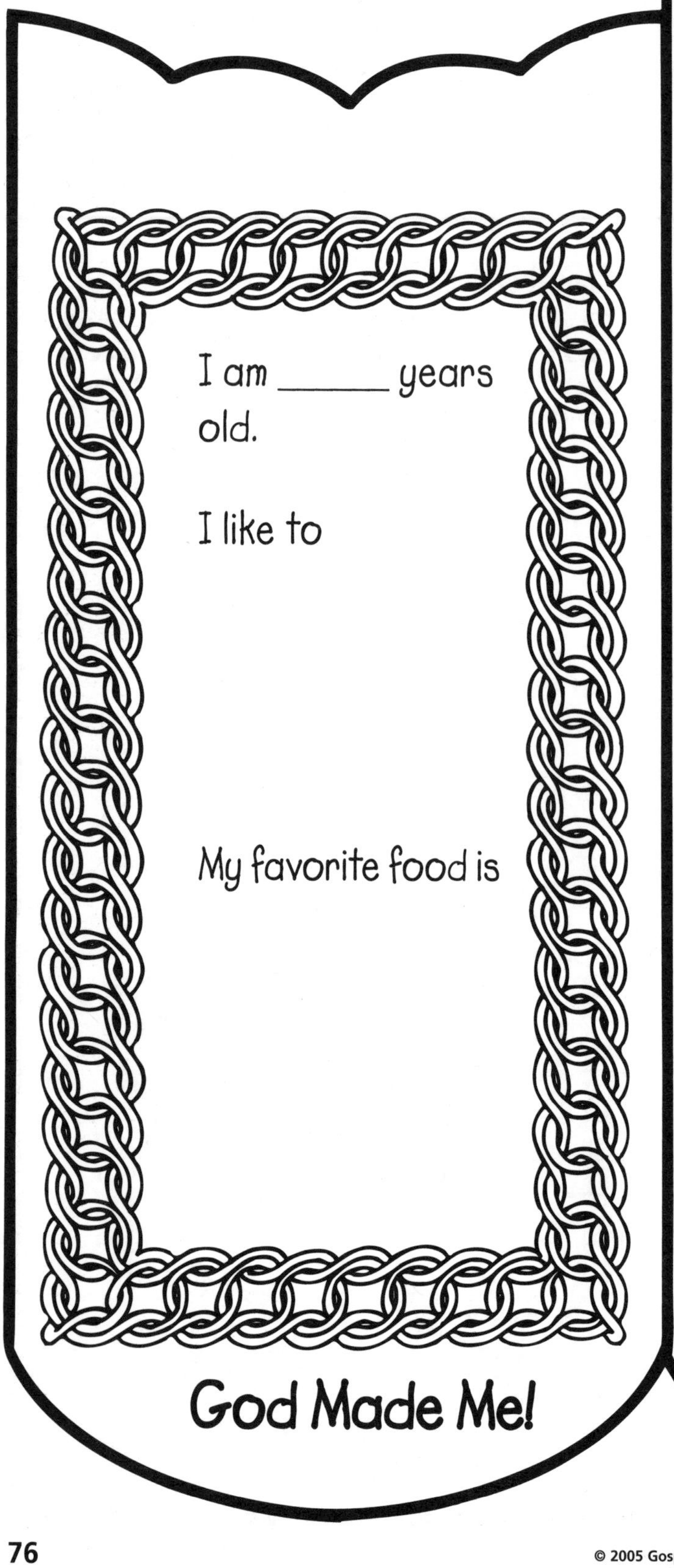
I am ______ years old.
I like to
My favorite food is
God Made Me!

MAKING MY MARK BOOKMARK
Older Elementary Bookmark Patterns

Bookmark Front

Bookmark Back

I am _____ years old.

I like to

My favorite food is

God Made Me!

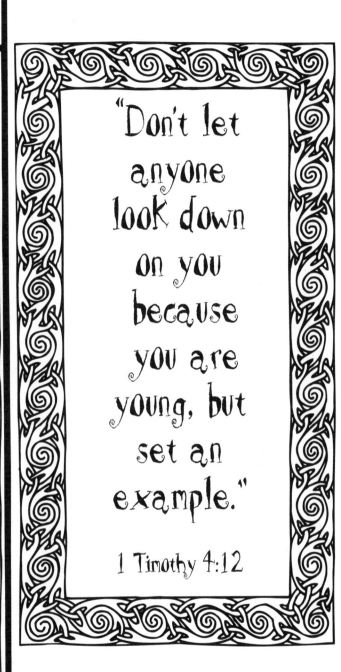

"Don't let anyone look down on you because you are young, but set an example."

1 Timothy 4:12

Bible Verse

Materials: Bibles, tempera paint in a variety of colors, paintbrushes, shallow containers, several kinds of discarded food containers (such as cereal or cracker boxes and milk cartons), cardboard, butcher paper, pencils, black felt pens, transparent tape, glue, craft knife, scissors, measuring stick, newspaper.

Preparation: Rinse out food containers and allow to dry. Cut cardboard into 1x2-foot (.3x.6-m) rectangles—one for each child. Cover work area with newspaper. Pour paint into shallow containers.

Instruct each child in the following procedures:

★ Choose several food containers to use for buildings.

★ With teacher's help, wrap each container in butcher paper or newspaper and secure with tape, as you would a gift (sketch a).

★ Paint each covered container to look like a house, store or other building.

★ Use felt pens to add familiar details so that buildings resemble structures in your town. Let dry.

★ Glue buildings onto cardboard base (sketch b).

★ Paint a street and sidewalk on cardboard base.

Simplification Idea: Use felt pens instead of paints to decorate buildings and street.

Enrichment Ideas: Use toilet paper tubes and construction paper to make trees, stop signs, traffic signals, vehicles and people figures to add to your city street. Children work in groups to make several streets, then place streets together to form a town.

Conversation:

What is on the street where you live? What do you like about your street? What do you dislike? Does everyone on your street get along? What might help people on your street be better friends? The Bible says to "love your neighbor as yourself" (Matthew 22:39). **Who are your neighbors? What is a way you can show love to them?**

a.

b.

Bible Verse

Materials: Bibles, gold metallic spray paint, ribbon, gold rickrack, acrylic jewels, construction paper, ruler, glue, scissors, newspaper. For each child—one cardboard tea box with flip-top lid, one round self-adhesive Velcro fastener.

Preparation: For each tea box—cut one construction paper rectangle measuring the width of tea box and the combined length of the back, top and an additional 1½ inches (3.75 cm). Cut one construction paper strip 1½ inches (3.75-cm) wide and 1½ inches (3.75 cm) longer than the construction paper rectangle. Photocopy Bible verses and cut apart into 2-inch (5-cm) strips. Children roll up scrolls and tie with yarn. Children fill trunks with verses.

Instruct each child in the following procedures:

★ Open box top and cut off side flaps. Bend top to form a curved "trunk" lid (sketch a).

★ Glue paper strip down the center of construction paper rectangle. One end of strip will extend 1½ inches (3.75 cm) past the edge of rectangle (sketch b).

★ Glue rectangle onto back of box and over lid. Construction paper should extend 1½ inches (3.75 cm) past the edge of lid (sketch c).

★ With teacher's help, lay box on newspaper in a well-ventilated area and spray entire box, inside and out, with gold spray paint. Allow to dry a few minutes.

★ Cut pieces of gold rickrack and ribbon, and glue pieces to box to decorate like a trunk (sketch d).

★ Attach the Velcro rounds together. Remove adhesive backing from both sides.

★ Attach one side of Velcro to underside of extending strip. Then press the other side onto the trunk front to close lid (sketch d).

Conversation:

Your Verse Trunk is your workmanship. You made it. You created it. The Bible says, "For we are God's workmanship, created in Christ Jesus to do good works" (Ephesians 2:10). What does the Bible mean when it says we are God's workmanship? (God made or created us.) **God created you to do good things. What are some good things you have done lately? What are some good things you have noticed other people doing?**

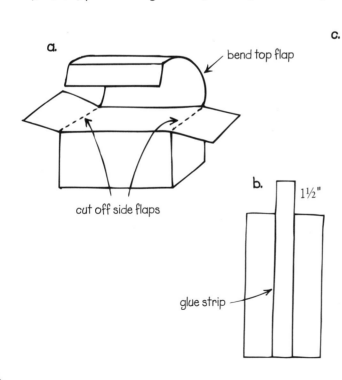

a.

bend top flap

cut off side flaps

b.

1½"

glue strip

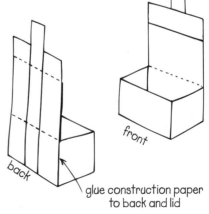

c.

back

front

glue construction paper to back and lid

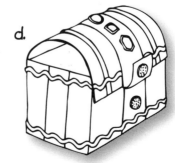

d.

Materials: Bibles, cinnamon-spice scented potpourri, coffee scoops or small-sized measuring cups, tan construction paper, toothpicks, hot glue gun and glue sticks, orange and brown felt pens or crayons, pencils, ruler, scissors, shallow containers.

Preparation: Cut construction paper into 5-inch (12.5-cm) squares—one for each child. Trace around a pie pan to make a circle on each tan square. In the center of each circle, use a brown felt pen to write the words "DO GOOD." Place potpourri in shallow containers. Plug in glue gun out of reach of children.

Instruct each child in the following procedures:

★ Cut out the construction paper circle.
★ With felt pens or crayons, draw short lines around the edge of circle to look like a baked crust (sketch a).
★ Use scoop or measuring cup to fill your pie pan with potpourri.
★ Teacher squeezes hot glue on edge of pie pan and glues tan circle on top for pie crust (sketch b). Allow glue to cool.
★ Use a toothpick to punch holes in the crust, on the lines of the words "DO GOOD" (sketch c).
★ Smell your pretend pie! Mmmmmm...

Enrichment Idea: Have children mix potpourri together using cinnamon sticks, wood shavings, scented oils, lavender, dried flowers, etc.

Conversation:

(Kristen), what is your favorite kind of pie? (Child responds.) **You can't eat your potpourri pie. It's just pretend. But it smells wonderful! Our Bible says, "God made us to do good"** (see Ephesians 2:10). **What is a way you can do good with your pie?** (Give to a friend.)

a. draw "crust" lines

DO GOOD

b. DO GOOD

potpourri

glue pie pan edge

c. punch holes with toothpick

DO GOOD

Bible Verse

Materials: Bible, salt or fine sand, electrical tape, clock or watch with a second hand, measuring cups, funnels, decorative cording or ribbon, fabric, 3-dimensional paints in metallic colors, rubbing alcohol, lightweight cardboard, pencils, hole punch, craft glue, scissors, paper towels, newspaper. For each child—one small bowl, two identical individual-sized clear plastic water bottles.

Preparation: Peel labels off plastic bottles. Apply rubbing alcohol with paper towels to remove any remaining adhesive. Cover work area with newspaper.

Instruct each child in the following procedures:

* Trace around the opening of a bottle onto lightweight cardboard. Cut out circle (sketch a).

* With hole punch, punch a hole in the middle of cardboard circle.

* Use funnel to fill bottle with two cups of salt or sand.

* Set bowl next to you. Hold cardboard circle firmly on top of bottle opening.

* Teacher uses watch to time two minutes. When teacher signals to start, turn bottle upside down over bowl, holding cardboard firmly against bottle opening (sketch b). Allow salt or sand to flow through cardboard hole into bowl for exactly two minutes. At teacher's signal, quickly turn bottle right side up.

* Discard sand that is left in bottle. Then use funnel to pour the sand from bowl back into the empty bottle.

* Glue cardboard circle to bottle opening. Then glue the opening of the second bottle on top (sketch c).

* Wrap electrical tape around bottle necks to secure.

* Tie or glue ribbon or cording over electrical tape to decorate. (Note: Keep sand glass upright while decorating so that sand does not stick to any wet glue.)

* Use metallic paints to decorate bottles. Write the words of Psalm 31:15 on the bottle. Use paint sparingly, so sand can still be seen through the bottles (sketch d). Allow paint to dry several hours or overnight.

* When paint and glue are dry, turn the sand glass upside down to time anything for two minutes. Use it for games, doing chores and taking turns.

Conversation:

Before people had clocks and watches, they used other ways to tell time. Sometimes people used hourglasses similar to the two-minute sand glass you made. They also used sundials, but not all the time. Why? (They could only be used when the sun was shining.) **Water clocks told time by how much water dripped into a jar, but they couldn't be used all the time either.** Read Psalm 31:15 aloud. **No matter how we tell time, King David said all our times are in God's hands. When we're hurried or worried, that's a good thing to remember!**

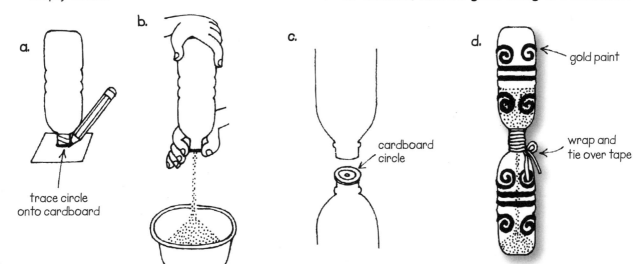

a. trace circle onto cardboard

b.

c. cardboard circle

d. gold paint

wrap and tie over tape

Bible Verse

EARLY CHILDHOOD • YOUNGER ELEMENTARY • OLDER ELEMENTARY

Materials: Bible, narrow ribbon, wide-tip felt pens in various colors, scissors, ruler. For each child—5¾x1-inch (1.9x2.5-cm) wooden spools, one chenille wire.

Preparation: Cut chenille wires into 6-inch (15-cm) lengths—two lengths for each child. Cut ribbon into 6-inch (15-cm) lengths—one for each child.

Instruct each child in the following procedures:

★ Use felt pens to decorate spools.

★ Thread three spools onto one piece of chenille wire. Allow about a 1-inch (2.5-cm) gap between top two spools. Bend each end of wire and tuck into spool to make a small loop at each end (sketch a).

★ Twist the second wire length horizontally to the vertical wire between top two spools (sketch b).

★ Thread one spool onto each end of second wire. Push spools toward center of cross until they nearly touch.

★ Bend and tuck each end of second wire into spool to make a loop on each end.

★ Thread ribbon through wire loop at top of cross, tie knot and trim ends (sketch c). Twist wire loop to secure.

★ Bend remaining loops on both sides and bottom to secure spools.

Simplification Idea: Leave spools uncolored.

Enrichment Idea: Glue strips of fabric or ribbon around spools.

Conversation:

What does the cross remind us about? (Children respond.) Read John 3:16 aloud. **Your Spool Cross can remind you that Jesus loved you so much that He died on a cross. He did it so that you can be part of God's family and have eternal life!**

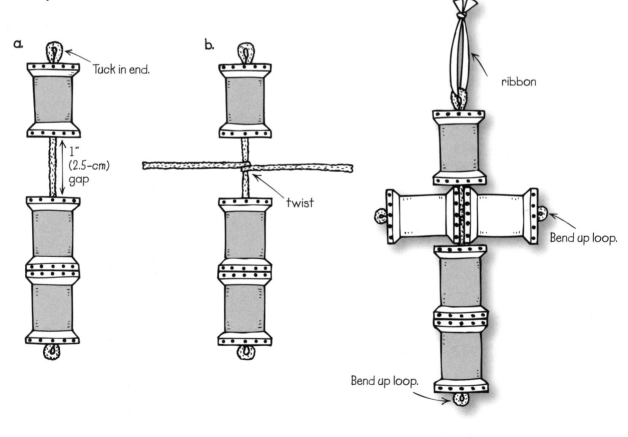

a. Tuck in end.

1" (2.5-cm) gap

b. twist

ribbon

Bend up loop.

Bend up loop.

Bible Verse

Materials: Bible; white paper; pencils; wide and fine-tip black permanent felt pens; food coloring in blue, red, yellow and green; white glue; paintbrushes; poster board; scissors; ruler; hole punch; ribbon; tape; shallow containers; newspaper. For each child—one overhead transparency or one 8½x11-inch (21.5x27.5-cm) sheet of heavy clear plastic. *Optional*—one suction hook for each child.

Preparation: For the frame, cut poster board into 10½x1-inch (26.25x2.5-cm) and 13x1-inch (32.5x2.5-cm) strips—four strips of each length for each child. Pour glue into shallow containers. Mix food coloring in glue to make several colors of glue paint. Cover work area with newspaper.

Instruct each child in the following procedures:

★ On paper, sketch a simple picture of a hot air balloon in the sky. Add a rainbow, clouds, landscape, etc.

★ Tape transparency on top of sketch (sketch a).

★ With wide-tip black felt pen, trace all lines of sketch onto transparency. Remove paper sketch.

★ With fine-tip felt pen, letter "Trust in the Lord and do good. Commit your way to the Lord. Psalm 37:3,5" on bottom of picture. Allow 1-inch (2.5-cm) margin for frame.

★ Glue four poster board strips around the edges of picture to make a frame on one side of transparency.

★ Turn picture over and glue remaining poster board strips to the back, aligning edges with front pieces (sketch b). Trim pieces if necessary.

★ Punch two holes in the top of the frame.

★ Cut a 12-inch (30-cm) length of ribbon and thread through holes. Knot ends to make hanger (sketch c).

★ Turn transparency over to backside and paint inside black outlines with colored glue. Allow to dry.

Simplification Idea: Eliminate poster board frame and punch holes directly in transparency for hanging.

Enrichment Idea: Give each child a suction hook to hang picture in a window.

Conversation:

Read Psalm 37:3,5 aloud from your Bible. **What do balloon pilots need to trust when they fly in hot air balloons?** (The weather, their equipment, their crew, their training, God.) **The Bible says that we can always put our trust in God. When we commit ourselves to doing the good things that God wants us to do, we can count on Him to help us follow through. We can trust God to help us do what's right.**

Bible Verse

Materials: Bible, Castle Picture, square-shaped cereal (such as Chex), 1-inch (2.5-cm) wide ribbon, photocopier, white Card stock, colored felt pens, ruler, fabric scissors, all-purpose scissors, glue, shallow containers. For each child—two craft sticks.

Preparation: Photocopy Castle Picture onto card stock—one for each child. Use all-purpose scissors to cut craft sticks in half—four halves for each child. Use fabric scissors to cut ribbon into 1½-inch (3.75-cm) pieces—two for each child. Cut half the ribbon pieces in half diagonally to make pennants—two pennants for each child. Cut the remaining ribbon pieces into banner shapes—one for each child (sketch a). Pour cereal into shallow containers. Pour glue into other shallow containers.

Instruct each child in the following procedures:

* Color the banner above the door with a light-colored felt pen.

* Glue craft sticks onto door of castle.
* Dip pieces of cereal into glue, one at a time, and stick on castle bricks.
* Glue ribbon pieces to flag poles to make pennants and banner (sketch b). Allow glue to dry.

Enrichment Idea: Fold back the sides of poster board to make castle stand.

Conversation:

The banner above your castle door says, God made us to do good (see Ephesians 2:10)**. (Laurin), what can you do to help (your mom/friend/teacher)?** (Child responds.) **When you (feed the cat) you are doing good. God wants us to do good things!**

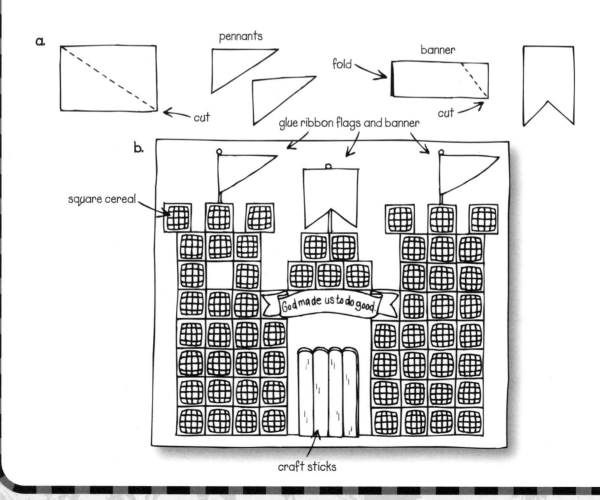

a.

pennants

fold

banner

cut

cut

glue ribbon flags and banner

b.

square cereal

God made us to do good.

craft sticks

STONE CASTLE PICTURE

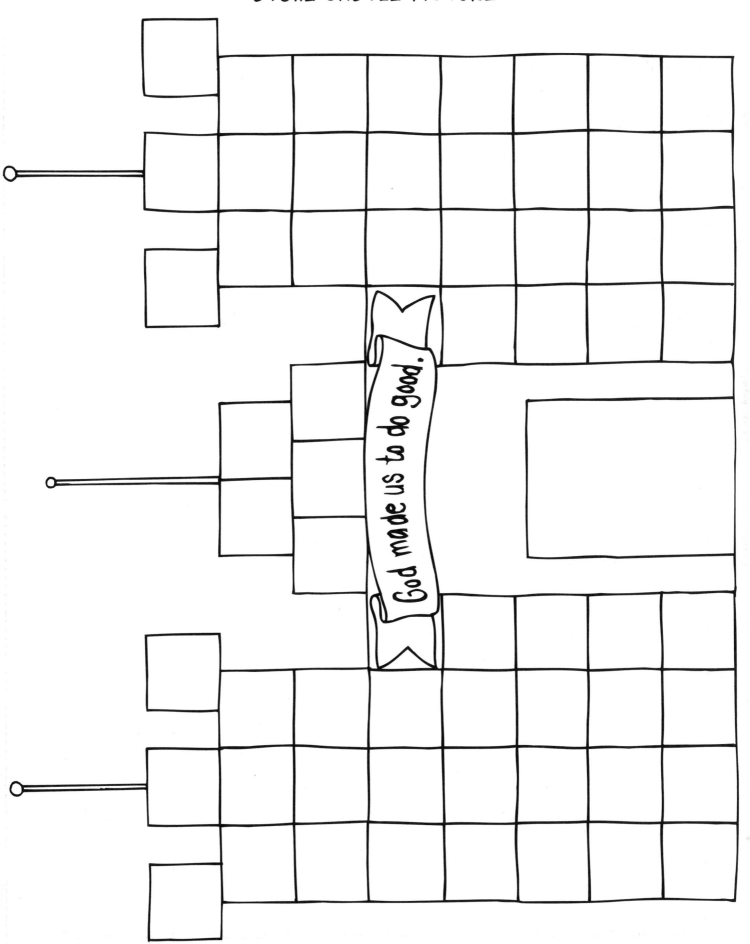

God made us to do good.

Bible Verse

Materials: Bible, paint pens in gold and white, damp paper towels, craft glue. For each child—five smooth flat stones (available in bulk at most garden centers), five ½-inch (1.25-cm) round, heavy duty magnets.

Instruct each child in the following procedures:

★ Use damp paper towels to clean off surface of stones.

★ Use white paint pen to write a memory verse, or significant words from a Bible verse (BELIEVE, OBEY, LOVE, PRAY, TELL OTHERS) on each stone. Use gold paint pen to decorate stones. Allow paint to dry.

★ Glue a magnet to the back of each stone. Allow glue to dry.

★ Display stones on your refrigerator or some other magnetic surface.

Conversation:

Read aloud a Bible verse you have selected. **What words from this verse can you write on your stones? Put your magnets in a place you see often to remind you of these five important nuggets of truth! It's a way to remind us of God, so we can grow in our relationship with Him.**

magnet

back of stone

Believe God's Promise

SPEAK TRUTH

God ♥ U!

LOOK UP!

Bible Verse

Materials: Bible, Storefront Patterns, corrugated cardboard, poster board in various colors, photocopier, card stock, wide- and fine-tip felt pens in various colors, pencils, glue, heavy-duty scissors, scissors, craft knife, ruler. For each child—two tongue depressors, five craft sticks, one self-adhesive picture hanger.

Preparation: Photocopy Storefront Patterns onto card stock and cut out several patterns. Use craft knife to cut cardboard into 8x10-inch (20x25-cm) rectangles—one for each child. Then cut a 2x3-inch (5x7.5-cm) opening on the right side of each cardboard rectangle, about 2 inches (5 cm) from bottom and 1 inch (2.5 cm) from right edge (sketch a). Use heavy-duty scissors to cut some of the craft sticks into 3-inch (7.5-cm) lengths—two for each child. Cut off rounded ends of additional craft sticks—one for each child (sketch b).

Instruct each child in the following procedures:

⋆ Trace Roof, Door and Sign Patterns onto poster board and cut out.

⋆ Fold and glue poster-board roof (sketch c).

⋆ Use wide-tip felt pens to color one side of each craft stick and tongue depressors.

⋆ Glue short craft sticks on top and bottom of window frame opening. Glue long craft sticks on each side of frame opening, overlapping short craft sticks (sketch d).

⋆ Use felt pen to draw door handle and details on poster-board door. Glue door onto bottom edge of frame approximately 1 inch (2.5 cm) from left side (sketch e).

⋆ Glue a tongue depressor on each side of door. Glue remaining craft stick at top of door.

⋆ Glue back edge of roof onto frame, right above door (sketch f).

⋆ Use felt pens to create a personalized store or business sign on poster board. Glue sign right above roof.

⋆ Attach picture hanger to back of frame, near the top.

⋆ At home, tape wallet-size photo to back of frame and hang.

Enrichment Idea: Use a thin-tip felt pen to make horizontal lines along the width of cardboard to make siding. Take photographs of each child; children tape photos to back of frames.

Conversation:

In many places, there are no malls or big stores. Instead, there is a general store. General stores carry a little bit of everything. Sometimes store owners build the fronts of their stores to look much taller than they actually are. Why do you think they do this? (To look more impressive.) **Because of this kind of building, we sometimes say a person is "putting up a front." What do you think this saying means?** (Pretending to be something that you're not.) **The Bible tells us, "Accept one another . . . just as Christ accepted you"** (Romans 15:7). **The more we accept others the way they are, the less likely they will be to want to "put up a front."**

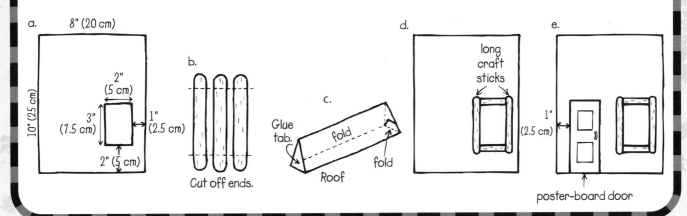

a. 8" (20 cm) / 10" (25 cm) / 2" (5 cm) / 3" (7.5 cm) / 1" (2.5 cm) / 2" (5 cm)

b. Cut off ends.

c. Glue tab. fold fold Roof

d. long craft sticks

e. 1" (2.5 cm) poster-board door

STOREFRONT PICTURE FRAME PATTERNS

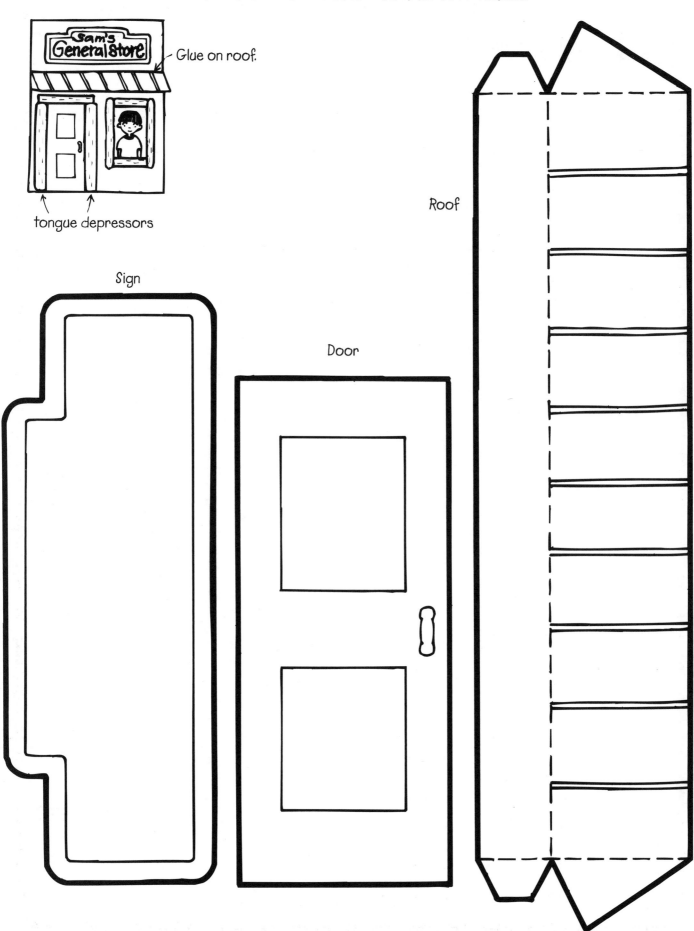

Glue on roof.

tongue depressors

Sign

Door

Roof

Bible Verse

Materials: Bible, Sunset Silhouette Patterns, colored ink stamp pads in a variety of sunset colors (orange, pink, lavender, red, blue), pencil, old sponges, 9x12-inch (22.5x30-cm) white construction paper, 12x18-inch (30x45-cm) black construction paper, scissors, glue, transparent tape, black felt pens, newspaper.

Preparation: Trace patterns onto black construction paper and cut out—one for each child. Tape two sheets of white construction paper together—one set for each child (sketch a). Cut additional white construction paper into rectangle pieces to use for writing verses—one for each child. Dampen sponges and cut into 2-inch (5-cm) squares. Cover work area with newspaper.

Instruct each child in the following procedures:

* Tear off bottom fourth of top sheet of white construction paper (sketch b).
* Press sponge piece onto ink pad. Beginning at torn edge of paper, press sponge onto exposed paper and rub downward (sketch c). Fill exposed area with ink color.
* Tape torn paper back in place to cover painted area (sketch d).
* Tear off another piece of top paper about the same width (sketch e).
* Choose another color of ink and paint second exposed section using same method as above.
* Repeat procedure to paint a total of four different sections of paper with four different colors.
* Take off taped sections of paper.
* Glue hot air balloon and rider silhouettes onto painted paper.
* Letter Bible verse onto construction paper rectangle.
* Glue painting and verse onto black construction paper (see sketch f).

Conversation:

Show Psalm 37 in your Bible. **The verse on your picture says, "Trust in the Lord and do good"** (Psalm 37:3). **When is it difficult to do good toward someone?** (Children respond.) **Your silhouette picture can remind you to ask God to help you (be kind to a friend who says mean things). You can trust God to help you do what is right.**

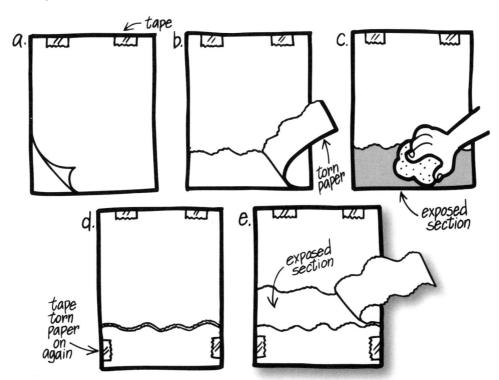

SUNSET SILHOUETTE PATTERNS

f.

"Trust in the Lord and do good." Psalm 37:3

BALLOON RIDER PATTERN

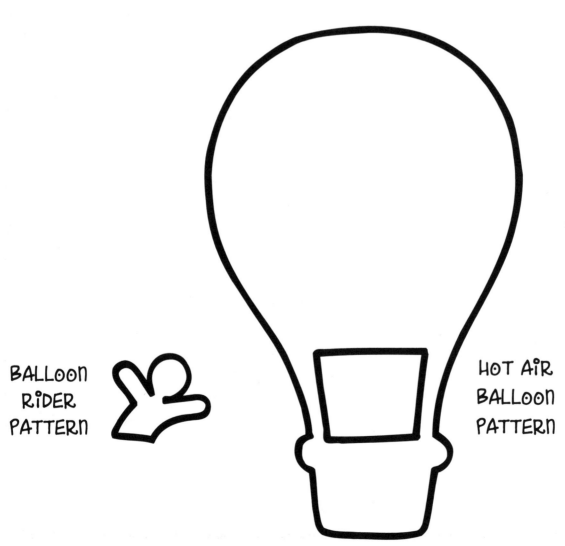

HOT AIR BALLOON PATTERN

Materials: Bible, brown acrylic paint, brown Fun Foam, black elastic, masking tape, scissors, hole punch, sponge brushes, ruler, shallow containers, newspaper. For each child—one plastic baby-wipe box with flip-up lid, one western concho (available at craft stores).

Preparation: Cut elastic into 3½-inch (8.75-cm) lengths—two for each child. Cut Fun Foam into 2-inch (5-cm) squares—one for each child. Use point of scissors to cut two vertical slits in front edge of each box lid, near the center (sketch a). Use scissors to poke a small hole in box front, near the center (sketch a). Cover work area with newspaper. Pour paint into shallow containers.

Instruct each child in the following procedures:

✶ Cover top and all four sides of box with short pieces of masking tape. Overlap and crisscross if desired.

✶ Use sponge brush to wipe paint over masking tape.

✶ Cut Fun Foam square into decorative shape. Punch two holes near middle of shape.

✶ Thread one elastic piece through slits in top. Tie ends of elastic together inside the box to make a loop in front.

✶ Thread second elastic piece through foam shape and concho and then through hole in front of box (sketch b). Tie ends together tightly, inside box.

✶ Close lid by stretching elastic loop over concho.

Simplification Idea: For younger children, tear masking tape into approximately 4-inch (10-cm) lengths ahead of time and stick to edge of table.

Conversation:

Your boxes look like wooden trunks. People used to pack their belongings in big trunks, load everything in wagons and travel for months to move to their new homes. Today, when we move, we pack boxes and suitcases. We probably have a truck to help us move. But no matter where we go, our Bible says, "The Lord himself goes before you and will be with you"(see Deuteronomy 31:8).

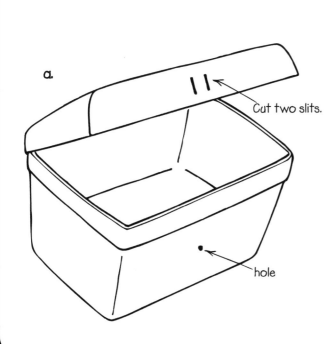

a.

Cut two slits.

hole

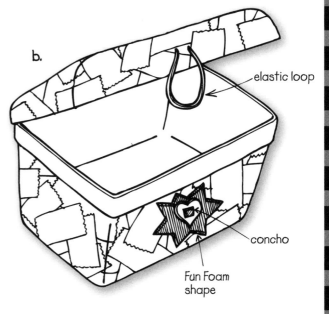

b.

elastic loop

concho

Fun Foam shape

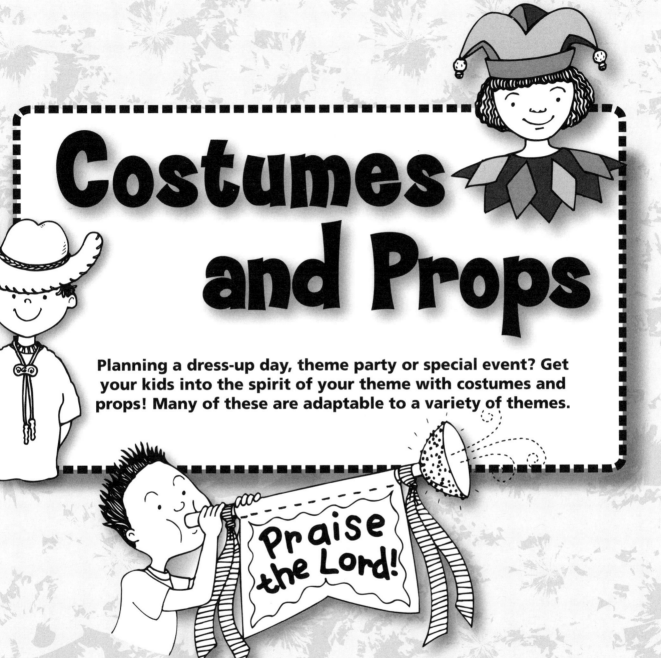

Costumes and Props

Planning a dress-up day, theme party or special event? Get your kids into the spirit of your theme with costumes and props! Many of these are adaptable to a variety of themes.

Praise the Lord!

Costumes and Props

Materials: Bolo Tie Patterns, white poster board, gold and silver crayons, aluminum foil, drinking straws, crayons in bright colors, pencil, transparent tape, scissors, ruler. For each child—one toothpick, one black or brown boot shoelace at least 18 inches (45 cm) long.

Preparation: Trace Bolo Tie Patterns onto poster board and cut out—one shape for each child. Cut foil into 1x3-inch (2.5x7.5-cm) rectangles—two for each child. Cut drinking straws into 1-inch (2.5-cm) lengths—one for each child.

Instruct each child in the following procedures:

★ Choose a bolo shape from poster board cutouts. Use a bright-colored crayon to color one side of poster board.

★ Rub a thick layer of silver or gold crayon on top of colored layer.

★ Use end of toothpick to scratch a design through crayon layer.

★ Tape straw piece to uncolored side of poster board (sketch a).

★ Fold shoelace in half. Thread folded side of shoelace through taped-on straw piece.

★ Wrap a piece of foil at each end of shoelace (sketch b).

★ Place bolo tie over your head. Adjust by sliding bolo up or down.

Simplification Idea: Instead of poster board cutouts, children use felt pens to decorate a wooden spool as the bolo. Girls may want to make a spool necklace instead of bolo tie.

Conversation:

Bolo ties were popular in the Old West. Many men still wear them when they dress up for church. What do you wear to church? What do you like best to do there?

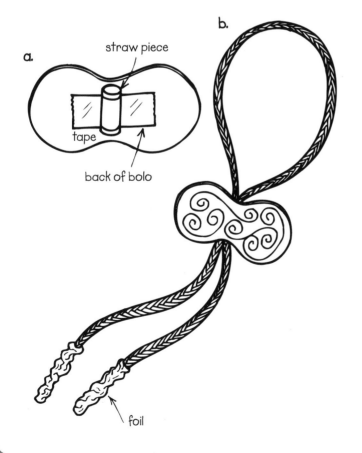

a. straw piece
tape
back of bolo

b.

foil

BOLO TIE PATTERNS

Costumes and Props

Materials: (makes two capes) Fabric 45 to 60 inches (1.12-to 1.5-cm) square (fake fur, velvet, brocade, satin, etc.), sewing machine and thread or craft glue, thin ribbon, fabric scissors, measuring stick, pen.

Instructions:

★ Fold fabric into fourths and cut the unfolded corner of fabric in a curve (sketch a). Open fabric. Cut circle in half. Use one half-circle for each cape.

★ In the center of the straight edge of cape, cut a half-circle about 6 inches (15 cm) wide for neckline (sketch b).

★ Sew or glue a hem along all edges.

★ Use scissors to make holes in corners of neckline.

★ Cut two 2-foot (60-cm) lengths of ribbon. Thread a ribbon through each hole, pull ends even and knot. Tie a knot in ribbon ends to keep them from unraveling.

★ Place cape around neck and tie ribbons together (sketch d).

Conversation:

What might you wear today in place of a cape? How is it better than a cape? How is a cape better? Let's thank God for the clothes He gives us!

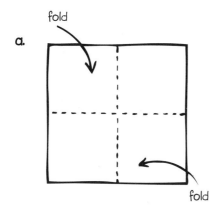

a.

fold

fold

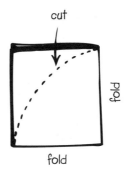

cut

fold

fold

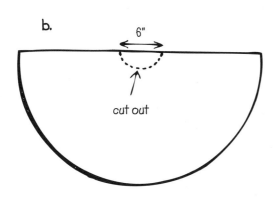

b.

6"

cut out

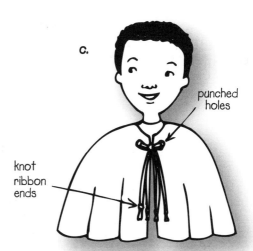

c.

punched holes

knot ribbon ends

Materials: Corncobs; fabric markers; acrylic paint in various colors; disposable plastic plates; solid, light-colored fabric; pencil; measuring stick; fabric scissors; paper towels; soap and water for cleanup; newspaper.

Preparation: Break large corncobs in half. Allow corncobs to dry out. Cut fabric into 18-inch (45-cm) squares—one for each child. Cover work area with newspaper. Pour small amount of paint onto disposable plates. Place a corncob on each plate.

Instruct each child in the following procedures:

✶ Use fabric marker to draw a design or write name around edge of bandana to make a border (sketch a).

✶ Roll corncob into paint and then roll across bandana (sketch b). Continue with various colors if desired. Allow paint to dry.

✶ Clean hands with soap and water and dry with paper towels.

Simplification Idea: Instead of using fabric markers, use cut vegetables such as mushroom halves, carrot pieces or celery stalks dipped in paint to make prints along the border.

Conversation:

(Andy), you listened to my directions. (Karina), you obeyed when I asked you to (put the corncob back on the plate). Thank you. You did what the Bible says to do. Our Bible says, "We will listen and obey" (Deuteronomy 5:27).

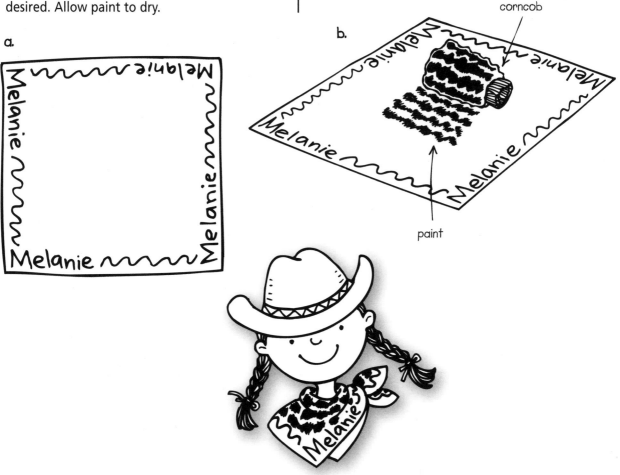

a.

b.

corncob

paint

Costumes and Props

Materials: Lightweight cardboard, yellow and orange tissue paper, solid-colored wrapping paper, squeeze bottles of colored glue, construction paper, pencil, glue sticks, transparent tape, scissors, hole punch, ruler. For each child—toilet paper tube, small solid-colored paper plate, drinking straw.

Preparation: Cut wrapping paper into 4½x6½-inch (11.25x16.25-cm) rectangles—one for each child. Place end of tube on center of paper plate and trace around it. Cut out traced circle from each paper plate. Cut construction paper into 2½-inch (6.25-cm) circles—one for each child. Punch a hole in center of each circle. Cut cardboard into shape of flame, approximately 1½x2 inches (3.75x5 cm) long (sketch a)—one flame for each child. Cut 3 inches (7.5 cm) off each straw. Cut two small slits at one end of each straw (sketch b). Insert cardboard flame into slits at end of straw and tape to secure (sketch c).

Instruct each child in the following procedures:

✶ With teacher's help, glue wrapping paper rectangle around tube (sketch d).

✶ Spread glue stick on one side of cardboard flame. Tear small pieces of yellow and orange tissue paper and press onto cardboard to cover flame (sketch e).

✶ Repeat to cover other side of flame; then trim edges with teacher's help.

✶ Insert end of tube through hole in paper plate. With teacher's help, tape tube onto plate to secure (sketch f).

✶ Tape construction paper circle over hole in plate (sketch g).

✶ Dribble glue all around outside top edge of candle. Allow glue to drip and dry for several hours to look like candle wax.

✶ Place straw into candle and through punched hole at bottom. Raise and lower flame by pulling straw up and down (sketch h).

Simplification Idea: Teacher uses hot glue to attach end of tube to top of uncut paper plate. Fill tube with candy or other goodies, insert straw and give to a neighbor.

Conversation:

What are candles used for? Back in the Old West, people used candles for light. They did not have lamps like we have today. There is a song called "This Little Light of Mine." Have you ever heard it? Sing one verse of song if possible. Raise and lower flame along with the song. **We are like candles shining when we show God's love to others.**

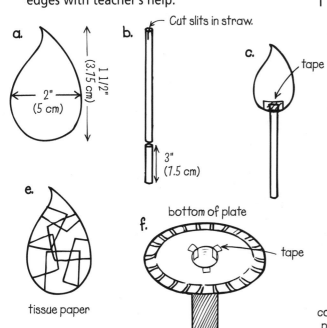

a. 2" (5 cm) 1 1/2" (3.75 cm)

b. Cut slits in straw. 3" (7.5 cm)

c. tape

e. tissue paper

f. bottom of plate — tape

g. Tape construction-paper circle.

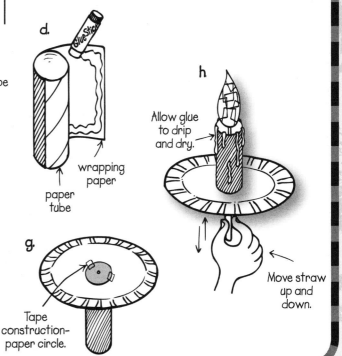

d. Glue Stick — wrapping paper — paper tube

h. Allow glue to drip and dry. — Move straw up and down.

Costumes and Props

Materials: Solid-colored fabric, fabric scissors, measuring stick, pencil.

Instructions:

★ Cut fabric into an 18x24-inch (45x60-cm) rectangle.

★ Fold the rectangle in half and cut out a half circle about 6 inches (15 cm) wide in the center on the fold (sketch a).

★ Cut a 3-inch (7.5-cm) slit in neck hole (sketch b).

★ Cut the shorter edges of collar in a jagged or scalloped pattern.

★ Place head through neck hole (slit in front) to wear collar.

Conversation:

Does your shirt have a collar? How is that collar like the one we're making? How is it different? What's your favorite piece of clothing? Let's thank God for clothes!

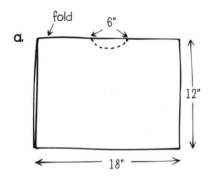

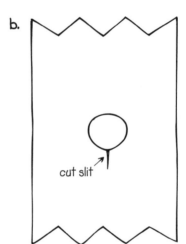

Costumes and Props

Materials: Tulle netting off the roll, assorted colors of curling ribbon, white electrical tape, white floral tape, white cloth-covered wire, sprays of silk flowers, wire cutter, pliers, scissors, measuring stick. For each child—thin wire clothes hanger.

Preparation: Straighten clothes hangers and cut with wire cutter to approximately 25 inches (62.5 cm). Cut ribbon into 6-foot (1.8-m) lengths—four for each child. Cut tulle into 2-foot (60-cm) lengths—one for each child. Use wire cutter to cut flowers apart, including a few inches of leaves and stems for each flower. Cut white cloth-covered wire into 6-inch (15-cm) lengths—one for each child.

Instruct each child in the following procedures:

★ Use pliers to bend both ends of hanger into small hooks. Join hooks together to form the hanger into a ring. Squeeze hooks closed with pliers.

★ Wrap a piece of electrical tape around hooks to cover ends (sketch a). This is the back of the garland.

★ Beginning at the center front of ring, lay a flower stem on the wire with flower facing toward the front. Wrap floral tape around stem and ring to secure. Then lay another flower stem next to the first one, facing front, and continue wrapping stem and ring (sketch b). Continue adding flowers until you reach the back of ring. Wrap end of tape around ring to secure. Repeat process on the other half of ring.

★ Fold tulle in half. Form a loop by twisting a length of white wire around tulle about 4 inches (10 cm) below the fold. Secure tulle to back of wreath by twisting remaining wire around ring (sketch c). Let ends of tulle fall freely from the back of garland.

★ Match the centers of four ribbon lengths to the front center of garland. Loosely wind ribbons around one side of garland, ending at the back (sketch d). Repeat on other side.

★ Knot ends of ribbon together on top of gathered tulle. Use scissors to gently curl ribbons and let them fall from back of garland.

★ You may wear your flower garland in your hair or hang it on a door for decoration.

Conversation:

People are always glad for springtime and warmer weather after a cold, dreary winter. People often weave garlands of flowers, herbs and leaves to wear in their hair to celebrate spring. What are some things God made in nature that you especially appreciate? How could you celebrate? (Thank God, praise Him, spend a day hiking, plant some flowers, share an outdoor hobby with a friend, etc.)

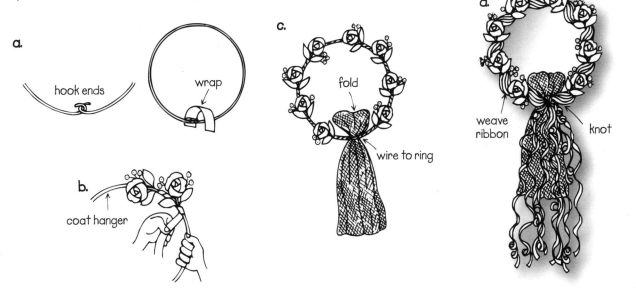

a. hook ends / wrap

b. coat hanger

c. fold / wire to ring

d. weave ribbon / knot

Materials: Envelope Pattern, white electrical tape, colored candles, matches, metal seals or embossed metal buttons with shanks, photocopier, ecru-colored copier paper, scissors, newspaper or butcher paper. For each child—one large feather, one thin ballpoint or felt-tip pen.

Preparation: Photocopy Envelope Pattern onto ecru paper—one copy for each child. Cover work area with newspaper or butcher paper.

Instruct each child in the following procedures:

★ Cut a length of white tape.

★ Hold pen next to the feather. Starting at the bottom of pen, wrap tape around pen and feather quill to hold together securely. Make sure you don't cover the tip of pen (sketch a).

★ Halfway up the pen, stop wrapping both the feather and pen together; but continue to wrap only the pen until it is covered (sketch b).

★ Cut out paper envelope.

★ Inside the dotted-line area of envelope, use your feather pen to write a message or draw a picture to give to someone. Or you may write on a separate piece of paper to tuck inside the envelope.

★ Fold envelope along dotted lines, with lines on the inside of envelope. If adding a separate note, fold so it fits and place inside. Fold all flaps down to close envelope (sketch c).

★ Turn envelope over and write the name of the person who will receive the letter.

★ Turn envelope back over. With teacher's help, light a candle and hold it over where the flaps meet. Allow candle wax to drip and form a circle. Let wax cool slightly and then press a metal seal or button into the wax to make a seal. Lift button off carefully to see the impression (sketch d).

★ Deliver your message personally or send a friend as a herald to deliver your message for you!

Conversation:

A long time ago, people used goose feathers called "quills" as pens. A small slit was cut in the end of the feather quill. When the pen was dipped in ink, the quill held a small amount of the ink. Since there wasn't a post office, a messenger or a herald delivered the message. Often the herald had to read the message aloud. Do you know why? (Many people couldn't read.) **In what ways do we send messages today?** (E-mail, telephone, mail, fax, etc.)

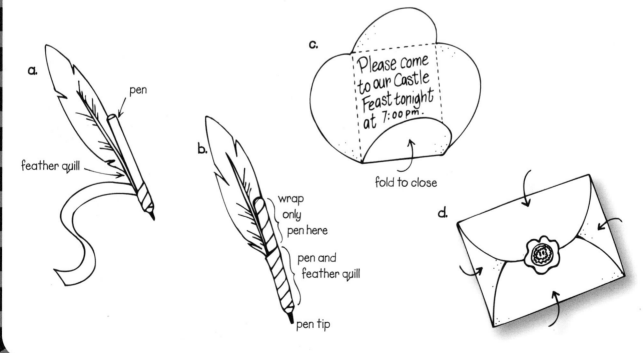

a. pen

feather quill

b. wrap only pen here

pen and feather quill

pen tip

c. "Please come to our Castle Feast tonight at 7:00 pm."

fold to close

d.

FEATHER PEN WITH SEALED MESSAGE
ENVELOPE PATTERN

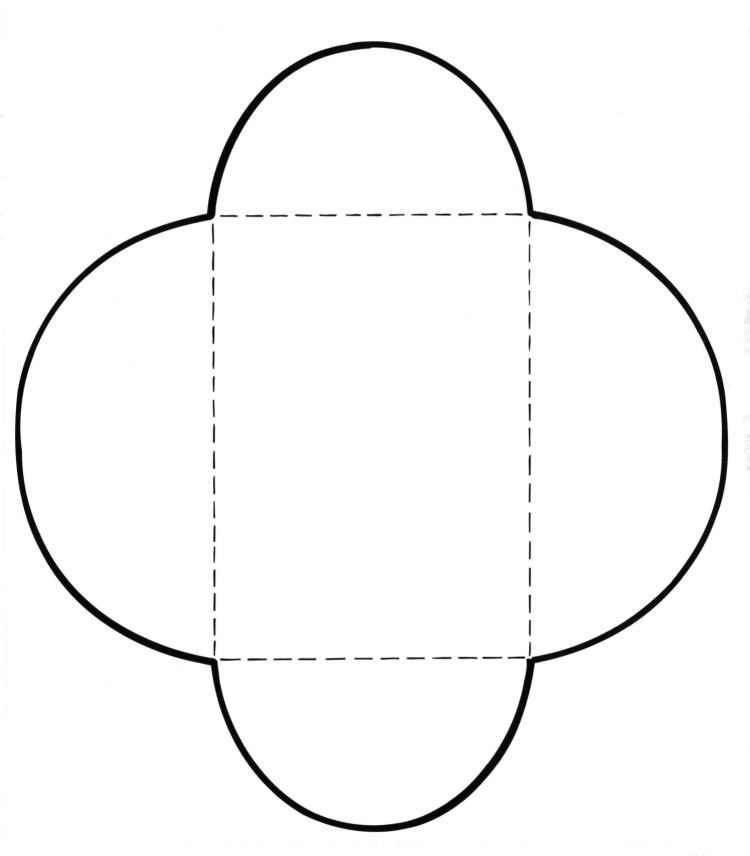

Costumes and Props

FELT HAT
(TWO-DAY CRAFT/ 15-20 MINUTES EACH DAY)

Materials: Brown felt, burlap, leather lacing, cotton string, plastic spoon, large shallow container, felt pens, glue, several pairs of fabric scissors, measuring stick, water, newspaper. For each child—large-sized whipped topping container.

DAY ONE Preparation: Cut felt into 22-inch (55-cm) squares—one for each child. Cut string into 28-inch (70-cm) lengths—one for each child. Cut burlap into 1x28-inch (2.5x70-cm) strips—one for each child. Cover work area with newspaper. Pour equal parts glue and water into large container and mix with plastic spoon.

Instruct each child in the following procedures:

- ✷ Immerse felt square in glue mixture. Carefully wring out excess liquid.
- ✷ Lay whipped topping container facedown on table.
- ✷ Drape felt over container and smooth material around the edges.
- ✷ Tie string around base of hat (sketch a). Set hat aside to dry for at least 4 hours.
- ✷ Use felt pens to decorate burlap strip.

DAY TWO Preparation: Cut leather lacing into 14-inch (35-cm) lengths—two for each child.

Instruct each child in the following procedures:

- ✷ When hat is dry, carefully remove from container, leaving string attached. Trim around edge of hat to make a 3-inch (7.5-cm) brim (sketch b).
- ✷ Glue burlap strip around base of hat to cover string.
- ✷ Use scissors to snip a small hole on each side of hat, near the base. Tie end of each leather lace in a knot and thread through each hole (sketch c).
- ✷ Put hat on head and tie laces together to fit under chin.

Conversation:

In the Old West, boys and men wore hats practically all the time to protect their faces from the sun and dust. One of the few times they took off their hats was when they were praying. Why do you think they took their hats off before praying? (To show honor and respect to God.) **What are some things we do to help us pray?** (Fold our hands. Close our eyes. Kneel.) **All these things help us to focus on God, but it's great to know that God wants us to talk to Him anytime and anywhere—hat or no hat!**

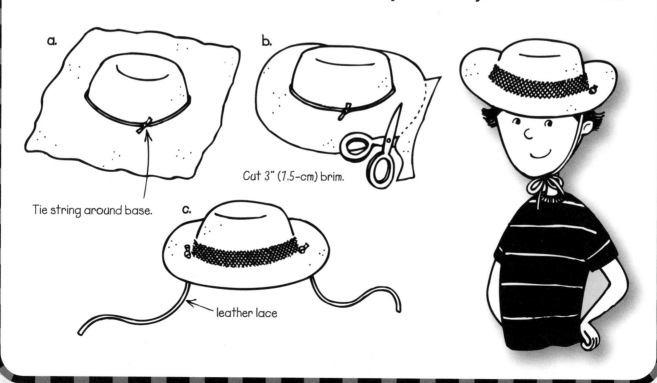

a. Tie string around base.

b. Cut 3" (7.5-cm) brim.

c. leather lace

Costumes and Props

Materials: Patch Patterns, photocopier and copier paper, crayons, glue sticks, masking tape, scissors. For each child—paper grocery bag.

Preparation: Cut grocery bags as shown in sketch a—one bag for each child. Turn bags inside-out so that printing is on the inside. Tape the sides closed. Attach masking tape around neck opening to reinforce and soften edges (sketch b). Photocopy Patch Patterns onto paper—one copy for each child.

Instruct each child in the following procedures:

★ Use scissors to cut fringe around bottom edge of vest (sketch b).

★ Color patches and cut out. (Younger children will need help with cutting.)

★ Glue patches to vest.

Enrichment Ideas: Paint vest before gluing on patches. Use glitter, decorative-edged scissors and felt pens to embellish patches.

Conversation:

Cowboys and cowgirls used to wear vests. What kinds of chores do you think they did? (Children respond.) **They took care of the cows and herded them to places to eat green grass. Who takes care of you and gives you good things to eat?** (Parents. God.) **God loves us and takes care of us. You can tell other people that God loves them, too. Let's read the good news on your vests. You can tell other people to read the words on your vests!**

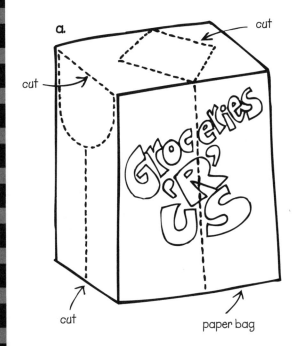

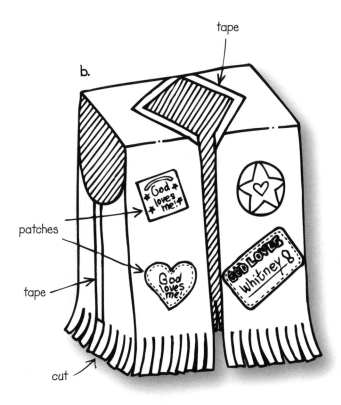

FRONTIER VEST PATCH PATTERNS

GOD LOVES

Costumes and Props

Materials: Bible, sandpaper, crepe paper streamers in a variety of colors, gold acrylic paint, gold glitter, duct tape, butcher paper, paintbrushes, scissors, colored felt pens, stapler and staples, measuring stick, newspaper. For each child—one 2-liter plastic soda bottle, one gift-wrap cardboard tube.

DAY ONE Preparation: With scissors, cut off the top third of each soda bottle (sketch a). Cut off bottom portion of soda bottles to make shallow containers. Pour paint into shallow containers. Cover work area with newspaper.

Instruct each child in the following procedures:

★ Use sandpaper to lightly sand outside of soda bottle top so paint will adhere to plastic.

★ Cut four small slits at one end of tube (sketch b).

★ Insert neck of bottle top into cut end of tube. Wrap duct tape around the slits to hold bottle securely in place.

★ Stand the trumpet on bottle end. Paint the entire trumpet with gold paint.

★ Brush a second coat of paint on only the bottle part of trumpet. While paint is still wet, sprinkle lightly with gold glitter. Set aside to dry.

DAY TWO Preparation: Cut butcher paper into 18x28-inch (45x70-cm) rectangles—one for each child. Fold each butcher paper rectangle in half and staple 3 inches (7.5 cm) from folded edge to make casing (sketch c). Cut streamers into 48-inch (1.2-m) lengths—two for each child. Write short Bible verses on additional butcher paper to display.

Instruct each child in the following procedures:

★ Cut unstapled edge of butcher paper banner into a V shape (sketch c).

★ Use felt pens to copy a Bible verse from display in front of class on one or both sides of banner. Decorate banner with felt pens.

★ Slide tube of trumpet through casing of banner (sketch d).

★ Tie streamers on both sides of banner.

Conversation:

In castle times, a herald's job was to deliver messages. Sometimes a herald blew a trumpet to get everyone's attention. Then he read the message aloud to all the people listening. A herald's job was important because most people couldn't read. They learned the latest news from the herald. How do we get news or messages from people today? (Telephone, e-mail, television, letters, etc.) **God has given us His messages. They are in the Bible. And the very best news is that God sent His Son, Jesus, to show us His love. That's good news we can announce to everyone!**

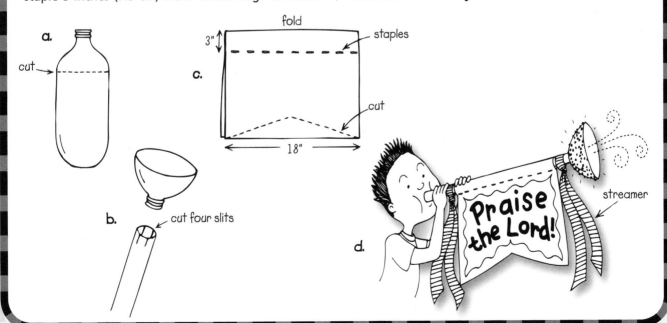

a. cut

fold

3"

staples

c.

cut

18"

b. cut four slits

Praise the Lord!

streamer

d.

Costumes and Props

Materials: 2x18-inch (30x40-cm) sheets of construction paper, colored felt pens, scissors, pen, measuring stick, glue, stapler and staples. For each child—one feather.

Preparation: On construction paper sheets, measure and draw triangles 16 inches (40 cm) wide and 9 inches (22.5 cm) tall (sketch a)—two triangles of the same color for each child. Cut out.

Instruct each child in the following procedures:

★ With teacher's help, stack two paper triangles together and fold the longer edges of triangles up diagonally (sketch b). This folded portion is the hat brim.

★ Separate the two papers. Fold one paper's brim back to the opposite side of paper.

★ Align the papers together, with brim sections facing out. Fold brims down. With teacher's help, staple hat sides together, stopping at fold (sketch c).

★ Fold brim up and staple the extending brim edges together (sketch d).

★ Decorate your hat with felt pens. Write your name on the hat brim.

★ Glue the feather inside hat brim (sketch d).

Enrichment Idea: Teacher makes hats out of felt instead of construction paper. Staple, sew or glue sides of hats together. Children decorate with felt pens, fabric paint or glued-on felt shapes.

Conversation:

(Evan), you can pretend that you live in Europe, long ago. Hunters wore hats like this. In those days, everyone wore hats. Their hats showed the kind of work they did. What work did God give you to do? How do you help at home? What do you sometimes have to hunt for?

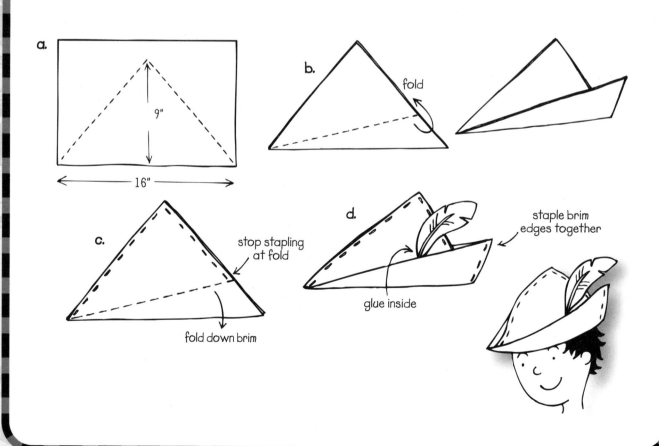

a.

9"

16"

b.

fold

c.

stop stapling at fold

fold down brim

d.

staple brim edges together

glue inside

Costumes and Props

Materials: Jester Collar and Diamond Patterns, black felt off the bolt, felt in assorted bright colors, ¼-inch (625-cm) satin ribbon, straight pins, fabric scissors, measuring stick, pen, craft glue.

Instruct each child in the following procedures:

★ Cut black felt into a 20-inch (50-cm) square.

★ Fold the felt square in quarters.

★ Pin Collar Pattern on felt with fold lines laying on folds of felt. Cut out through all thicknesses (sketch a).

★ Remove pattern and pins. Open felt collar.

★ Cut through one point of collar to open (sketch b).

★ On either side of collar opening, cut a small slit ½ inch (1.25 cm) from neckline corner (sketch c).

★ Cut two 2-foot (60-cm) lengths of ribbon. Thread a ribbon through each slit and pull ends even.

Knot ribbons to make collar ties. Tie a knot in each of the ribbon ends to keep them from unraveling (sketch d).

★ Choose the colors you would like to use for the diamonds on your collar. Lay diamond pattern on felt, trace and cut out. Cut out eight felt diamonds in two or four colors.

★ Glue each diamond between black collar points, with top of diamonds touching the neckline (sketch e).

★ When glue is dry, tie collar around neck, with ties in back.

Conversation:

Jesters often told stories and sang songs. What's a story you can tell? A song about God you can sing? Who do you know needs to hear the good news of God's love?

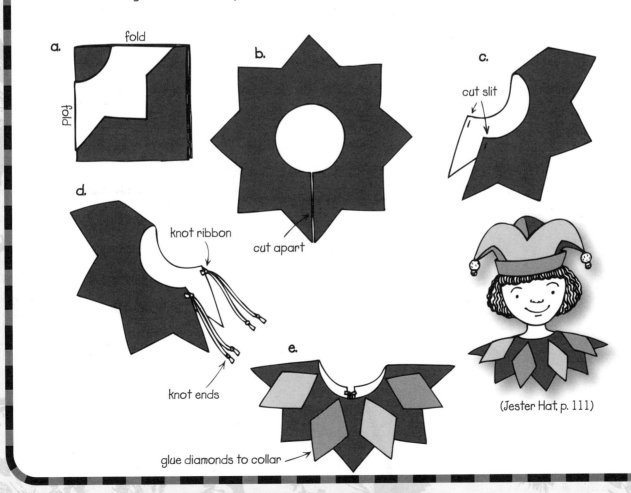

a. fold / fold

b. cut apart

c. cut slit

d. knot ribbon / knot ends

e. glue diamonds to collar

(Jester Hat, p. 111)

JESTER COLLAR PATTERN

Place on fold

DIAMOND PATTERN

Costumes and Props

Materials: Jester Hat Pattern, felt in a variety of colors, black felt off the bolt, straight pins, sewing machine and black thread, three jingle bells, three large black pom-poms, fabric scissors, pen, measuring stick. Optional—black crochet thread, crewel needle.

Instruct each child in the following prcedures:

✶ Trace Jester Hat Pattern onto three different colors of felt and cut out.

✶ Sew the three hat pieces together only on the sides indicated on pattern, using a ¼-inch (.625-cm) seam (sketch a). Turn hat right side out.

✶ Cut black felt into a 21½x3-inch (53.75x7.5-cm) strip.

✶ To make the band of the hat, sew the short ends of the black felt strip together with a ¼-inch (.625-cm) seam. Place the band inside the hat with the right side of band facing the inside (sketch b). Sew the band to the hat with a ¼-inch (.625-cm) seam.

✶ Pin one triangle of the hat to an adjoining different-colored triangle, matching the edges and the points. Pin the remaining triangles to adjoining triangles to make three pinned sections

✶ Sew the pinned edges of the triangle sections with sewing machine and thread (sketch c).

✶ *Optional:* Hand-sew edges together using crewel needle and black crochet thread.

✶ Cut three 6-inch (15-cm) lengths of crochet thread. Thread the ends through the shanks of jingle bells and knot securely (sketch d).

✶ Tie each bell around the diameter of a pom-pom and knot securely. Trim ends of thread.

✶ Glue each pom-pom and bell to the pointed ends of hat. Allow to dry. Turn band up along seam.

Conversation:

What other kinds of hats do you wear? What's a story about Jesus you can tell? A song about Jesus you can sing? Who will you invite to hear you tell a story, dressed in your jester hat?

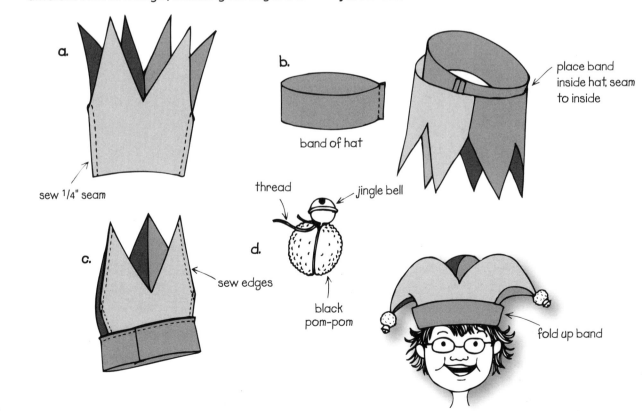

a. sew ¼" seam

b. band of hat | place band inside hat, seam to inside

c. sew edges

thread — jingle bell

d. black pom-pom

fold up band

JESTER HAT PATTERN

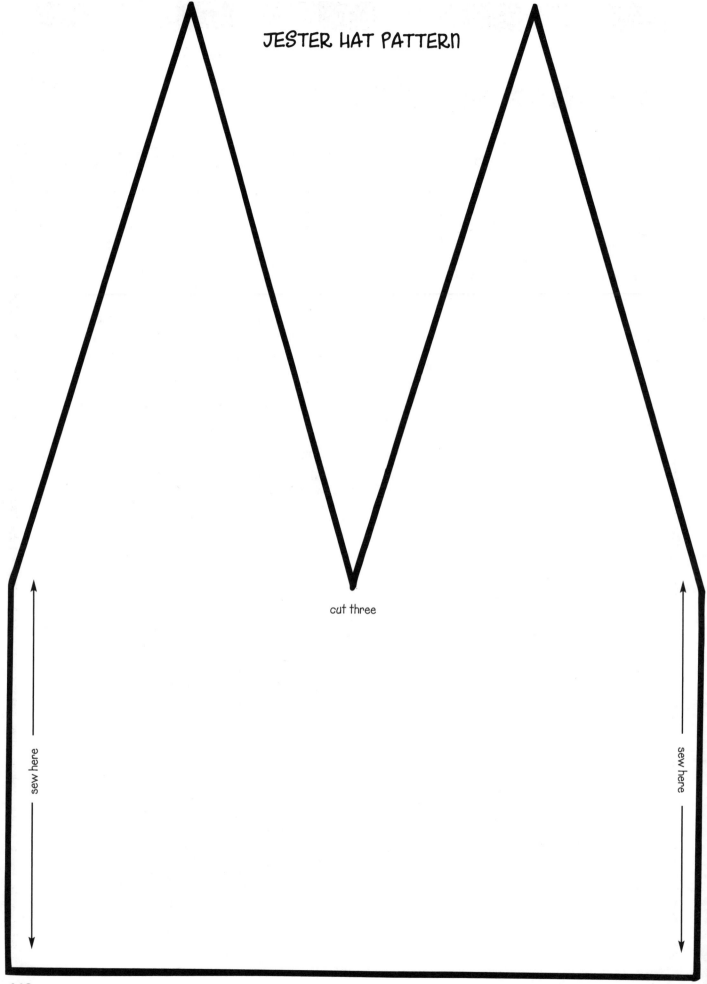

cut three

sew here

sew here

Costumes and Props

Materials: Several magazines, brightly colored fabric, aquarium rocks, 1-inch (2.5-cm) diameter wooden dowels, funnels, saw, colored felt pens, shallow containers, craft glue, scissors, fabric scissors, ruler. For each child—one plastic water bottle with wide base, three jingle bells.

Preparation: Cut large facial features out of magazines—two eyes, one nose and one mouth for each child. Cut fabric into 2x8-inch (5x20-cm) triangles as shown in sketch a and glue a jingle bell on the end of each triangle—three triangles for each child. Cut dowels into 1-foot (30-cm) lengths—one for each child. Place aquarium rocks in shallow containers.

Instruct each child in the following procedures:

⭐ Decorate the dowel with felt pens.

⭐ Lay bottle on table, with opening facing you. Glue magazine cutouts onto bottle to make jester face (sketch b).

⭐ Use funnel to pour a small amount of aquarium rocks into bottle.

⭐ Glue one end of dowel into the opening of bottle.

⭐ Glue the wide end of each fabric triangle to top of bottle and allow glue to dry (sketch c).

⭐ When glue has dried, use your Joyful Jester Shaker to cheer up someone!

Simplification Ideas: For younger children, cut circles out of construction paper and have them draw faces. Glue faces onto bottles.

Conversation:

In a castle, the jester worked for the king. The jester's job was to tell funny jokes and riddles and make people laugh. What makes you laugh? (Volunteers respond.) **Sometimes people like to be cheered up when they are sad or tired. (Katie), what are some things you can do to make your mom smile?**

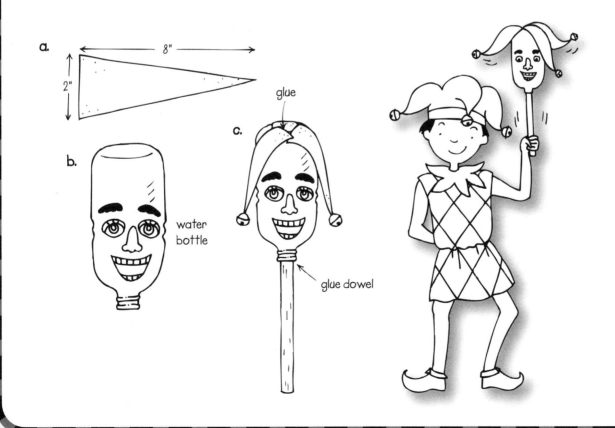

a.
8"
2"
glue

b.
water bottle

c.
glue dowel

Costumes and Props

Materials: Brown or tan fabric (simulated suede or cotton/polyester blend), straight pins, fabric scissors, butcher paper, pencil, scissors.

Instruct each child in the following procedures:

★ To make shoe pattern, trace around your foot on butcher paper, adding about 3 inches (7.5 cm) all around (sketch a). Cut out pattern.

★ Pin pattern to a double thickness of fabric. Cut out two shoes.

★ Cut ½-inch (1.25-cm) slits about 1 inch (2.5 cm) apart all the way around each shoe, ½ inch (1.25 cm) from the edge (sketch b).

★ Cut two 6-inch (15-cm) circles from fabric scraps. Make laces by cutting a strip ½ inch (1.25 cm) wide starting at the outside edge of each circle and spiraling to the center (sketch c).

★ Starting at the heel of shoe, thread lace through the slits, evening out the ends of lace.

★ Place your foot in the center of shoe piece and pull lace to gather shoe around foot. Crisscross lace around ankle and calf and tie in the back (sketch d).

Conversation:

Where are some places you would not want to walk in these shoes? Why? How are your shoes different from the ones you wore today? No matter what shoes you wear, God is with you wherever you go!

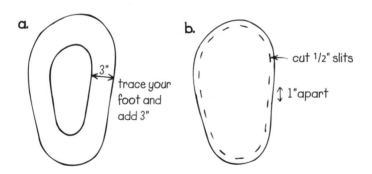

a. trace your foot and add 3"

b. cut ½" slits — 1" apart

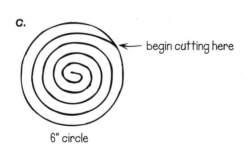

c. begin cutting here — 6" circle

Costumes and Props

Materials: Pouch Flap Pattern, brown fabric-backed vinyl, leather punch or heavy-duty paper hole punch, yarn, fabric scissors, pen, crayons or felt pens, measuring stick. For each child—thirteen ½-inch (1.25-cm) brass paper fasteners, two jingle bells, small wood or cardboard circle shapes for coins (Woodsie brand available at craft stores).

Preparation: Cut vinyl into 6x15-inch (15x37.5-cm) rectangles—one for each child. Lay Pouch Flap Pattern at one end of each rectangle. Trace around pointed end of pattern only. Cut on line (sketch a). This is the pouch back and front. Trace Pouch Flap Pattern onto vinyl and cut out—one flap for each child. Cut remaining vinyl into 1x28-inch (2.5x70-cm) strips for pouch straps—one strap for each child.

Fold each vinyl rectangle as shown in sketch b. Using a leather punch or hole punch, punch six holes through both thicknesses along each side of pouch, 1 inch (2.5 cm) apart. Punch one hole at each end of strap and two holes where indicated on flap pattern. Cut a 6-inch (15-cm) length of yarn for each child. Tie bells onto ends of yarn.

Instruct each child in the following procedures:

★ Fold pouch rectangle so that the holes match, right side out. Push paper fastener through both layers of the first hole (sketch c). Turn pouch over and open paper fastener. Press firmly.

★ Insert paper fasteners through all holes from front to back along both sides of pouch. Open and press firmly (sketch d).

★ With teacher's help, fold strap so holes are even. Place strap holes over hole at the top of pouch. Then place flap on top of straps, with all holes lined up. From front, push a paper fastener through all four layers of holes. Turn over, open fastener and press firmly.

★ With teacher's help, fold yarn piece in half. Push the fold of yarn through lower hole in flap. Then pull bells through the loop to attach to flap (sketch e).

★ Use crayons or felt pens to decorate wooden or cardboard circle shapes to use as coins in your pouch.

Enrichment Idea: Children place real coins in their pouches.

Conversation:

All through history, people have carried money and other important things in pouches made of cloth or leather. What will you carry in your pouch?

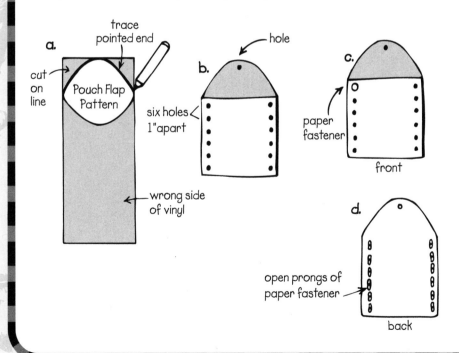

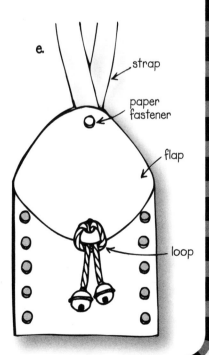

"LEATHER" POUCH

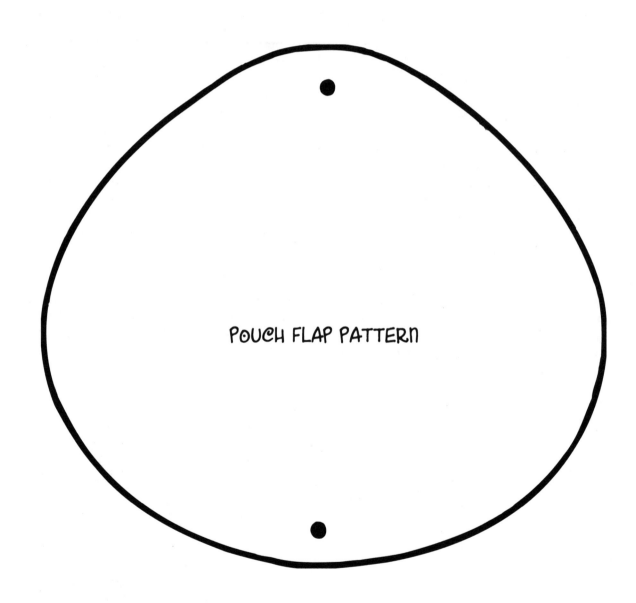

POUCH FLAP PATTERN

Costumes and Props

Materials: Looking Glass Patterns, poster board, aluminum foil or silver-coated card stock, yarn, colored felt pens, glue, hole punch, pencil, measuring stick, scissors.

Preparation: Trace Looking Glass Back and Front Patterns onto poster board and cut out—one back and front for each child. Cut aluminum foil or silver-coated card stock into 2½-inch (6.25-cm) squares—one for each child. Cut yarn into 2-foot (60-cm) lengths—one length for each child.

Instruct each child in the following procedures:

★ Use felt pens to decorate one side of both pieces of looking glass.

★ Glue the foil square, shiny side up, on the undecorated side of looking glass back (sketch a).

★ Spread glue on the undecorated side of looking glass front piece. Then place glued side down onto looking glass back, with the silver showing through the frame (sketch b).

★ With teacher's help, punch a hole near bottom of handle.

★ Thread yarn through hole and tie ends in a knot (sketch c).

★ Wear your looking glass around your neck or tie to your belt like the ladies and lords did in castle times!

Enrichment Idea: Children may glue on a variety of materials to decorate their looking glasses.

Conversation:

(Mickey), who do you see in your looking glass? (Child responds.) **What color of eyes do you have? What color of hair?** (Child responds.) **God made you special. Our Bible says, "God made me"** (see Job 33:4). **What else did God make?**

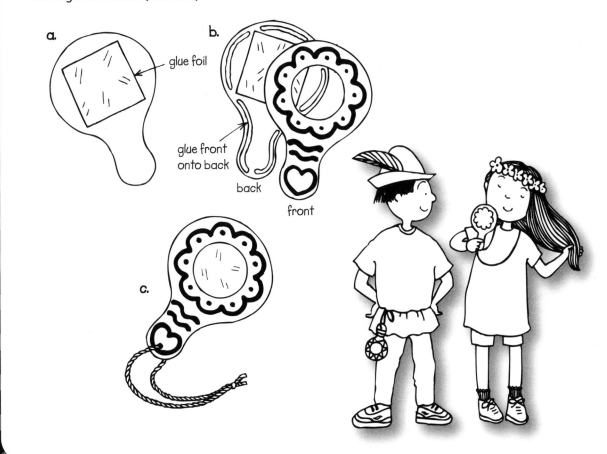

a.

glue foil

b.

glue front onto back

back

front

c.

LITTLE LOOKING GLASS PATTERNS

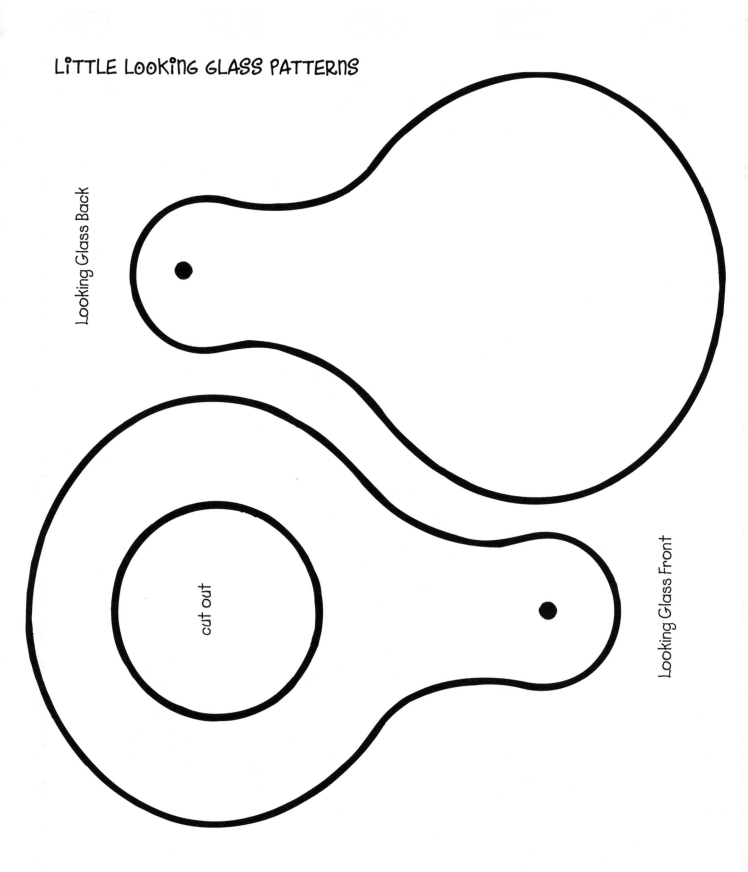

Looking Glass Back

Looking Glass Front

cut out

Costumes and Props

Materials: Gray or silver poster board, 1-inch (2.5-cm) wide belting (available at fabric stores), 3/4-inch (1.9-cm) wide self-adhesive Velcro stripping, gold glitter glue, jute twine, sewing machine and thread, craft glue, fabric scissors, stapler and staples, measuring stick. For each child—small disposable aluminum pie pan, paper towel tube, one sock.

Preparation: Cut belting into 26-inch (65-cm) lengths—one for each child. Use sewing machine to finish ends of each belt to keep it from unraveling. Cut additional belting into 2-inch (5-cm) lengths and staple one end to edge of each pie pan (sketch a). Cut poster board into 5-inch (12.5-cm) squares—one for each child. Cut off tops of socks to make socks about 6 inches (15 cm) long (sketch b). Discard top portion of sock. Cut five small snips evenly spaced around top of sock (sketch b). Cut twine into 12-inch (30-cm) lengths—one for each child. Cut Velcro into 1-inch (2.5-cm) strips—three for each child. Cut additional Velcro into 3½-inch (8.75-cm) strips—one for each child.

Instuct each child in the following procedures:

★ To make gold pouch, thread twine through slits in sock (sketch c). Pull ends of twine together and tie to close pouch.

★ Squeeze a few drops of glitter glue inside pie pan and allow glue to dry.

★ To make shovel, flatten paper towel tube for handle. With teacher's help, cut a ½-inch (1.25-cm) slit on each side of one end of paper tube (sketch d). Insert poster-board square in slits and glue in place.

★ To make belt closure, remove backing from long strip of Velcro. Place one side of Velcro on inside edge at one end of belt. Place other side of Velcro on outside edge at other end of belt (sketch e).

★ Attach one side of each small strip of Velcro to each tool.

★ Attach the other side of each small strip of Velcro to three different places on belt (sketch e). Attach tools to belt.

Simplification Idea: Instead of Velcro, use small clothespins to attach tools.

Enrichment Idea: Paint rocks with gold spray paint and give one to each child to place in pouch.

Conversation:

Miners in the Old West used tools like the ones we made today to search for gold. What do you think a (shovel) was used for? Allow volunteers to answer, describing what each tool was used for.

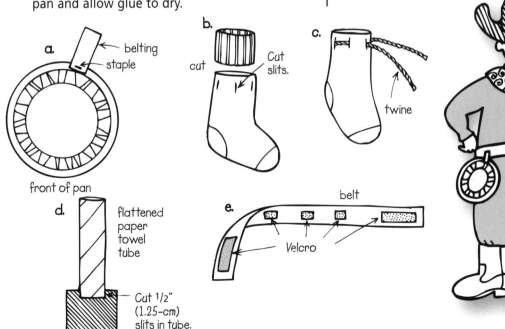

a. belting / staple / front of pan

b. cut / Cut slits.

c. twine

d. flattened paper towel tube / Cut ½" (1.25-cm) slits in tube.

e. belt / Velcro

Costumes and Props

Materials: Solid-colored cotton or muslin fabric, sewing machine and thread or craft glue, cording or thick yarn, fabric scissors, measuring stick.

Instruct each child in the following procedures:

★ Cut fabric into a 15x36-inch (37.5x90-cm) rectangle.

★ Sew or glue a ½-inch (1.25-cm) hem along the two short sides and one long side of fabric (sketch a).

★ Fold rectangle in half, right sides together, and sew or glue a seam along the unhemmed edge of fabric. This is the back of hood. Turn hood right side out (sketch b).

★ Place hood over head with the fold of fabric on top and the seam to the back (sketch c). Fold front opening of hood back, if needed, to fit. Tie hood loosely around neck with cord or yarn.

Conversation:

In most parts of the world, people wear hoods or hats to protect their heads from heat or cold. What do you wear?

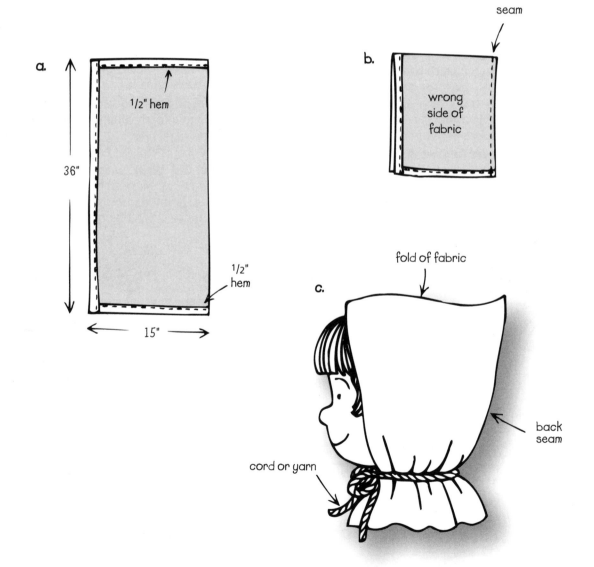

a. 36" 15" ½" hem ½" hem

b. seam wrong side of fabric

c. fold of fabric back seam cord or yarn

The Really Big Book of Cool Crafts for Kids

Materials: Pocket Pattern, velvet or synthetic suede fabric, embroidery floss in a variety of colors, satin rat-tail cord or gold or silver cord (available at fabric or craft stores), straight pins, gold or silver pony beads, photocopier and paper, glue sticks, measuring stick, fabric scissors. For each child—one crewel needle.

Preparation: Cut fabric into 4x5-inch (10x12.5-cm) pieces—one for each child. Photocopy Pocket Pattern—one copy for each child. Cut cord into 18-inch (45-cm) lengths—two for each child.

Instruct each child in the following procedures:

★ Cut out pocket pattern and pin onto fabric. Cut fabric along pattern edge. Remove pins and paper pattern.

★ Rub glue stick on top and bottom edges of wrong side of fabric piece. Fold each edge over to make ¼-inch (.625-cm) hems (sketch a).

★ If desired, decorate the top half of fabric pouch by stitching a simple design or your initials using embroidery floss. Or sew a small shape cut from contrasting fabric to the top half of pocket (sketch b).

★ Fold pocket in half, with right side out and edges even. Pin sides in place.

★ Knot one end of a cord length. Place knot inside bottom corner of pocket (sketch c).

★ Thread needle with embroidery floss. Knot end.

★ Starting at bottom inside corner of pocket, begin stitching sides together by sewing through the cord near bottom of pocket to secure cord in place (sketch d).

★ Lay cord along edge of pocket. Sew overcast stitches up the side of pocket and around cord (sketch e). When complete, tie a knot on the inside of pocket and trim ends.

★ Sew the other side of pocket in the same manner, using another length of cord.

★ Thread one or two beads onto each cord. Knot ends of cord together.

★ You can wear your pocket around your neck or hang it from your belt.

Conversation:

Years ago, people didn't have pockets in their clothes! They had separate pouches or pockets that they attached to their clothing, hung on their belts or hung around their necks. Small pockets like these carried precious items, such as stones or jewels. Men and women often put sweet-smelling herbs and flowers in pockets and wore them as perfume. What will you keep in your pocket?

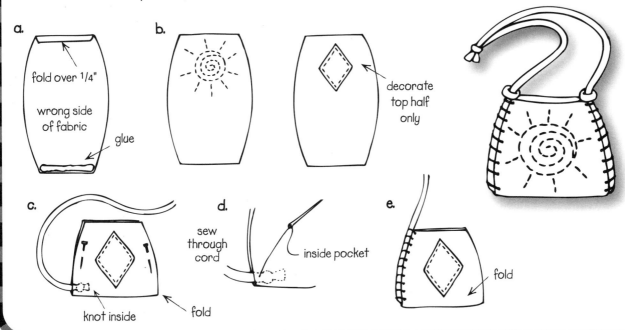

a. fold over ¼"
wrong side of fabric
glue

b. decorate top half only

c. knot inside / fold

d. sew through cord / inside pocket

e. fold

POCKET ON A STRING PATTERN

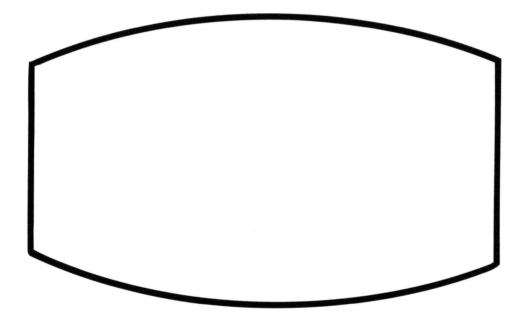

Costumes and Props

Materials: Felt, sewing machine and thread or crewel needle and yarn, cotton balls, one sock to fit, fabric scissors, pen.

Instruct each child in the following procedures:

★ Lay sock on felt and trace around it, adding a 2-inch (5-cm) border all around, stopping at ankle height (sketch a). Make the toe long and pointed. Cut out.

★ Trace around felt shoe shape on additional felt and cut out. Repeat to make four felt shoe pieces.

★ Place two sides of a shoe together and sew with sewing machine or needle and yarn. Do not sew ankle opening.

★ Sew other shoe in the same manner (sketch b).

★ Stuff ends of shoes with cotton balls.

Simplification Idea: Cut two identical long triangles from construction paper or felt. Cut the short edges of triangles in a curve. Punch holes along the curved edges of triangles and lace with yarn (sketch c). To wear, tie the yarn around ankles with the triangles covering the tops of shoes (sketch d).

Conversation:

Where are some places you would not want to walk in these shoes? Why? How are your shoes different from the ones you wore today? No matter what shoes you wear, God is with you wherever you go!

a.

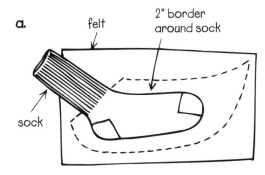

felt   2" border around sock

sock

b.

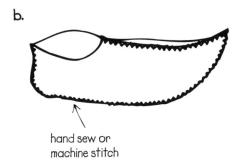

hand sew or machine stitch

c.

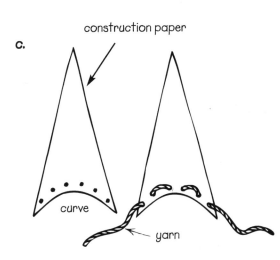

construction paper

curve

yarn

d.

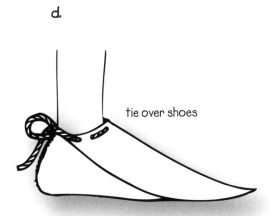

tie over shoes

Costumes and Props

Materials: Poster board, tulle, glitter glue pens, hole punch and elastic cord or hairpins, scissors, felt pens, measuring stick, stapler and staples.

Instruct each child in the following procedures:

★ Draw and cut a 14-inch (35-cm) quarter circle out of poster board (sketch a).

★ Decorate poster board with felt pens and/or glitter glue pens. Allow glitter glue to dry.

★ Bend poster board into a cone shape to fit the top of your head. Leave a small opening at the tip of cone. Staple in place (sketch b).

★ Cut tulle into a 12x30-inch (30x75-cm) rectangle.

★ Gather one end of tulle together and push inside small end of cone. Staple in place (sketch c).

★ Secure hat to head with hairpins. Or punch holes on each side of hat, ½ inch (1.25 cm) from edge. Tie a length of elastic cord to each hole, to fit under chin.

Conversation:

If you have joined God's family, the Bible says you are part of the royal family. (See 1 Peter 2:9.) **You're a princess! Now you can even look like one!**

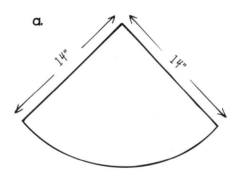

a.

14"   14"

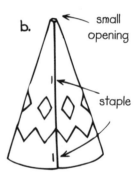

b.   small opening

staple

c.

Costumes and Props

Materials: Key Pattern, Fun Foam in a variety of colors (available at craft stores), dry rigatoni and wagon wheel pasta, rubbing alcohol, food coloring in three colors, gold metallic spray paint, yarn, gold glitter squeeze-tip fabric paint, glue, shallow containers, hole punch, scissors, pencils, measuring stick, newspaper.

Preparation: Cover work area with newspaper and spray wagon wheel pasta with gold spray paint. Dye rigatoni three different colors as follows: Pour some rubbing alcohol into shallow containers. Add several drops of food coloring to each container. Soak rigatoni in alcohol mixture just long enough for color to be absorbed. Spread rigatoni on newspaper to dry.

Cut yarn into 1-yard (.9-m) lengths—one for each child. Dip both ends of each yarn length into glue and allow to dry stiff. Trace Key Pattern onto Fun Foam—one key outline for each child.

Instruct each child in the following procedures:

★ Cut out Fun Foam key shape. Punch a hole near top of key with hole punch.

★ Fold the yarn in half. Push doubled yarn loop through key hole. Then thread both ends of yarn though the loop and pull to secure (sketch a).

★ Thread pasta pieces onto yarn. Complete both sides of necklace (sketch b).

★ Tie ends of yarn together. Cut off stiffened ends.

★ Use fabric paint to write the initial of your first name on key. Decorate key with painted dots and/or lines.

★ Allow pendant to dry a few hours or overnight before wearing necklace.

Conversation:

Many years ago, kings depended on special helpers called stewards. A steward would take care of the castle and make sure everyone did their jobs and that everything got done. Who takes care of your home? What can you do to help? (Child responds.) **Your Steward's Pendant can help you remember that it's important to help and do your part, whether you live in a castle, a house or an apartment!**

KEY PATTERN

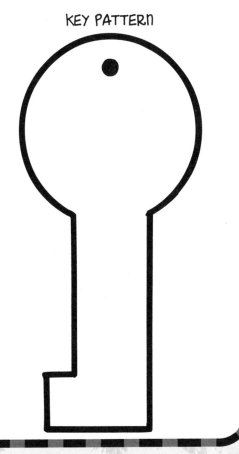

a.　b.

Costumes and Props

STICK HORSE
(25-30 MINUTES)

Materials: Horse Ear Pattern, brown paper grocery bags, photocopier, colored copier paper, one sheet white copier paper, fine-tip black felt pen, wide-tip colored felt pens, scissors, ruler, stapler and staples. For each child—one gift-wrap paper tube, one brown lunch bag, two sheets newspaper.

Preparation: Trace Horse Ear Pattern onto brown paper grocery bags and cut out—two ears for each child. Fold the sheet of white paper in half lengthwise. With black felt pen, mark lines 1/2 inch (1.25 cm) apart stopping 1/2 inch (1.25 cm) from fold (sketch a). Unfold paper. Copy onto colored copier paper—one for each child. Fold each copy lengthwise with lines on the outside. Cut a slit in paper tubes the same measurement as the width of the lunch bag. Flatten the slit part of tubes (sketch b).

Instruct each child in the following procedures:

★ Cut the folded paper on the lines to make horse's mane.

★ Crumple sheets of newspaper and stuff into bag.

★ With teacher's help, pinch lunch bag closed so pleats are on the inside. Staple mane to top of bag as in sketch c. Both rows of fringe are on one side of bag.

★ Insert stapled part of mane into tube slit. Staple three or four times along slit (sketch d).

★ Fold bag back against the tube so mane sticks out. Fold the extending part of mane to turn the corner and fit into the end of tube. Staple top of mane in place.

★ Staple bag to the other edge of flattened tube (sketch e).

★ Pinch lower edge of ears in half (sketch f). With teacher's help, staple to top of paper bag head.

★ With felt pens, draw eyes, nose and mouth on bag.

★ Decorate paper tube with felt pens.

Conversation:

For many, many years, there were no cars. People often rode horses. (Justin), what could you name your horse? (Child responds.) **You can pretend your horse is galloping if you hold on to your horse and run fast. God gave you strong legs to run. What other things can you do with your legs?**

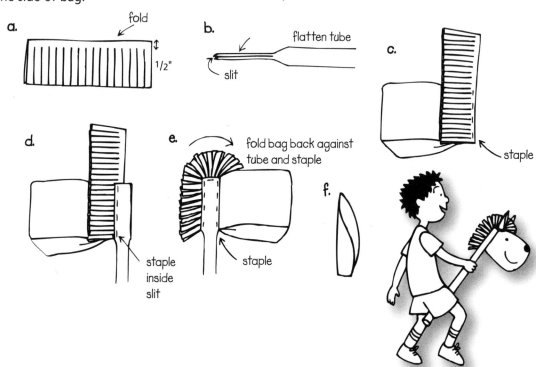

a. fold 1/2"

b. flatten tube / slit

c. staple

d. staple inside slit

e. fold bag back against tube and staple / staple

f.

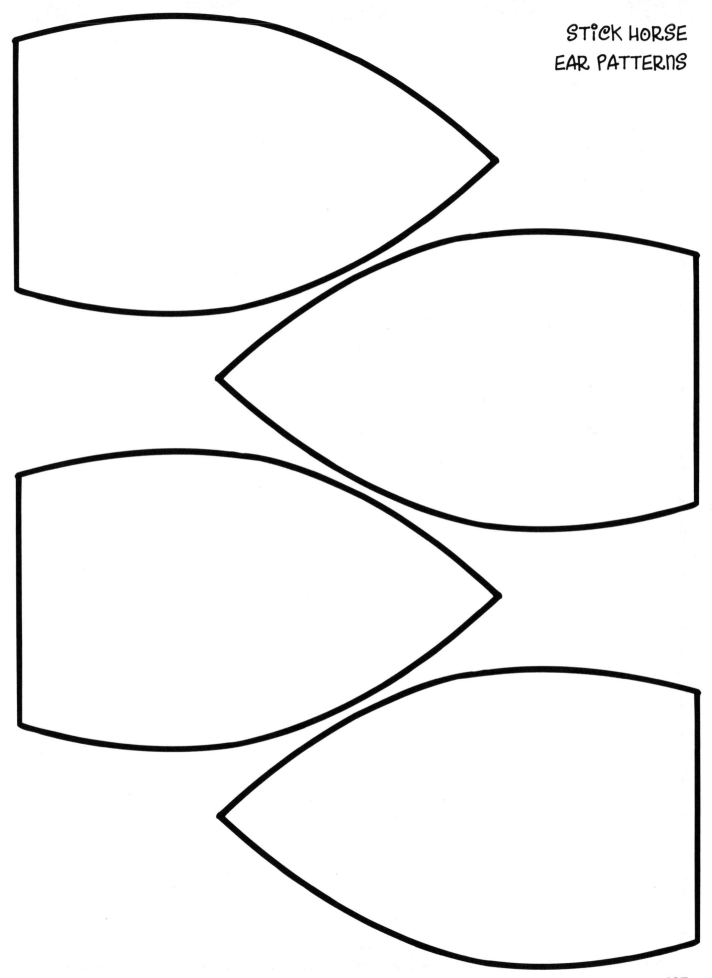

STICK HORSE
EAR PATTERNS

Costumes and Props

Materials: Bonnet Pattern, poster board, calico or gingham fabric, ribbon, lace, rickrack, large sheet of construction paper, pen, glue sticks, craft glue, several pairs of fabric scissors, scissors, hole punch, stapler and staples, measuring stick.

Preparation: Fold construction paper in half, place Bonnet Pattern on fold, trace around pattern and cut out (sketch a). Unfold construction paper pattern and trace onto poster board—one bonnet for each child. Mark position of holes on Bonnet Pattern on each poster-board bonnet. Cut fabric into 16-inch (40-cm) squares—one for each child. Cut ribbon into 8-inch (20-cm) and 18-inch (45-cm) lengths—two of each length for each child. Cut lace into 30-inch (75-cm) lengths—one for each child.

Instruct each child in the following procedures:

★ Lay poster-board bonnet on flat surface with hole marks facedown. Apply glue stick over entire surface and along edges.

★ Lay fabric piece flat on table, wrong side up.

★ Press sticky side of poster-board bonnet onto fabric (sketch b). Turn over and smooth fabric.

★ Trim excess fabric along poster-board edges.

★ Punch a hole at each end of bonnet as indicated on pattern. Tie a short ribbon to each hole (sketch c).

★ With teacher's help, put bonnet on head and tie ribbons in back to fit appropriately. Teacher marks a hole on each side of bonnet, near the child's chin.

★ Remove bonnet, punch holes and then tie a long ribbon to each new hole (sketch c).

★ Staple lace along rim of bonnet on the poster-board side (sketch d). Trim ends of lace, if necessary.

★ Use craft glue to glue rickrack or ribbon along rim to cover staples on the fabric side of bonnet.

★ Put bonnet on head and tie front ribbons (sketch e).

Simplification Idea: Instead of covering bonnets with fabric, children use felt pens to decorate poster-board bonnets.

Conversation:

Most girls in the Old West wore sunbonnets to protect their faces from the sun and dust. Your sunbonnets are made from colorful fabric. Pioneer women made dresses out of similar fabrics, but bonnets were usually made of brown, gray or black fabric. Why do you think bonnets were those colors? (Dark colors didn't show dirt and dust. Brightly colored bonnets weren't considered appropriate.)

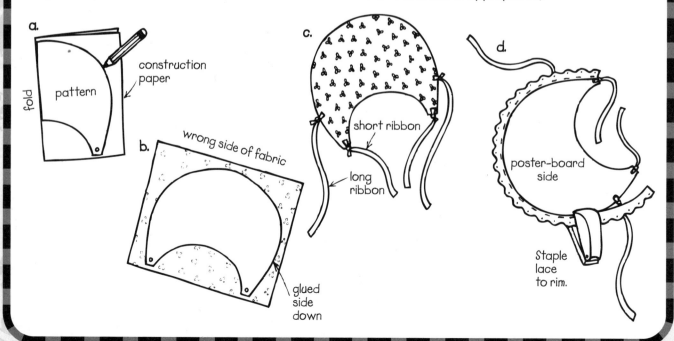

a. construction paper / fold / pattern

b. wrong side of fabric / glued side down

c. short ribbon / long ribbon

d. poster-board side / Staple lace to rim.

SUNBONNET PATTERN

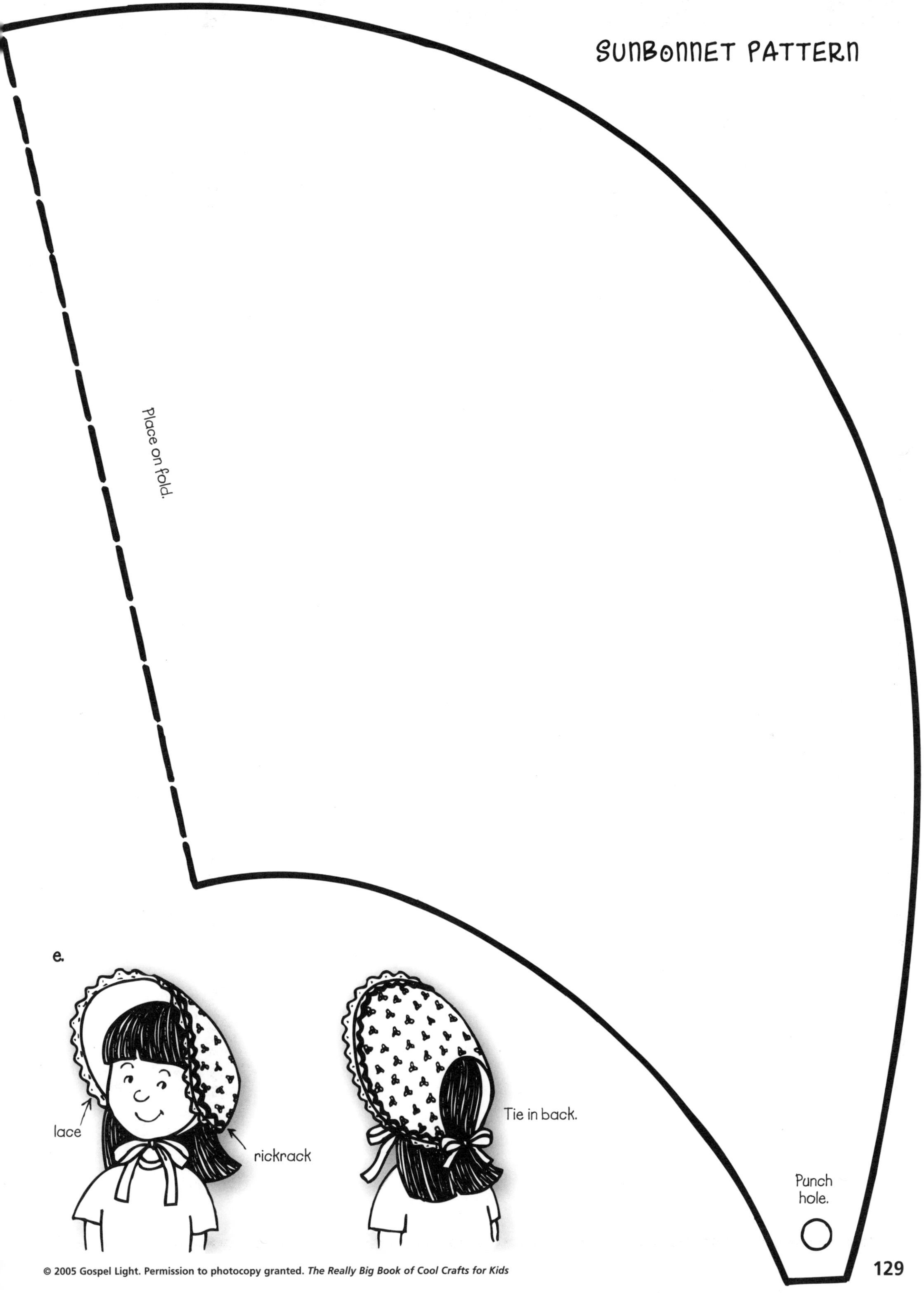

Place on fold.

Punch hole.

e.

lace

rickrack

Tie in back.

Costumes and Props

EARLY CHILDHOOD • YOUNGER ELEMENTARY • OLDER ELEMENTARY

Materials: White poster board, wrapping-paper in various colors, coaster-sized doilies, wide ribbon in various colors, narrow ribbon in various colors, artificial flowers, pencil, glue, scissors, measuring stick.

Preparation: Cut poster board into 12-inch (30-cm) circles—one for each child. Using a poster-board circle, trace circles onto wrapping paper—one wrapping paper circle for each child. Cut doilies in half—about 10 halves for each child. Cut wide ribbon into 3-foot (.9-m) lengths—one for each child. Cut narrow ribbon into 12-inch (30-cm) lengths—one for each child.

Instruct each child in the following procedures:

★ Glue wrapping-paper circle onto poster-board circle.

★ Glue doily halves evenly around outer edge of paper circle (sketch a).

★ Teacher cuts two 2-inch (5-cm) slits on opposite sides of circle (sketch a).

★ Thread wide ribbon through slits and pull until ends are even (sketch b).

★ With teacher's help, slide narrow ribbon under wide ribbon on top of hat (sketch c).

★ Lay a bunch of flowers on ribbon. With teacher's help, tie and knot narrow ribbon around flowers and then tie ribbon in a bow.

★ Wear your Sunday Hat by tying large ribbon under your chin.

Simplification Idea: Use large colored paper plates instead of poster board and wrapping paper.

Conversation:

In the Old West, folks dressed up in their very finest hats and clothes to go to church. Sundays were a special time for families to spend together learning more about God. How does your family like to spend time together?

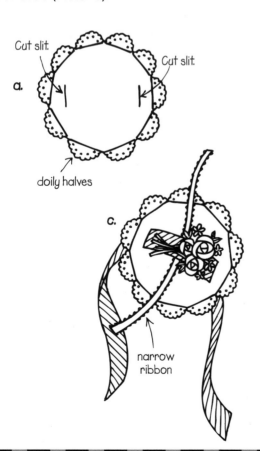

Costumes and Props

Materials: Banner Symbol Patterns, Stiffened Eazy Felt in a variety of colors (available at craft stores), narrow gold cord, ½-inch (1.25-cm) dowels, saw, embroidery floss in a variety of colors, craft glue, lightweight cardboard, pencil, measuring stick, scissors, fabric scissors, hole punch. For each child—two clothespins, two gold-toned buttons, one crewel needle.

DAY ONE Preparation: Trace Banner Symbol Patterns onto lightweight cardboard and cut out. Cut felt into 12x18-inch (30x45-cm) rectangles — one for each child.

Instruct each child in the following procedures:

★ With pencil, draw a line at the bottom of felt rectangle to make a curved, scalloped or pointed edge (sketch a). Cut along line.

★ Use pencil to trace desired symbol patterns onto additional felt pieces and cut out. Glue felt symbols on banner.

★ Squeeze a line of craft glue around the edge of each felt symbol. Lay a length of gold cord onto glue outline (sketch b). Trim cord to fit and glue ends of cord under felt symbol.

DAY TWO Preparation: Cut additional felt into 1½x5½-inch (3.75x13.75-cm) strips—two for each child. Saw dowels into 16-inch (40-cm) lengths—one for each child. Cut cardboard into 5-inch (12.5-cm) squares—one for each child. Cut embroidery floss into 5-yard (4.5-m) lengths—one for each child. Cut gold cord into 18-inch (45-cm) lengths—two for each child.

Instruct each child in the following procedures:

★ Fold each felt strip in half. Glue strips near top edge of banner, with banner sandwiched between strip ends to make hanging tabs. Use clothespins to hold in place until dry (sketch c).

★ Punch a hole at the bottom of banner with hole punch.

★ To make a tassel, wrap the length of floss around cardboard square. Thread needle with a length of gold cord. Slide needle under floss and tie a knot that gathers all strands together (sketch d). Slide embroidery floss off cardboard.

★ While cord is still threaded on needle, insert needle through the hole in banner (sketch e). Wrap cord around the tassel several times to tightly bind floss together (sketch f). Push needle and cord underneath the wrapped cording and up through the top of tassel to secure. Trim both ends of gold cord.

★ Cut looped ends of tassel and trim ends to make even (sketch g).

★ Slip the dowel through felt tabs. Place a drop of glue about 1-inch (2.5-cm) from each end of dowel and tightly tie the other length of gold cord over glued areas to make hanger.

★ Remove clothespins from tabs. Glue one gold-toned button on top of each tab for decoration. Lay flat to dry.

Simplification Idea: Buy pre-made tassels. Children tie to bottoms of banners.

Enrichment Idea: Paint dowel with gold or silver paint.

Conversation:

In castle times, people who were talented at certain crafts could belong to a guild. A guild was a group of craftspeople who all did the same type of work. There were guilds for candlemakers, glassmakers, wheelmakers, pastrymakers and many others. Often all the members of a guild celebrated feasts, holidays and weddings together. Each guild had its own uniform and banner. On the banner were symbols to represent the guild's work. If you joined a guild today, what type of guild would you like to belong to? What would your banner look like?

TAPESTRY BANNER

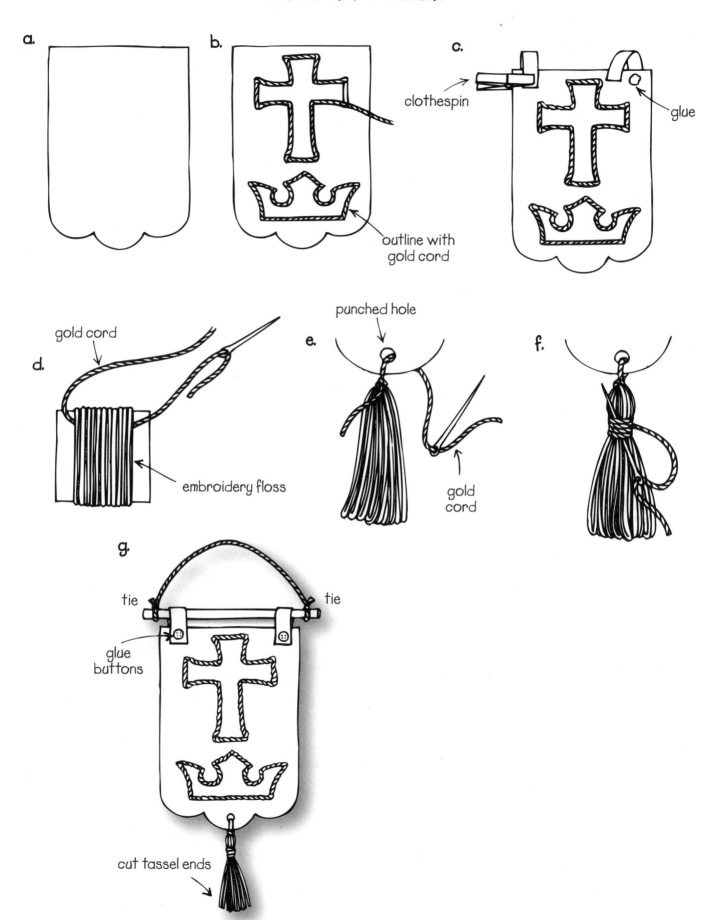

a.

b.

c.

clothespin

glue

outline with
gold cord

d.

gold cord

embroidery floss

e.

punched hole

gold
cord

f.

g.

tie   tie

glue
buttons

cut tassel ends

TAPESTRY BANNER
SYMBOL PATTERNS

TAPESTRY BANNER
SYMBOL PATTERNS

Costumes and Props

Materials: 18-gauge wire, wire cutters, several needle-nose pliers, can opener, candlestick adhesive (available at craft stores), freezer, baking sheet, sink or plastic tub, several beach or bath towels, paper, pencils, tape, measuring stick, water. For each child—hammer or mallet, long nail, empty 16 oz. soup can, 8 oz. tuna can, votive candle.

Preparation: Fill soup cans almost full with water and place on baking sheet. Place baking sheet in freezer, making sure it's level. Freeze until solid. Take out just before children are ready to do craft. (This makes cans solid for easier punching.) Cut paper into 4x10-inch (10x25–cm) rectangles—one for each child. Cut wire into 30-inch (75-cm) lengths—one for each child. Use nail and hammer to punch a hole on each side of tuna can, near top (sketch a). Cover work area with layer of towels. (Note: This craft requires plenty of adult supervision to ensure tools are used properly.)

Instruct each child in the following procedures:

★ On piece of paper, draw a design pattern for your lantern.

★ Tape pattern in place on soup can (sketch b).

★ Lay can on its side on towels.

★ Following your pattern, carefully punch holes in can with hammer and nail (sketch c). Remove paper when finished.

★ Use hammer and nail to punch holes on both sides of can, ½ inch (1.25 cm) from top of can and ½ inch (1.25 cm) from bottom (sketch d).

★ Dump ice from can into sink or tub.

★ Use can opener to cut off bottom of can.

★ Fasten one end of wire through one hole in tuna can. Use needle-nose pliers to pinch end closed or curl wire up to secure. Starting from inside of soup can, thread wire through bottom hole, up the outside and through top hole. Be careful! Edges of holes inside can are sharp. Bend wire to make lantern handle. Thread remaining wire through opposite top hole of can from the inside, down the outside and in through bottom hole. Fasten end of wire through remaining hole in tuna can and pinch or curl wire up to secure (sketch e).

★ Use candlestick adhesive to attach votive candle to bottom of tuna can. Slide soup can down wire, toward tuna can, as far as it will go.

★ At home, hang lantern on nail or hook. With adult supervision, tilt soup can back to light candle. Once candle is lit, do not try to carry lantern as wire and cans get hot. (Safety Note: Never use candle without adult supervision.)

Conversation:

What would it be like if the electricity in your home went out tonight? What things would you not be able to do? People who don't have electric lights use lanterns that burn candles or oil. Jesus said that we should be like light to the people around us. That means that we can help others see God's love by the way we act. What are some ways that you can show God's love to the people around you?

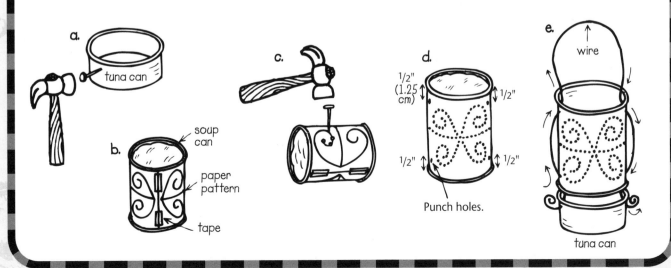

a. tuna can

b. soup can / paper pattern / tape

c.

d. 1/2" (1.25 cm) / 1/2" / 1/2" / 1/2" / Punch holes.

e. wire / tuna can

Costumes and Props

Materials: Tissue paper in a variety of colors, narrow gift-wrap ribbon, hole punch, scissors, glue, measuring stick, shallow containers. For each child—one 9-inch (22.5-cm) paper plate, one light-colored crayon.

Preparation: Cut a 6-inch (15-cm) circle out of the center of each paper plate. Then trim ½ inch (1.25 cm) off the outside rim, leaving a narrow ring (sketch a). To make flowers, cut tissue paper into 3-inch (7.5-cm) squares—approximately 20 squares for each child. Stack several squares together and fold them in quarters. Cut the unfolded corner, rounding it off to make a petal shape (sketch b). Unfold tissue flowers. Cut ribbon into 24-inch (60-cm) lengths—three for each child. Pour glue into shallow containers.

Instruct each child in the following procedures:

★ Lay paper plate ring on work surface, bottom facing up.

★ Place the flat end of crayon in the center of a tissue paper flower. Smooth tissue over the crayon and hold it while dipping the end in glue. Press glued end of tissue onto paper plate ring. Remove the crayon, leaving the flower (sketch c).

★ Continue gluing flowers onto paper plate ring until completely covered.

★ Use hole punch to punch a hole near edge of paper plate ring at center back. (Note: If a child does not glue flowers all the way around ring, center the flowers in front.)

★ With teacher's help, fold lengths of ribbon in half, push through the hole to form a loop and pull ribbon ends through loop (sketch d).

★ After glue has dried, gently open and fluff flowers.

Enrichment Idea: Provide two bobby pins to secure garland to child's hair.

Conversation:

All through history, men and ladies sometimes wore rings of flowers in their hair. You may wear your flower garland on your head or you may hang it on the wall for a pretty decoration. God made many different colors of flowers. What is your favorite color? What is your favorite kind of flower?

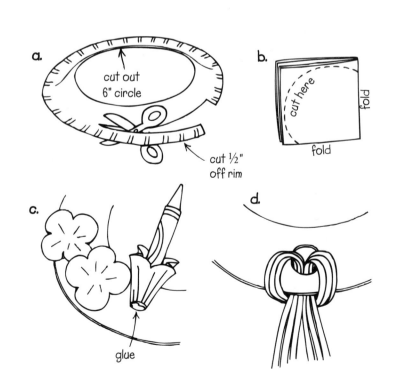

Costumes and Props

Materials: Traveler's Bag Patterns, brown sheets of Fun Foam, brown embroidery floss, jute twine, pencils, scissors, measuring stick. For each child—craft needle, wooden bead, approximately 1 inch (5 cm) long.

Preparation: Fold sheets of Fun Foam in half and place Patterns 1 and 2 along fold as indicated on patterns. Trace around patterns and cut out—one of each pattern for each child. Place Pattern 1 on another sheet of Fun Foam, not folded, and cut out for bag front—one for each child. Cut embroidery floss into 1-yard (.9-m) lengths—two each for each child. Cut jute twine into 1-yard (.9-m) lengths—one for each child.

Instruct each child in the following procedures:

★ Thread needle with embroidery floss and knot the end. Line up edge of Pattern 2 piece (sides and bottom of bag) along one side of large Pattern 1 piece (back and flap of bag) as shown in sketch a. Stitch pieces together with a whip stitch and finish with a knot.

★ Line up smaller front piece along unstitched edge of Pattern 2 piece (sketch b). Stitch pieces together with a whip stitch and finish with a knot.

★ Use scissors to snip a hole in center of bag flap (sketch c). Make hole wide enough for bead to thread through it.

★ Fold flap down over front of bag. Use a pencil to mark flap hole on bag front.

★ Knot thread and pull needle from inside of bag through mark on front of bag. String wooden bead on thread; then pull needle back through foam to secure bead onto bag. Tie knot on inside of bag and trim thread.

★ Use scissors to make a small hole on each side of bag, about 1 inch (2.5 cm) from top (sketch d). Thread ends of jute through holes and knot ends inside bag to form a strap.

Enrichment Ideas Use black permanent felt pen to write name on front of bag. Make bag out of leather and thin leather lacing instead of Fun Foam.

Conversation:

When people traveled on foot or horseback, they wore bags to keep their valuable items next to them at all times. There is one thing we can carry with us wherever we go, and we don't need a bag to carry it—it's God's Word! When we memorize Bible verses, we carry God's Word in our hearts. What is a verse that you always remember?

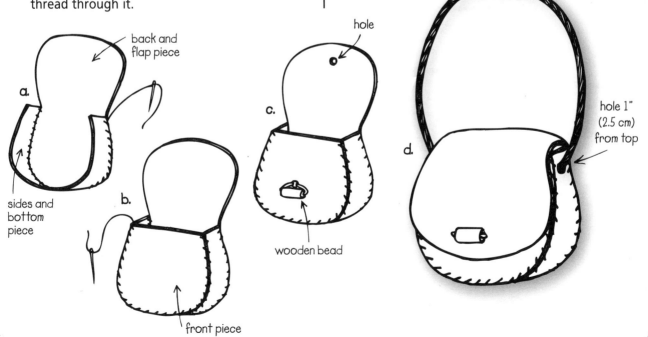

a. back and flap piece
sides and bottom piece

b. front piece

c. hole
wooden bead

d. hole 1" (2.5 cm) from top

TRAVELER'S BAG PATTERNS

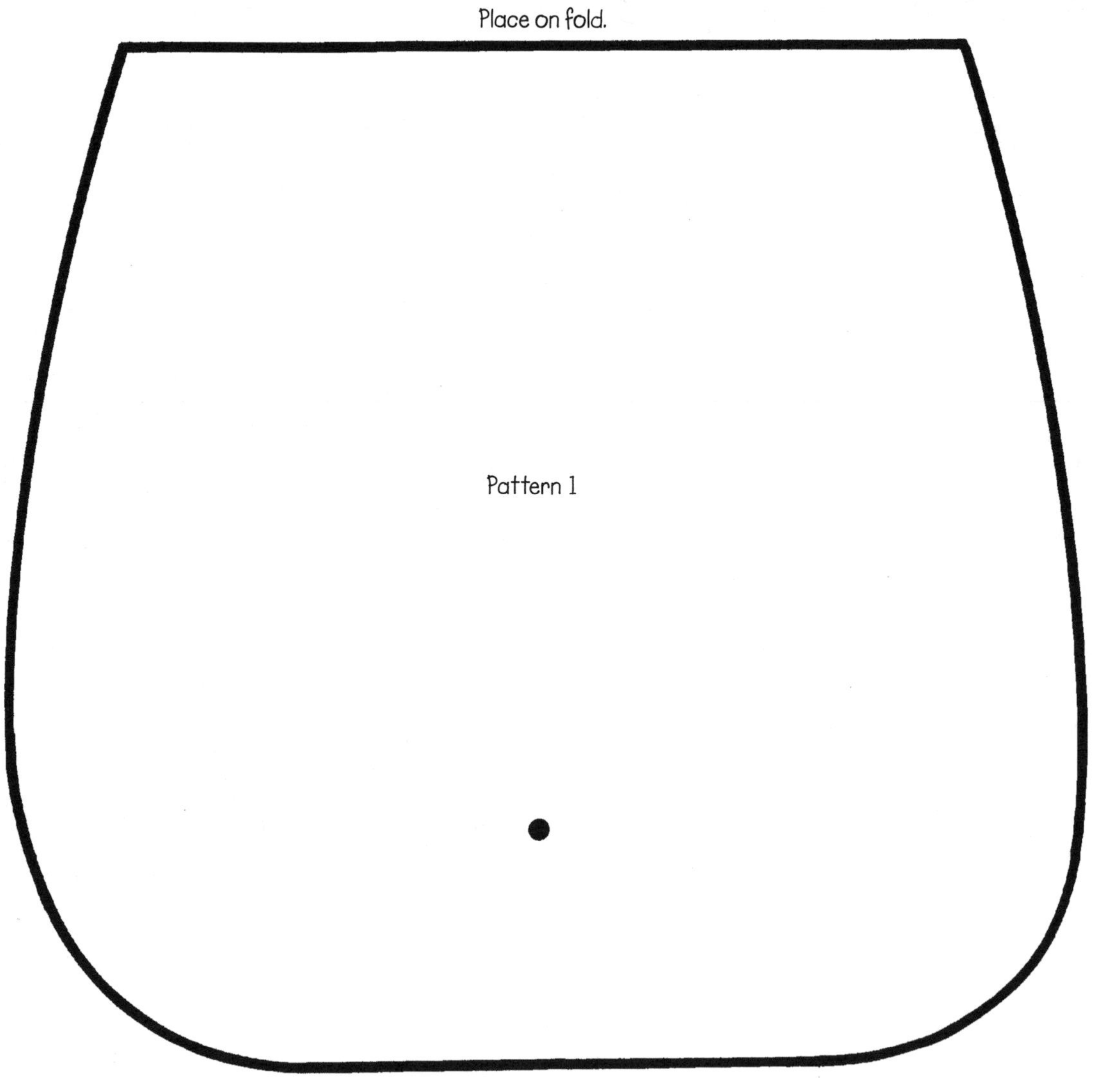

Place on fold.

Pattern 1

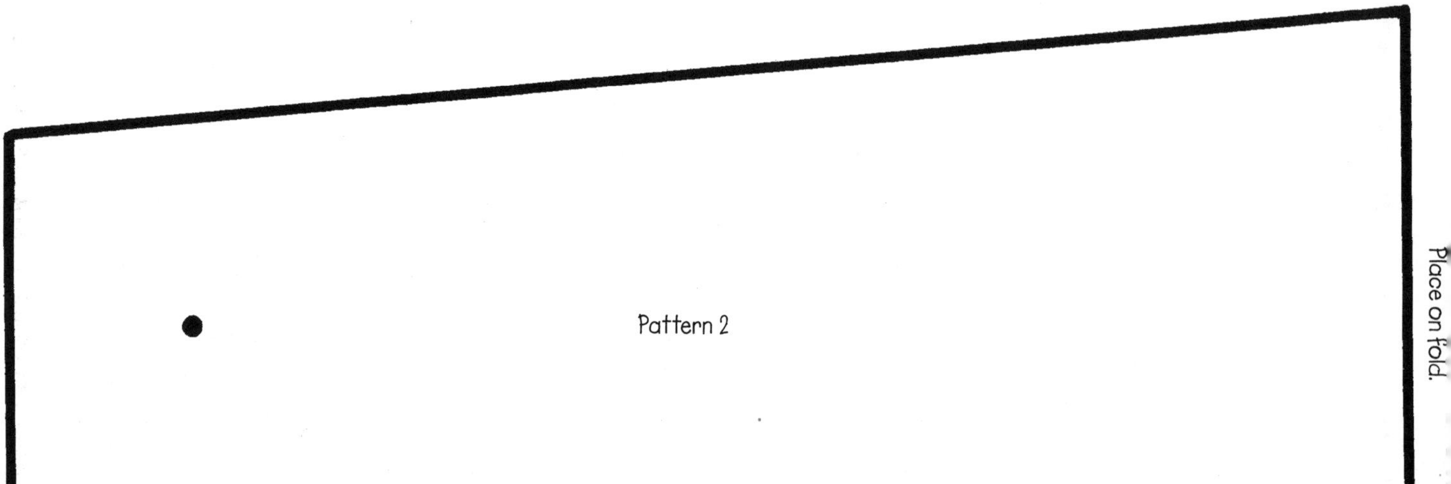

Pattern 2

Place on fold.

Costumes and Props

Materials: Solid-colored fabric or bed sheet, sewing machine and thread, fabric marking pen, thick satin cord or rope, fabric scissors, tape measure.

Instruct each child in the following procedures:

✶ Measure from your shoulder to the length you want your Tunic or Gown to be. Multiply the number by two.

✶ Cut fabric the length of the number.

✶ With right sides together, fold fabric with the top and bottom edges together. Then fold again with the folds to the top and the left (sketch a).

✶ Measure 9 inches (22.5 cm) from the left fold and 9 inches (22.5 cm) from the top fold and mark with fabric marking pen. (This measurement fits an average-size woman. Adjust as needed.)

✶ For Tunic: Draw a line from the mark straight down. Then draw another line from the mark straight to the right for sleeve (sketch b). For Gown: Draw an angled line from the mark to the bottom right corner of fabric and another line at an angle to the right for sleeve (sketch b).

✶ Cut out on lines through all thicknesses of fabric.

✶ Cut a neck opening 3 inches (7.5 cm) from folded corner (sketch c).

✶ Unfold costume and pull on over head. Adjust length of sleeves or costume, if necessary.

✶ Fold costume, right sides together with fold at top of sleeves. Sew side seams and under arms (sketch d).

✶ Turn costume right side out. You may cut neckline in a V shape for gown.

✶ Tie a satin cord around waist for a royal costume. Tie rope around waist for a peasant or craftsperson costume.

Simple Tunic or Gown for a Small Child

Use a solid-colored pillow case for costume. Cut a neckhole in the short seam of pillowcase. Cut arm holes in both sides near the top corners (sketch e). Cut open end in a jagged pattern. Child slips costume on through open end of pillow case, puts head through neckline hole and arms through arm holes. Tie with cord or rope around waist.

a. fold   fold

b. ←9"→   9"↓   ←9"→   9"↓   c. ←3"→ 3"

Tunic   Gown

d. right sides together

Simple Child's Tunic

cut neckhole

cut armhole   fold   cut armhole

e.

open end   pillowcase

Daily Life

Here are crafts that kids can make to use every day at home!

Daily Life

Materials: Acrylic paint in a variety of bold colors, clear acrylic spray paint, small paintbrushes, shallow containers, pencils, newspaper. For each child—one 8-inch (20-cm) square clay tile (available at building supply stores), one plate hanger.

Preparation: Cover work area with newspaper. Pour paint into shallow containers.

Instruct each child in the following procedures:

★ Use pencil to sketch address number on tile. Make numbers large enough to cover most of tile space.

★ Sketch a simple border around edge of tile.

★ Attach plate hanger to tile using manufacturer's instructions. (Note: If tile is too heavy for plate hanger, drill a small hole in back of tile and hang on a nail.)

★ Paint numbers and border. (Bold colors will show up best.) Let dry.

★ In well-ventilated area, spray tile with clear spray and allow to dry.

★ Ask parent's permission to hang tile on the front of house or apartment.

Simplification Idea: Use crayons instead of acrylic paint.

Conversation:

Knowing a person's address can help you find his or her house or apartment, even if you've never been there before. What is your address? I'm glad that God knows where each of us lives. He doesn't need to look up our addresses to find us. He is with us all the time.

paint

283

clay tile

283

Daily Life

Materials: Old maps or map-design wrapping paper, scissors, yarn, hole punch or awl, felt pens, glue, water, paintbrushes, shallow containers, sharp pencils. For each child—one box with lid (such as shoe boxes, laundry-detergent boxes, papier mâché boxes purchased in craft stores, etc.), one small unlined index card. *Optional*—clear acrylic spray.

Preparation: Cut maps or wrapping paper into large pieces that are easy to handle. With hole punch or awl, make holes in opposite sides of boxes just below where the lid will lie (sketch a). Cut yarn into lengths suitable for box handle—three equal lengths for each child. Pour glue into shallow containers and dilute with a small amount of water.

Instruct each child in the following procedures:

* Tear map into various sized strips and pieces, no smaller than 2x2 inches (5x5 cm).
* Brush glue on outside of box and place map pieces over glue, overlapping pieces. Brush glue on edges of pieces to smooth down (sketch b).
* Continue in this manner, smoothing map pieces around corners and edges of box and lid. Cover top and sides of lid. Cover sides of box. Let dry.
* Find the holes on the box sides and use a sharp pencil to poke through the map-covered holes.

* Push three lengths of yarn through one hole and knot inside box (sketch c).
* Braid lengths of yarn.
* Push ends of yarn through opposite hole and knot inside box to form handle.
* Letter your name and "Adventure Kit" on index card and glue to box front or top of lid.
* Put lid on box.
* *Optional*—Teacher may spray boxes with clear acrylic spray before inserting yarn handle, to give Adventure Kits a more durable finish.

Simplification Idea: Use thick yarn or cording for handle instead of braided yarn.

Enrichment Idea: Letter Bible verses on additional index cards and place inside Adventure Kit.

Conversation:

Your Adventure Kit can hold items you would like to bring on your next adventure. If you could travel anywhere, where would you like to go? What would you bring on your trip? (Children respond.) **Wherever you go, God is always with you. The Bible says He will watch over and take care of you.** (See Joshua 1:9.)

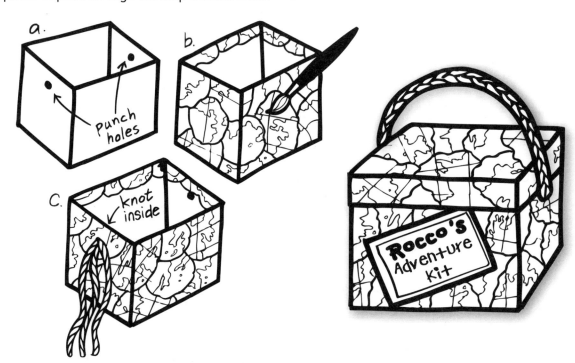

Materials: Hot Air Balloon, Basket, Cloud and Mountain Patterns, fabric scraps, old buttons, fabric scissors, glue, thin black felt pens, pencils, tagboard. For each child—one solid-color gift bag with handle (found at craft or party stores).

Preparation: Trace patterns onto tagboard and cut out—one set of patterns for every four children.

Instruct each child in the following procedures:

★ Trace patterns onto fabric scraps and cut out.

★ Arrange fabric cut-outs on gift bag and glue in place (see sketch).

★ With thin black felt pen, draw short dashes around shapes, outlining to look like stitching.

★ Glue buttons on balloon, basket or mountains to decorate.

Enrichment Idea: Use your bag as a gift bag. Cut a long length of matching fabric and tie into a bow around the handle.

Conversation:

You can use your tote bag to carry special papers and other favorite things. We each have our own favorites because God made everyone unique. That's what makes our world so interesting! And God loves each of us!

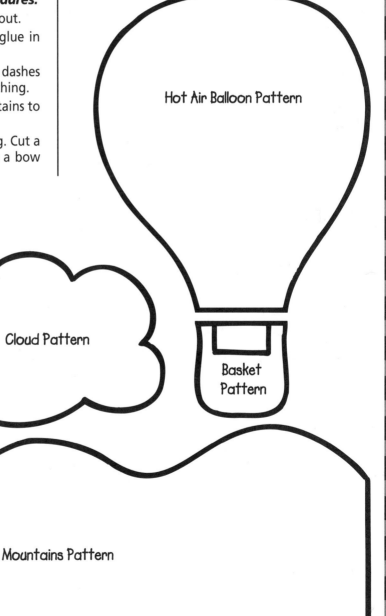

Hot Air Balloon Pattern

Cloud Pattern

Basket Pattern

Mountains Pattern

Daily Life

Materials: Plaster of paris, water, wire ornament hangers, variety of used greeting cards and/or wrapping paper, construction paper in a variety of colors, raffia, hammer, nail, piece of wood scrap, scissors, glue, pencils. For each child—one large can (such as a coffee can), a small tree branch with several limbs, one medium-size paper sack, three frozen-juice can lids (any size), paint stirring stick.

Preparation: Place juice can lids on scrap-wood surface. Use hammer and nail to make a hole at top of each lid (sketch a).

Instruct each child in the following procedures:

★ Fill can two-thirds with plaster of paris and one-third with water. Use paint stirring stick to stir until creamy. (Note: Work rapidly, as mixture begins to harden very quickly.)

★ Insert end of tree branch into center of can (sketch b). Hold in place until plaster begins to harden.

★ Make ornaments for tree to celebrate your favorite holidays. Cut out pictures from greeting cards and wrapping paper, cut shapes from construction paper, or draw your own pictures to glue onto lids (sketch c).

★ Insert end of wire hanger through hole in each juice can lid.

★ When plaster is fairly dry, place can inside bag. Fold down top edge of bag (sketch d).

★ Take several strands of raffia and tie around can to secure bag in place (sketch d).

★ Make additional ornaments at home. Place ornaments on tree according to celebration. Or, glue photographs of family members onto juice can lids to create a "family tree."

Simplification Ideas: Use jars filled with gravel instead of plaster. Use chenille wire to make ornament hangers.

Enrichment Ideas: Cover can with wrapping paper or colorful self-adhesive paper. Paint tree branches using acrylic paint in a variety of bright colors. Make a chain of garland to decorate tree using interlocking strips of construction paper.

Conversation:

What occasions does your family like to celebrate? How do you celebrate birthdays? How do you decorate for each celebration? Families are unique in the ways that they celebrate. Sometimes celebrations are based on traditions, passed on from generation to generation. And sometimes we make up our own ways to celebrate. You can decorate and redecorate your celebration tree to liven up any special occasion. Or add photos to it and use it for a "family tree"!

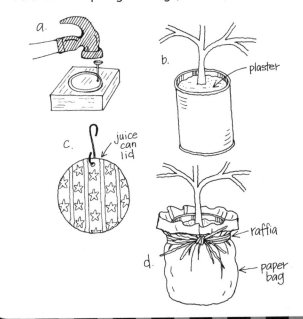

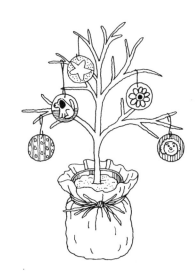

Materials: Thin adhesive-backed corkboard, cardboard, felt, drill, ¼-inch (.625-cm) drill bit, pencil, glue, scissors, measuring stick. For each child—three metal binder rings.

Preparation: Cut cardboard into 9x12-inch (22.5x30-cm) rectangles—two for each child. Cut cork into 12x19-inch (30x47.5-cm) rectangles—one for each child. Cut felt into 12x19-inch (30x47.5) rectangles—one for each child. Save felt scraps.

Instruct each child in the following procedures:

★ Peel adhesive backing from cork piece. Line up edges of cardboard pieces onto cork piece, leaving a 1-inch (2.5-cm) gap in the center (sketch a).

★ Glue large felt piece onto cardboard pieces, on side opposite of cork.

★ Fold book in half and mark three evenly spaced holes as shown in sketch b. With teacher's help, drill holes through cardboard, felt and cork.

★ Attach metal rings through holes.

★ Cut felt shapes into letters and shapes. Glue onto corkboard to decorate scrapbook (sketch c).

Simplification Ideas: Cover both sides of cardboard with felt instead of using cork. Or, cover cardboard with self-adhesive paper.

Enrichment Idea: Use scribble pads or brown paper bags cut into 12x19-inch (30x47.5-cm) sheets for scrapbook pages.

Conversation:

Why do people make and keep scrapbooks? Scrapbooks are good places to keep pictures, cards, awards and other special reminders of the good times we've had with our families and friends. What is a special time with your family you'll never forget?

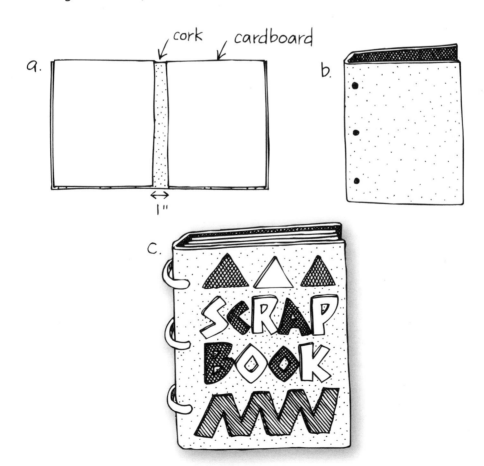

Daily Life

DENIM BIBLE BAG
(25-30 MINUTES)

Materials: Discarded adult-sized denim jeans with back pockets—one pair for every two children, embroidery floss, embroidery needles, ¼-inch (.625-cm) rope, bandanas, fabric glue or fusible webbing and iron, decorative buttons, grommet pliers (available at fabric stores), sewing machine and thread, 3-dimensional fabric paint in a variety of colors, including gold, fabric scissors, measuring stick. For each child—four grommets

Preparation: Cut legs off jeans just above the knee and just below the crotch to make a 14-inch (35-cm) long section (sketch a). Turn this section inside-out and stitch bottom closed to make bag. Turn right-side out. Cut entire back two pockets out of jeans (sketch b). Attach pocket to one side of jeans bag using fabric glue, fusible webbing or sewing machine. Cut embroidery floss into 24-inch (60-cm) lengths—one for each child. Cut rope into 22-inch (55-cm) lengths—two for each child. Cut bandanas into four quarters—one quarter for each child.

Instruct each child in the following procedures:

★ Fold down to the inside about ½ inch (1.25 cm) of top edge of bag. Thread needle with embroidery floss and knot one end. Sew a whip stitch around top edge of bag (sketch c).

★ Fold and tuck cut end of bandana into pocket.

★ Sew buttons onto bandana and through front of pocket to hold bandana in place (sketch d).

★ With teacher's help, use grommet pliers to insert two grommets on each side of top of bag, 1 inch (2.5 cm) from top (sketch e).

★ Thread ends of rope through front of grommets. Tie a large knot at each end, inside bag. Repeat with second length of rope to make handles (sketch f).

★ Use fabric paint to write name below pocket and to decorate rest of bag. Allow paint to dry.

★ Take denim bag home and use it to hold your Bible. (*Note:* Some children may not own a Bible. Be prepared ahead of time to give Bibles to those who need them.)

Simplification Idea: Use store-bought canvas bags to decorate with jeans pocket and fabric paint.

Conversation:

If you were traveling to a new place and could only bring three of your belongings, what would you bring? The Bible is one of the most valuable items we can own, because it's God's letter to us. When we read His Word, we learn the answers to our most important questions. Now you can use your Denim Bible Bag to carry your Bible with you!

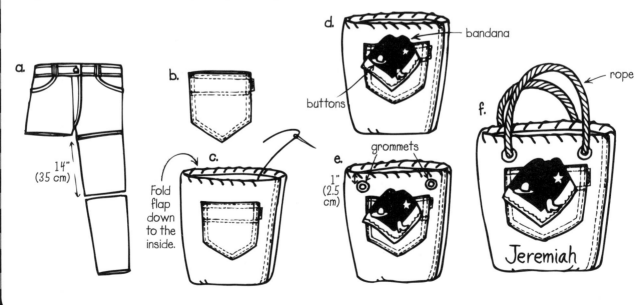

a.

14" (35 cm)

b.

c. Fold flap down to the inside.

d. bandana — buttons

e. grommets — 1" (2.5 cm)

f. rope — Jeremiah

Materials: Felt pens in a variety of colors, drill, ⅛-inch (.32-cm) drill bit, narrow ribbon or raffia, wood glue, measuring stick. For each child—three tongue depressors, two craft sticks.

Preparation: Cut ribbon into 14-inch (35-cm) lengths—one for each child. Drill hole at one end of each tongue depressor.

Instruct each child in the following procedures:

★ Use felt pens to color and decorate tongue depressors and craft sticks.

★ With teacher's help, glue craft sticks directly on top of each other.

★ Thread ribbon or raffia through holes in tongue depressors. With teacher's help, secure ribbon with a knot or a bow (sketch a).

★ Separate top two tongue depressors from the third one. Glue edge of craft sticks onto tongue depressors as shown in sketch a. Allow glue to dry.

★ Arrange ends of tongue depressors in a triangular shape. Use easel to display postcards, greeting cards or photographs (sketch b).

Enrichment Ideas: Use acrylic paints instead of felt pens. Letter words of a memory verse on a large index card to display on easel.

Conversation:

Artists use large easels to hold pictures and paintings. What do you like to paint pictures of? Who in your family is a good artist? What are you good at doing? Some people may be good artists and some may be good at sports, music or something else. We use the word "talent" to describe something a person is good at. God gave each person in your family a talent. Every person is special in his or her own way. Let's thank God for making each one of us special!

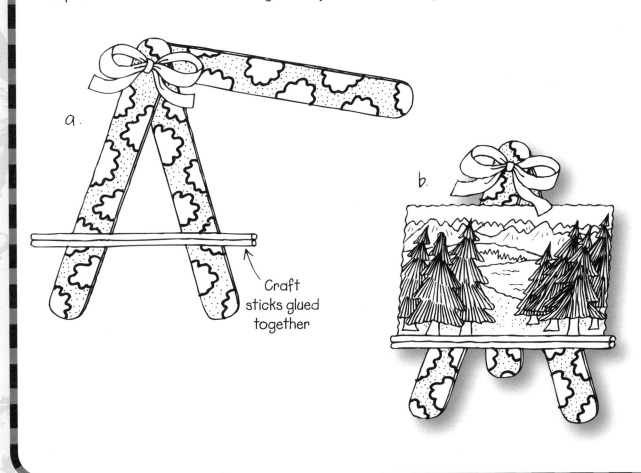

a.

Craft sticks glued together

b.

Daily Life

Materials: Tempera paint in a variety of bright colors, paintbrushes, shallow containers, heavy white cardboard or foam-core board, wide magnetic strips, pencils, craft knife, glue, scissors, rulers, newspaper. For each child—three to five wooden clothespins (spring-type).

Preparation: Cut cardboard or foam-core board into 9x12-inch (22.5x30-cm) rectangles—one for each child. Cut magnetic strips into 5-inch (12.5-cm) lengths—two for each child. Cover work area with newspaper. Pour paint into shallow containers. Optional: Ask children to bring in small household items that would make good prints.

Instruct each child in the following procedures:

✶ Paint each clothespin a different color—one for each family member. Let dry.

✶ Glue magnet strip at top and bottom on back of message board.

✶ Dip ends of various items such as pencil erasers, rulers or forks into paint and press onto front of board to make prints (sketch a).

✶ Glue clothespins onto message board (sketch b).

✶ Place message board on refrigerator or other metal appliance at home. Clip drawings or notes of thanks, love, encouragement to a specific family member by attaching message to his or her colored clothespin.

Simplification Idea: Provide stickers instead of paint or ask children to bring in their favorite stickers to decorate message boards.

Enrichment Ideas: Cover cardboard with wrapping paper or self-adhesive paper. Glue sequins or jewels onto message board. With teacher's help, write names of family members on clothespins. Or draw shapes of plants and animals on poster board. Cut out shapes and glue onto front of clothespins (sketch c).

Conversation:

What can you clip onto your message board? How do you feel when you get a kind card or picture from someone in your family? We can let our family members know we love them by writing messages, by drawing pictures, or by telling them!

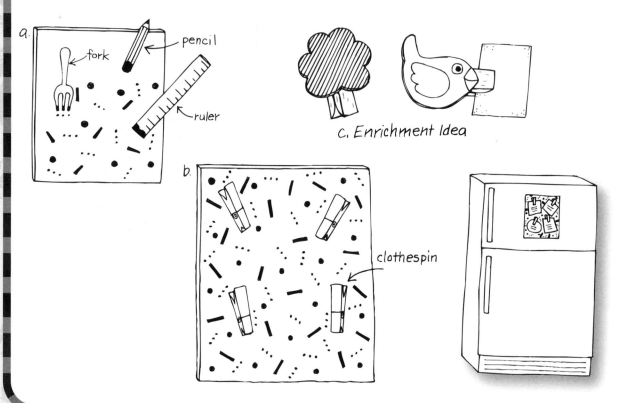

a. fork   pencil   ruler

c. Enrichment Idea

b. clothespin

Daily Life

Materials: Bible, brown and yellow Fun Foam or felt, Fun Foam or felt scraps in various colors, gold glitter glue stick, yarn, writing paper, pencils, crayons, glue, masking tape, scissors, hole punch, measuring stick.

Preparation: Cut brown Fun Foam or felt into 5x12-inch (12.5x30-cm) rectangles—one for each child. Fold bottom third of rectangle up to make a pocket. Punch through both layers eight evenly spaced holes along the three outside edges of pocket (sketch a). Cut an X in top third portion of rectangle for doorknob opening. Cut yarn into 2-foot (60-cm) lengths—one for each child. Wrap the end of each yarn length with tape to make a needle. Cut yellow Fun Foam or felt into star shapes approximately 2½ inches (6.25 cm) in diameter—one for each child. Cut a variety of geometric shapes out of Fun Foam or felt scraps—several for each child.

Instruct each child in the following procedures:

★ With teacher's help, fold rectangle and hold pocket together with holes aligned. Thread yarn through top hole and tie a knot (sketch b).

★ Lace yarn through holes around all edges of pocket.

★ Tie a knot at the last hole and trim excess yarn.

★ Spread gold glitter glue stick on front of yellow star shape. Use white glue to attach star to center of pocket.

★ Decorate pocket by gluing other shapes onto pocket.

★ With teacher's help, write or draw a message on paper to give to a special person. Put paper in pocket.

★ Take door hanger home and hang on a door knob where your special person will find it.

Enrichment Idea: Write or photocopy a memory verse or special message on pieces of paper. Place in door hangers for children to look at later.

Conversation:

What special message will you leave in your door hanger? This is a good place to leave a happy message or to share good news with everyone. God wants us to share His good-news message with everyone too. What is God's good news? (God loves us!) **We can put this good news in our door hanger!**

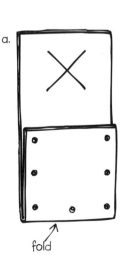

a.

fold

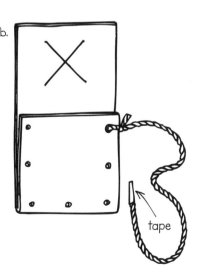

b.

tape

To MOM

"HAMMERED METAL" FLOWER POT
(TWO-DAY CRAFT/20-25 MINUTES EACH DAY)

Materials: Black acrylic paint, permanent felt pens, heavy-duty aluminum foil, thick cotton string, craft glue, pencils with erasers, sponge brushes, rulers, paper towels, scissors, shallow containers, newspaper. For each child—one 4- or 5-inch (10- or 12.5-cm) light-colored plastic plant pot with or without saucer.

DAY ONE

Instruct each child in the following procedures:

★ With permanent felt pen, draw simple shapes such as hearts, crosses, flowers, large initials or borders onto plastic pot.

★ Squeeze glue on felt pen lines.

★ Cut several lengths of string. Carefully lay string on glue to follow design lines. Trim excess string and allow to dry (sketch a).

DAY TWO

Preparation: Cover work area with newspaper. Pour black paint into shallow containers.

Instruct each child in the following procedures:

★ Measure and cut enough foil to fit around the entire pot, with about 1 inch (2.5 cm) for overlap and an extra 5 inches (12.5 cm) above top of pot. Crumple foil slightly and then smooth out.

★ Using a sponge brush, coat the outside of pot with glue.

★ With shiny side out, wrap foil around the pot with at least 3 inches (7.5 cm) extending above the top of pot and some foil extending at the bottom. Carefully smooth foil over the string by pressing the pad of your finger or a pencil eraser along edges of string designs (sketch b). Take care not to puncture or tear foil.

★ Apply glue to inside and bottom of pot. Press down excess foil over glue (sketch c).

★ If a saucer accompanies pot, cover saucer with foil in the same manner.

★ Brush black acrylic paint onto pot and saucer. Use paper towels to lightly wipe off excess paint, leaving some paint in the wrinkles. Let dry (sketch d).

Conversation:

Long ago, people who made things out of metal were called "smiths." There were tinsmiths, goldsmiths, silversmiths, etc. Often a man came to be known by the name of his trade. A worker in metals might be known in town as John the smith, and the baker known as James the baker. Today we would call them John Smith and James Baker. Many families have last names that came from these trade names. What other names can you think of that might have come from trade names? (Carpenter, Miller, Shoemaker, etc.)

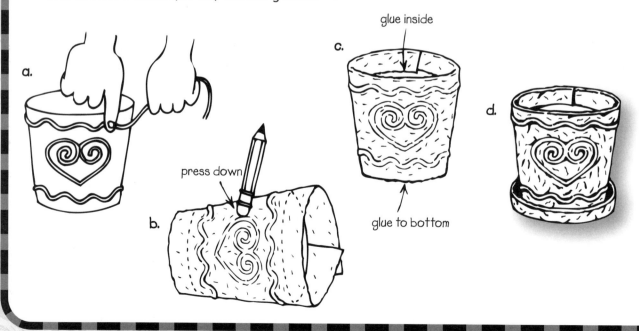

a.

b. press down

c. glue inside

d.

glue to bottom

Daily Life

Materials: Black or navy felt, fabric scraps and ribbons in a variety of colors, white fabric, silver or gold sequins, ½-inch (1.25-cm) dowels or sticks, saw, sewing machine or needle and thread, yarn, permanent fine-tip felt pens, pencil, glue, scissors, ruler.

Preparation: Cut felt into 9x12-inch (22.5x30-cm) rectangles—one for each child. Fold over top of each felt rectangle about 1 inch (2.5 cm) and stitch to make a casing (sketch a). Cut ribbon into 5-inch (12.5-cm) lengths—three for each child. Saw dowels or sticks into 12-inch (30-cm) lengths—one for each child. Draw 3- to 4-inch (7.5- to 10-cm) stars onto white fabric and cut out—one for each child.

Instruct each child in the following procedures:

★ Cut and glue fabric scraps onto felt banner to look like your home (sketch b).

★ Use felt pen to letter a message on the star, such as "God bless our home."

★ Choose three ribbons. Glue star at top corner of banner, attaching ends of ribbons underneath star.

★ Glue sequins onto banner for additional stars.

★ Slide dowel or stick through casing at top of banner.

★ Cut yarn to desired hanging length. Tie one end of yarn to each side of dowel to make a hanger.

Simplification Idea: For younger children, cut fabric scraps into a variety of geometric shapes ahead of time.

Enrichment Idea: Children hand-stitch the casing.

Conversation:

What does your home look like? Some people live in houses. Other people live in apartments, mobile homes or even boats! No matter what your home is like, it is a special place where you sleep, eat and spend time with your family. What else do you like to do at home? Let's ask God to bless us and keep us safe in our homes.

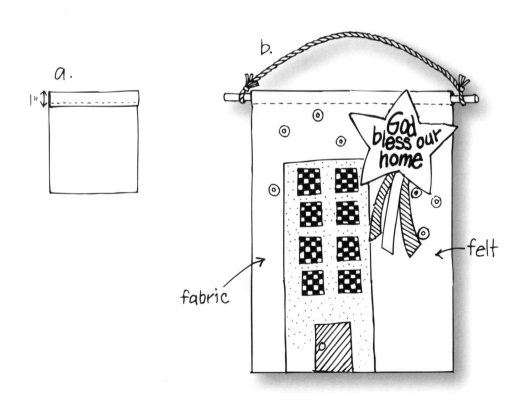

a.

1"

b.

God bless our home

fabric

felt

Materials: Graham crackers, powdered sugar, lemon juice, eggs, salt, medium-size bowl, measuring cups and spoons, electric mixer, plastic sandwich bags, colorful candies such as Skittles® or M&Ms®, sturdy cardboard, aluminum foil, glue, scissors or craft knife, ruler.

Preparation: Cut cardboard into 2½-inch (6.25-cm) squares and 12-inch (30-cm) squares—one of each for each child. Cover larger square with aluminum foil to make a platform for the house. The following recipe will make enough icing for eight children: Beat 3 cups powdered sugar, 2 egg whites, ¼ teaspoon salt and 2 teaspoons lemon juice for five minutes or until fluffy. Pour equal amounts of icing into eight sandwich bags. Squeeze icing into corner of bag and tie top of bag in a knot (sketch a).

Instruct each child in the following procedures:

★ Glue small cardboard square onto foil-covered platform.

★ Cut a small piece off the corner of bag of icing.

★ Squeeze a generous line of icing around edges of small cardboard square (sketch b).

★ Stand up half a graham cracker in icing to form front of house (sketch c).

★ Add sides and back to house in same manner, squeezing icing in between crackers (sketch d).

★ Use icing to attach two crackers on top of house to form roof.

★ Use icing and candy pieces to customize house with a door, windows, shingles, a walkway leading to the house, etc.

Simplification Ideas: For younger children, build houses ahead of time and allow children to decorate. Or cut off top half of milk carton (half-gallon size) and use icing to glue graham crackers onto edges of carton.

Enrichment Ideas: Cut two triangles from brightly colored paper to fill in front and back roof spaces. Provide a variety of healthy food items such as raisins, nuts and cereal to decorate houses.

Conversation:

What would your dream house be like? What do you like about the home you live in now? What have you and your family done to make the place where you live better? How do you help take care of your home? Let's thank God for giving us a place to call home!

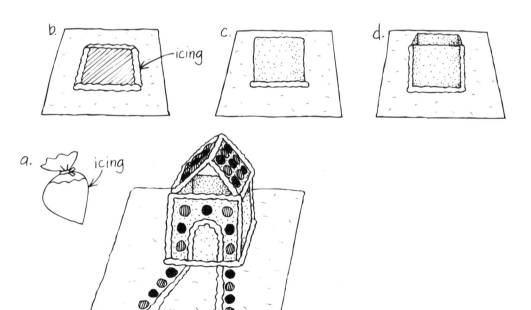

b.   icing

c.

d.

a.   icing

Daily Life

EARLY CHILDHOOD • YOUNGER ELEMENTARY • OLDER ELEMENTARY

Materials: Tempera paint in a variety of colors, shallow containers, several cookie sheets, white or beige card stock, thin yarn, hole punches, plastic spoons, paper towels, transparent tape, scissors, measuring stick, newspaper. For each child—one marble, five resealable plastic sandwich bags.

Preparation: Cut the card stock into 7-inch (17.5-cm) squares—two for each child. Cut yarn into 18-inch (45-cm) lengths—one for each child. Wrap small piece of tape around one end of each yarn piece to make a needle. Pour thin layer of paint into shallow containers. Place a spoon in each color of paint. Line cookie sheets with newspaper. Cover work area with newspaper.

Instruct each child in the following procedures:

★ Place card stock squares in cookie sheet.

★ Dip marble in paint. Use spoon to remove marble and place marble on cookie sheet. Move cookie sheet around so that marble rolls over card stock to make a design (sketch a).

★ Wipe paint off marble and repeat process with another color. Allow paint to dry.

★ Lay sandwich bags directly on top of one another with openings facing same direction.

★ Place one card stock square under sandwich bags and one on top, aligning all sides. Punch three evenly spaced holes on side opposite of bag openings (sketch b).

★ Thread yarn up through bottom hole leaving about 4 inches (10 cm) of slack at bottom.

★ Weave yarn through other holes as shown in sketch c.

★ Thread yarn around spine of book and through holes as shown in sketch d.

★ Tie loose ends of yarn together tightly at bottom of book (sketch e). Cut off excess yarn.

★ Place postcards, leaves, photographs and other memorabilia in resealable bags.

Simplification Idea: Punch holes in covers and bags ahead of time.

Enrichment Idea: Use felt pens to write title on front cover. Add more resealable bags.

Conversation:

When you buy or collect things from a trip or special event they are called "souvenirs" or "keepsakes." What kinds of souvenirs have you saved? Souvenirs and keepsakes help us remember special places and events. When you're much older, you can look through your Keepsake Book to remind you of good times you had with your family and friends. Let's thank God for special memories!

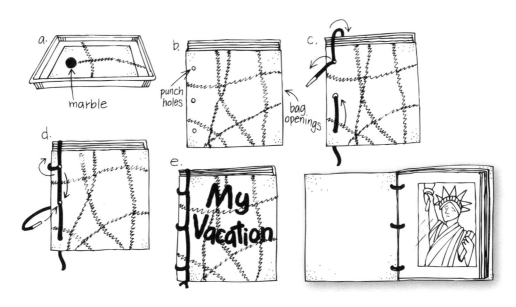

Daily Life

Materials: 18-gauge wire, wire cutters, needle-nose pliers, raffia, sand, gold glitter, plastic scoops, scissors, measuring stick. For each child—one pint-sized mason jar with lid, one votive candle.

Preparation: Cut wire into 20-inch (50-cm) lengths—two for each child. Cut raffia into 18-inch (45-cm) lengths—several strands for each child.

Instruct each child in the following procedures:

★ Curl one end of wire length into a small loop. Student may use pliers to make tighter loops.

★ Starting ⅓ of the way up from bottom of jar, use your thumb to hold looped end of wire against jar and wrap wire halfway around width of jar. Bend wire down and wrap wire under jar until it meets the starting loop (sketch a).

★ Hook wire through loop and wrap remaining wire around other half of jar (sketch b). Wrap the end of wire under the intersecting wire and curl end into a loop.

★ Make a handle with the second wire by threading ends through loops of first wire (sketch c). Curl ends.

★ Wrap raffia tightly around neck of jar to hold handle in place. Tie ends of raffia in a bow and trim excess.

★ Use scoop to fill jar halfway with sand. Sprinkle gold glitter over sand. Push bottom of votive candle into sand (sketch d). Screw on lid.

★ Use candle under adult supervision. Remove lid and have an adult use a long matchstick to light the candle inside jar. Do not touch wire handle or place lid on jar until candle is extinguished.

Enrichment Ideas: Use glass paint to decorate jar. Use acrylic paint to paint jar lid, or glue fabric circles on top of lid and trim with ribbon. Instead of sand, fill jar with small pebbles spray-painted gold.

Conversation:

Imagine what it was like before electricity was invented. For most people, a single candle or lantern was all the light they had at night. The Bible often refers to our faith in Jesus as a light that shines to others. What does that mean? What are some ways we can show our families, friends and neighbors God's love?

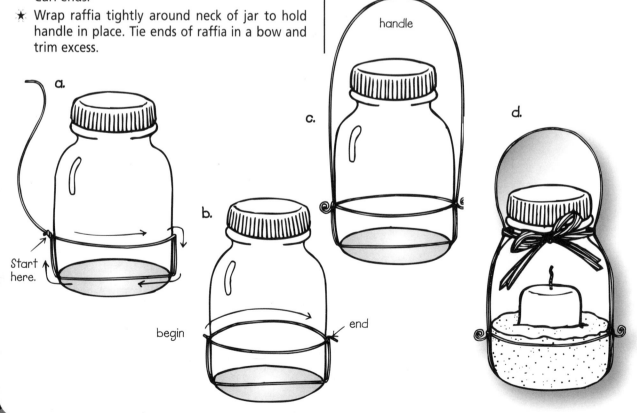

a.

Start here.

b. begin

c. handle

d. end

Materials: Fruity Pebbles or other colored rice cereal, poster board, self-adhesive magnet strips, clear acrylic spray, paper plates, craft glue, wide paintbrushes, shallow containers, ruler, pencils, scissors, newspaper.

Preparation: Cut poster board into 5-inch (12.5-cm) squares—one for each child. Cut magnet strips into 3-inch (7.5-cm) lengths—one for each child. Pour cereal into containers. Lay newspaper in a well-ventilated area

Instruct each child in the following procedures:

★ Use a pencil to draw a simple design on poster-board square.

★ Remove adhesive backing from the magnet strip and press onto back of the poster-board square (sketch a).

★ Put a handful of cereal onto paper plate. Separate the different colors on the plate.

★ Brush a thick layer of craft glue on poster-board design, working on one section at a time.

★ Press cereal into glue to create your mosaic. Use different colors of cereal in different sections of your design (sketch b).

★ Continue adding cereal until poster board is covered. Allow glue to dry.

★ In well-ventilated area, teacher sprays finished mosaic with clear acrylic spray.

★ Put your Mosaic Magnet on your refrigerator at home.

Conversation:

Your mosaic design is made with many small pieces of cereal. Most mosaics are made using many small pieces of tile, glass or stone. Talented artists have made mosaics on floors, walls or even furniture. What are some things you like to make? What are some other talents you have?

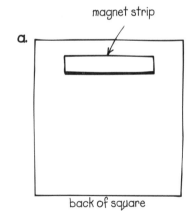

magnet strip

a.

back of square

b.

glue

Daily Life

Materials: Fabric and felt scraps in various colors, rick rack, buttons, pen, craft glue, fabric scissors. For each child—one 9x12-inch (22.5x30-cm) felt rectangle.

Preparation: Cut 10 to 15 geometric shapes for each child. Make two sample Quilt Mats, placing pattern shapes in simple designs that children can imitate.

Instruct each child in the following procedures:

★ Arrange and glue felt and fabric shapes onto felt rectangle to make a quilt pattern. Follow the pattern on one of the samples or make a crazy quilt using your own design.

★ Glue rickrack and buttons on quilt to decorate.

Simplification Idea: Use construction paper instead of felt and fabric.

Conversation:

In the Old West, people made big quilts out of little pieces of fabric. The quilts were very warm blankets. Today we made little quilts. What will you do with your quilt? (Use as a placemat, hang on a wall, give to someone, etc.) **(Seth's) quilt looks a little different from (Sam's) quilt. They are both very special. God made all of us a little different from each other, too. He loves each one of us very much!**

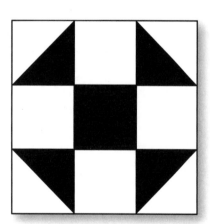

Shoofly

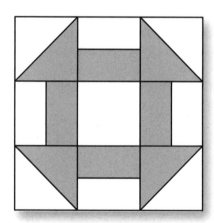

Churn Dash

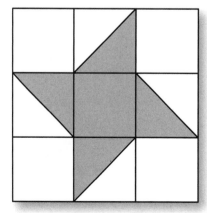

Friendship Star

Materials: Sampler Pattern, muslin fabric, embroidery floss in various colors, narrow ribbon, cardboard, pencil, craft glue, fabric scissors, measuring stick. For each child—embroidery needle, eight craft sticks, eight large paper clips.

Preparation: Cut fabric into 4-inch (10-cm) squares—one for each child. Lay fabric square over Sampler Pattern. Trace letters and design from pattern onto fabric with pencil—one for each child. Cut ribbon into 6-inch (15-cm) lengths—one for each child. Glue ends of eight craft sticks together to make square frame—one frame for each child (sketch a). Cut cardboard into 4½-inch (11.25-cm) squares—one for each child. Cut embroidery floss into 18-inch (45-cm) lengths.

Instruct each child in the following procedures:

★ Use large paper clips to secure fabric behind craft stick frame (sketch b). Pull fabric taut, so frame acts as embroidery hoop.

★ With teacher's help, thread embroidery floss onto needle and knot one end. Starting at top of first letter, make simple running stitches to stitch letters and design onto fabric (sketch c). Knot end of floss and trim excess.

★ Remove paper clips and fabric from frame.

★ Squeeze glue along edges of cardboard square and glue to back of fabric square.

★ Form ribbon into a loop for hanger. Glue loop onto top of sampler (sketch d).

★ Glue frame over fabric and ribbon. Allow to dry.

Simplification Idea: Paper-clip fabric to frame ahead of time. Use fabric paint pens instead of embroidery floss.

Enrichment Idea: For a two-day craft, children assemble and decorate frames with acrylic paint one day and stitch sampler the next day.

Conversation:

All through the world, girls are often taught how to stitch at a very young age. They often keep little boxes with all their stitching supplies and fabric scraps in them. They use the materials in their boxes to practice their handiwork. What kind of hobbies do you practice at home? (Volunteers respond.)

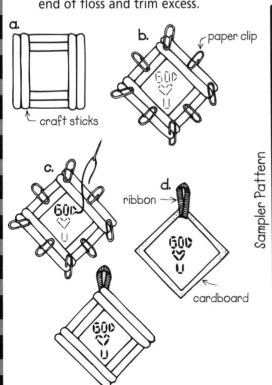

a.

craft sticks

b.

paper clip

c.

d.

ribbon

cardboard

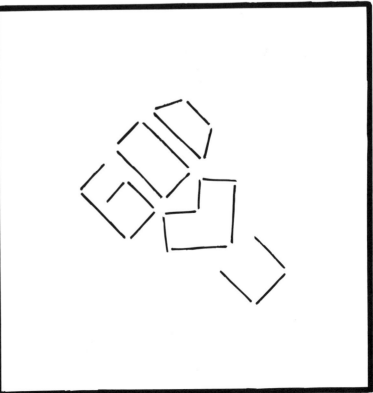

Sampler Pattern

Daily Life

Materials: Sturdy wallpaper in a variety of colors and patterns, rickrack in a variety of colors, hole punch, pencil, glue, scissors, measuring stick. For each child—three brads.

Preparation: Cut wallpaper into 12x19-inch (30x47.5-cm) rectangles—one for each child.

Instruct each child in the following procedures:

★ Fold wallpaper in half to make book cover.

★ With teacher's help, punch three evenly spaced holes in left margin of book.

★ Secure a brad through each hole.

★ With teacher's help, use pencil to write the initial of your last or first name.

★ Cut and glue rickrack onto pencil lines.

Enrichment Idea: Use scribble pads or brown paper bags cut into 12x19-inch (30x47.5-cm) sheets for scrapbook pages.

Conversation:

What is a scrapbook? A scrapbook is a special book with lots of pages. We glue or tape things that we want to save onto the pages so that they don't get lost or damaged. In your scrapbook, you can save pictures, awards, cards, letters or anything else that will help you remember special times you had with your families and friends. When did you have a fun time with your family?

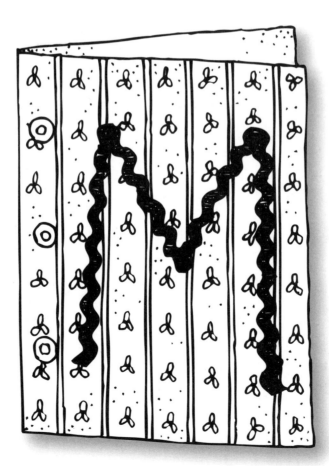

Daily Life

Materials: Light blue acrylic spray paint, white and yellow acrylic paint, sponges, prepasted wallpaper scraps in green and tan small prints, water, sponge brushes, scissors, hot air balloon stickers, ¼-inch (.625-cm) cording, ruler, ice pick or awl, pie tins, shallow containers, newspaper. For each child—one clean laundry detergent box (approximately 5x8½x8½ inches [12.5x21.5x21.5 cm]) with flip-top lid.

Preparation: With ice pick, poke holes on the opposite sides of each box, 1½ inches (3.75 cm) from the top edge (sketch a). Widen hole to about a ¼-inch (.625-cm) opening. Spray boxes with blue spray paint. Cut green and tan wallpaper into hill shapes with a straight edge at the bottom (sketch b). Cut damp sponges into cloud shapes and round suns. Cut cording into 2-foot (60-cm) lengths—one for each child. Pour white and yellow paint into pie tins. Pour water into shallow containers. Cover work area with newspaper.

Instruct each child in the following procedures:

★ With sponge brush, brush water onto the back of wallpaper mountain and hill shapes to activate wallpaper paste.

★ Place wallpaper shapes at the bottom of each side of the box to make the land (sketch c). Smooth wallpaper down.

★ Press cloud-shaped sponge in white paint. Then press sponge onto the blue part of box to make a cloud. Repeat sponging to make clouds on every side of box.

★ Press circle sponge in yellow paint and then press onto box to make a sun in the sky. Allow paint to dry.

★ Place hot air balloon stickers in the sky.

★ For carrying handle, poke the cording into one of the holes on the side of the box and pull through to the inside. With teacher's help, tie a large knot at the end of cording inside the box to secure. Repeat for the other hole.

Enrichment Idea: Older children may cut out their own wallpaper mountain and hill shapes. They may cut out wallpaper house and tree shapes to add to their landscape.

Conversation:

There are many things you can do with your travel tote. You can carry things that are special to you. You can use your tote to hold your Bible and other books. What will you put in your travel tote, (Eric)?

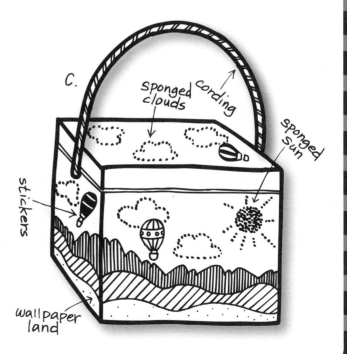

Materials: Several new large shoe insoles, rubber cement, colored ink pads, disposable wet tissues, writing paper, ballpoint pens, scissors. For each child—two medium-size jar lids or small wood blocks.

Preparation: Cut insoles into three even pieces—one piece for each child.

Instruct each child in the following procedures:

★ Draw a simple shape, such as a heart, star, initial, flower, onto smooth latex side of each insole piece. (Note: Letters and shapes are reversed when stamped—draw initials backwards.)

★ Cut out shapes (sketch a).

★ Glue cutouts onto jar lids or wood blocks to make rubber stamps (sketch b). Allow glue to dry.

★ Press rubber stamp onto ink pad and then onto paper.

★ Wipe stamps clean using disposable wet tissues.

Enrichment Ideas: Children work in groups and share rubber stamps and ink pads to decorate stationery, greeting cards and envelopes.

Conversation:

What are your initials? Some people's first, middle and last initial, when put together, form a new word. Initials are a quick way to identify your name. Do you know why your parents gave you your name? What does your name mean? Many names used today can be found in the Bible. What are some you can think of?

a.

jar lid

b.

Daily Life

Materials: Yarn in various colors, ribbon, craft glue, masking tape, scissors, measuring stick. For each child—seven medium-sized wooden spools, one chenille wire.

Preparation: Cut yarn into 18-inch (45-cm) lengths—seven for each child. Cut ribbon into 18-inch (45-cm) lengths—one for each child. Tear masking tape into 1-inch (2.5-cm) pieces and place on edge of table—seven for each child.

Instruct each child in the following procedures:

★ With teacher's help, tape one end of a length of yarn to the middle of a spool (sketch a). Wrap yarn around spool.

★ Glue down end of yarn to secure (sketch b). Repeat with the six remaining spools.

★ Thread spools onto chenille wire and bend into a wreath shape.

★ With teacher's help, twist ends of wire together to close wreath. Teacher ties ribbon at bottom of wreath.

Simplification Idea: Color spools with felt pens instead of wrapping them with yarn.

Conversation:

When people don't have many things to decorate their houses with, they use what they have to make simple decorations. This wreath is made from leftover spools. Hanging a wreath on your door is a way to welcome guests to your home. What are other ways we welcome guests?

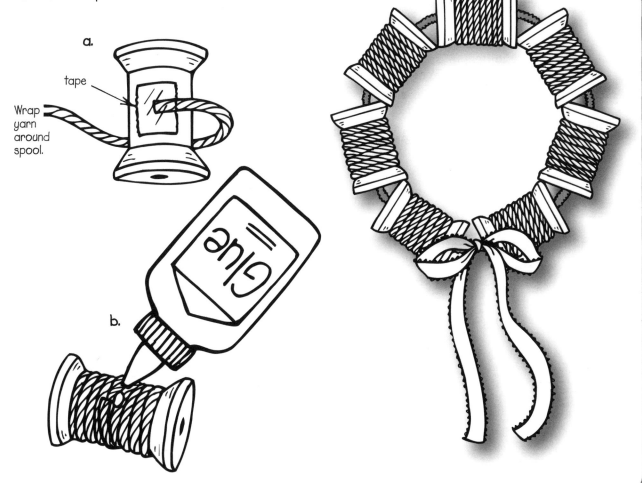

a.

tape

Wrap yarn around spool.

Glue

b.

Materials: Stained Glass Patterns, several squeeze bottles of simulated liquid lead (available at craft stores), glass paints in a variety of colors, small plastic bottle caps, photocopier and paper, thin paintbrushes, crayons, shallow containers, water, paper towels, scissors, newspaper. For each child—one inexpensive 4-inch (10-cm) tall clear glass jar candle (found in kosher food or candle sections of grocery stores).

DAY ONE Preparation: Photocopy one copy of Stained-Glass Patterns for each child. Set out shallow containers filled with water. Cover work area with newspaper.

Instruct each child in the following procedures:

★ Cut out the pattern(s) you want to use on your candle.

★ Dip paintbrush in water and lightly dampen a pattern with water.

★ Stick wet pattern on glass. Trace around pattern with a crayon. Remove pattern (sketch a).

★ Trace the same pattern again to repeat the design or trace different patterns on glass. Smaller shapes such as diamonds, circles and squares may also be drawn on glass.

★ Squeeze a thin line of liquid lead over crayon outlines. Be careful not to smear lead on the opposite side of glass while working (sketch b).

★ Allow to dry overnight.

DAY TWO Preparation: Pour small amounts of glass paints into bottle caps (paint dries out quickly)—one color in each lid. Set out paper towels and shallow containers filled with water.

Instruct each child in the following procedures:

★ With paintbrush, brush a thin coat of paint inside leaded lines of each shape. If coated too thick, paint will run (sketch c).

★ Clean brush in water before using another color of paint. Use paper towels to dry brush as needed.

★ If desired, paint the rest of glass as well.

★ As time allows, add a second coat of paint to create more vivid color.

Simplification Ideas: Younger children may decorate only one side of glass or they may draw leaded lines on glass to make geometric designs instead of using paper patterns.

Conversation:

Your Stained-Glass Candleholder can be used again and again. When your candle has burned away, you can put another one inside. The talents and abilities we have can be used again and again too. What are some talents that you have? What are some different ways a (musical) talent could be used?

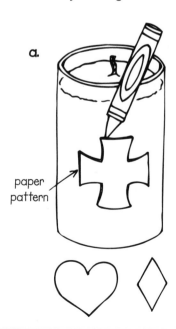

a.

paper pattern

b.

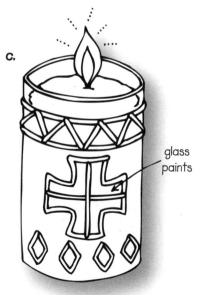

c.

glass paints

STAINED-GLASS CANDLEHOLDER PATTERNS

Daily Life

Materials: Poster board, white corrugated cardboard (found at craft or school supply stores), pencil, colored felt pens, paper clips, ruler, scissors, craft knife, white glue, glue sticks, colored poster-board scraps.

Preparation: Cut poster board into 9x22-inch (22.5x55-cm) rectangles—one for each child. Begin at one end and measure 4-inch (10-cm), 7-inch (17.5-cm), 7-inch (17.5-cm) and 4-inch (10-cm) sections (sketch a). Lightly score along these lines. Cut 7x9-inch (17.5x22.5-cm) rectangles from the corrugated cardboard—two for each child. Cut out a centered 3x5-inch (7.5x12.5-cm) opening from half of the corrugated pieces for photo frames (sketch c).

Instruct each child in the following procedures:

★ Fold poster-board piece on scored lines to make a triangle shape.

★ Glue overlapping bottom sections together to make triangle board stand. Use paper clips to hold until glue has dried (sketch b).

★ With felt pens, color each rib of corrugated pieces a different color to make stripes.

★ Glue cutout corrugated piece to one side of triangle board. Glue only the side edges and bottom, leaving the top unglued so a photo can be inserted (sketch c).

★ Glue second corrugated piece to the back of triangle board.

★ Cut poster board scraps into triangles, squares, circles or other shapes.

★ Using glue stick, glue poster board shapes around the photo frame.

Enrichment Idea: Take a horizontal photo of each child and develop ahead of time to insert into frame.

Conversation:

Whose picture are you going to put in your frame? God takes care of us by giving us special people who love us. When you look at the picture in your frame, you can remember that (your dad) loves you and that God loves you, too!

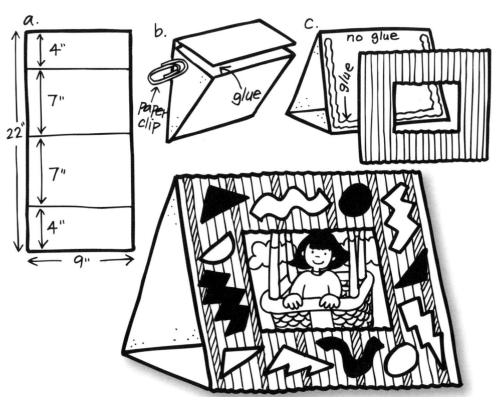

Materials: Ivory Snow detergent, water pitcher, water, measuring cup and spoons. For each child—one margarine tub or small bowl, plastic spoon, small plastic animal or toy figure (such as math counters found in school supply stores), plastic sandwich bag.

Preparation: Fill pitcher with water.

Instruct each child in the following procedures:

★ Measure ½ cup detergent and pour into bowl.

★ Teacher measures 1½ teaspoon water and adds to the detergent.

★ Mix soap with spoon. Then knead mixture with your hands. Teacher adds more water by the half-teaspoonfuls if needed.

★ Mold soap mixture around small toy figure. Smooth soap into a ball. Let dry to harden.

★ Take home soap ball in sandwich bag. Use soap in the bathtub or to wash hands.

Enrichment Idea: Have children make more than one soap ball and give one to a friend.

Conversation:

Do you like surprises? When was a time you were surprised by something special, (Daniel)? God loves us. He even gives us things that surprise us! He loves to give us good things.

Daily Life

Materials: Camera, film, heavy cardboard, toilet paper tubes, craft knife, ruler, scissors, hole punch, masking tape, pencils, shallow containers, white glue, water, aluminum foil, white acrylic spray paint, acrylic craft paint in blue, green, white, yellow and various other colors, paintbrushes, poster board or tagboard, ⅛-inch (.31-cm) satin ribbon, newspaper. For every two children—one 3-inch (7.5-cm) Styrofoam egg. Optional—clear acrylic spray, black medium-tip permanent felt pen.

DAY ONE Preparation: Take a photo of each child standing up. Develop film same day. Cut cardboard into 6x8-inch (15x20-cm) rectangles—one for each child. Cut a scalloped edge at the top of each frame (sketch b). Punch hole in center top of each frame. Cut toilet paper tubes open and cut into 1½-inch (3.75-cm) sections—one section for each child (sketch a). Cut Styrofoam egg lengthwise in half. Mix equal parts of glue and water in shallow containers, making more as needed. Tear newspaper into strips 1 inch (2.5 cm) wide and 4 inches (10 cm) long. Cover the work area with newspaper.

Instruct each child in the following procedures:

★ Fold ends of toilet paper tube section back to make 1-inch (2.5-cm) tabs. Tape to the center bottom of the frame to make balloon basket (sketch b).

★ Stuff opening with newspaper strip.

★ Glue Styrofoam egg half onto frame just below punched hole, with narrow end of egg pointing down. Tape to frame to hold in place.

★ Dip strips of newspaper into glue, removing excess glue by pulling strips between fingers. Lay strips over Styrofoam egg and paper tube. Cover the entire front and back of frame, wrapping strips around edges and smoothing out wrinkles and bubbles. Cover with three layers of newspaper strips.

★ With a pencil, poke a hole to uncover the punched hole. Smooth strips around hole, leaving hole open.

★ Allow to dry on a length of foil that has been loosely gathered and formed into a circle (sketch c).

DAY TWO Preparation: Spray all frames with white acrylic paint, front and back. Allow to dry. Pour acrylic paint into shallow containers. Cut ribbon into 10-inch (25-cm) lengths—four for each child. Cover work area with newspaper.

Instruct each child in the following procedures:

★ Paint the sky blue.

★ Paint the balloon and basket solid colors.

★ Allow a few minutes to dry.

★ Paint green hills, carefully painting around the basket.

★ Paint designs on the balloon and the balloon basket (sketch d).

★ Paint clouds and/or sun in the sky.

★ Paint small house, if desired.

★ Glue photo to tagboard. Carefully cut out your image, cutting off legs. Glue to frame, at the top of basket (sketch d).

★ Glue four ribbons from the center top of the balloon to the basket rim, spacing them evenly (sketch d). Cut ribbons to fit if necessary.

Enrichment Idea: When paint is dry, students outline designs on frame with medium-tip permanent felt pen to give a "coloring book" look. Then finish with clear acrylic spray.

Conversation:

Your frame can remind you that you are a special person to God. He loves you, just for being you. When you believe in Jesus and accept His love and forgiveness, you become a part of God's family. He loves you so much, He sent His Son, Jesus, to die for you.

a.
cut
cut

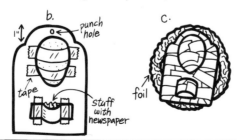

b.
1"
punch
hole
tape
stuff
with
newspaper

c.
foil

d.

Daily Life

Materials: Acrylic paint in a variety of colors, paintbrushes, shallow containers, jute, craft glue, craft knife, scissors, ruler, newspaper. For each child—15 tongue depressors.

Preparation: Use craft knife to score and break tongue depressors into 4-inch (10-cm) pieces—six for each child. Cut fabric scraps into 1x3-inch (2.5x7.5-cm) strips—eight for each child. Cut jute into 10-inch (25-cm) lengths—two for each child. Pour paint into shallow containers. Cover work area with newspaper.

Instruct each child in the following procedures:

★ Place cut ends of tongue depressor pieces together to make three vertical rows as shown in sketch a.

★ Glue a whole tongue depressor on top of each vertical piece (sketch b).

★ Turn vertical pieces over. Place six whole tongue depressors horizontally across rows to make four windows (sketch c). Glue in place and allow to dry.

★ Paint front of frame to look like an apartment building or house. Let dry.

★ Glue one end of each jute piece onto top of frame. Tie loose ends of jute together in a bow.

★ At home, glue four photographs onto back of frame. Hang picture frame on a hook or nail.

Simplification Idea: Decorate with felt pens instead of paint.

Enrichment Idea: Glue fabric scrap pieces onto sides of each window to make curtains (sketch d).

Conversation:

What did you look like when you were a baby? Videos and photographs are some ways to see what you really looked like when you were younger. What did people do before the camera was invented? (Drew sketches or painted portraits of family members.) **What pictures will you put in your frame?**

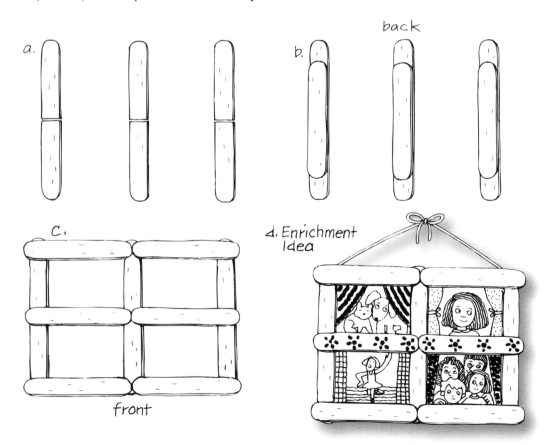

a.

b.

back

c.

front

d. Enrichment Idea

Games and Toys

Nothing is more fun than a game or toy you make yourself!

Games and Toys

Materials: Balloon Pattern, white tagboard, pencil, tempera paints in various bright colors, corn syrup, paintbrushes, bright-colored embroidery floss, scissors, measuring stick, hole punch, shallow containers, newspaper, disposable wipes. For each child—three ½-inch (1.25-cm) wooden beads.

Preparation: Trace Balloon Pattern onto tagboard and cut out—one balloon for each child. Punch six holes in balloon as shown in sketch a. Cut embroidery floss into 4-foot (1.2-m) lengths—one for each child. Cover work area with newspaper. Pour paint into shallow containers.

DAY ONE *Instruct each child in the following procedures:*

- ✶ Teacher pours a drop of corn syrup on the center of the balloon.
- ✶ With paintbrush, add paint to corn syrup to make shiny paint. Use fingers or paintbrush to mix paint and spread mixture around balloon shape. Allow paint to dry overnight.
- ✶ Use disposable wipes to clean hands.

DAY TWO *Instruct each child in the following procedures:*

- ✶ Fold embroidery floss in half. With teacher's help, thread folded floss through bead (sketch b). Slide bead down about 3 inches (7.5 cm).
- ✶ With teacher's help, tie a double knot above bead leaving loop at top for hanging (sketch b).
- ✶ Thread one end of floss through punched holes on one side of balloon as shown in sketch c. Repeat with other end of string on opposite side of balloon.
- ✶ Thread a bead on each end of string. With teacher's help, tie a double knot below each bead.
- ✶ Place loop around doorknob or other hook. Slide balloon up and down strings to make your balloon "take off" or "land."

Conversation:

(Karina), how do you think it would feel to go up, up in the sky in a hot air balloon? (Child responds.) **Some people might be afraid to be high in the sky. Some people might think it is fun to be up in the clouds. Wherever we are, we can know that God is always with us. The Bible says, "Do not be afraid; God is with you."** (See Deuteronomy 31:6.)

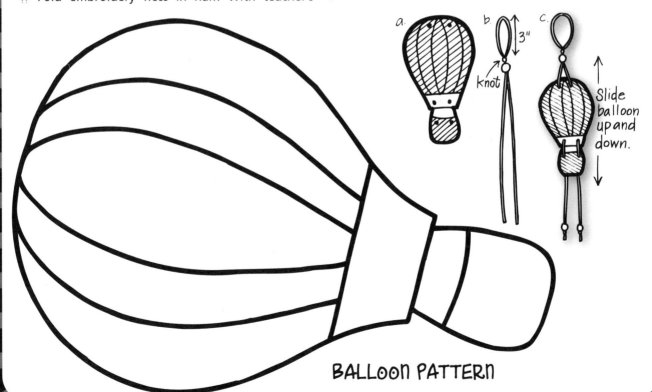

BALLOON PATTERN

Materials: Fish Pattern, plain or print fabric, narrow ribbon, pinking shears, thread, dry beans, pencil, glue, fabric scissors, ruler. For each child—one sewing needle, two small wiggle eyes, two hole reinforcements.

Preparation: Trace Fish Pattern onto folded fabric and use pinking shears to cut out—one fish for each child. Cut ribbon into 8-inch (20-cm) lengths—one for each child.

Instruct each child in the following procedures:

★ Fold fabric fish in half so that pointed ends are lined up and wrong sides of fabric are together. Use needle and thread to sew pieces together with a running stitch around edge, leaving a 2-inch (5-cm) opening (sketch a). (Note: Younger children will need assistance.)

★ Insert dry beans into fish through opening until loosely full.

★ Finish stitching to close fish shape and knot thread securely.

★ Tie ribbon near back of fish to form tail (sketch b).

★ Place a hole reinforcement on each side of fish for eyes. Glue a wiggle eye in center of each hole reinforcement.

Conversation:

You followed my instructions to make your fish. The Bible says, "Blessed . . . are those who hear the word of God and obey it" (Luke 11:28). **God has given us His Word, the Bible, as our instructions to follow. Knowing God's Word helps us do what is right.**

a.

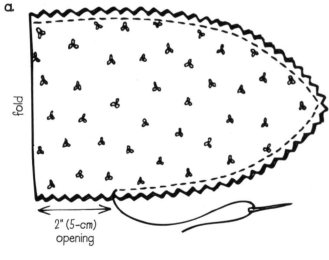

fold

2" (5-cm) opening

b.

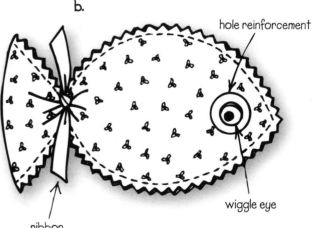

hole reinforcement

wiggle eye

ribbon

BEANBAG FISH PATTERN

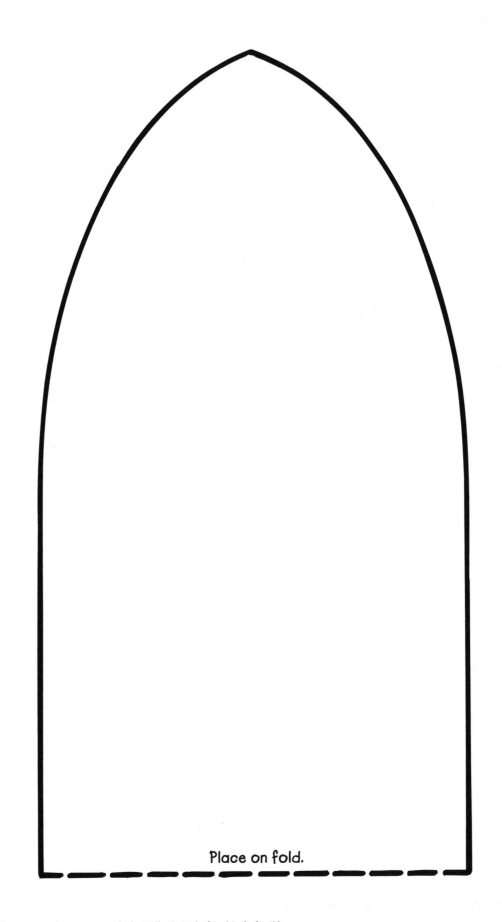

Place on fold.

Games and Toys

Materials: String or yarn, clear packing tape, decorative stickers, scissors, measuring stick. For each child—clean, empty medium-sized tin can, one ¾-inch (1.9-cm) wooden bead.

Preparation: Remove labels from cans. Cut string or yarn into 14-inch (35-cm) lengths—one for each child.

Instruct each child in the following procedures:

* Thread bead onto string. With teacher's help, tie bead to end of string.
* Tape other end of string to inside rim of can (see sketch).
* Decorate outside of can with stickers.
* Hold can in one hand, flip bead up and try to catch it inside can.

Enrichment Idea: Wrap and tape construction paper around can. Decorate with felt pens.

Conversation:

Children had simple, homemade toys back in the Old West—like this Catch Can. Catching the ball in the can looks simple, but it takes practice. And the more you practice, the easier it gets. What are your favorite toys?

tape

stickers

bead

Games and Toys

Materials: Thin plywood, saw, sandpaper, twill tape (available at fabric stores), hot glue gun and glue sticks or staple gun and staples, scissors, measuring stick.

Preparation: Saw the wood into 2½x3½-inch (6.25x8.75-cm) blocks—seven for each child. Cut twill tape into 28½-inch (71.25-cm) lengths—two for each child. Cut additional twill tape into 21½-inch (53.75-cm) lengths—one for each child.

Instruct each child in the following procedures:

* ★ Use sandpaper to smooth rough edges on blocks.
* ★ Lay long pieces of twill tape parallel to each other, about ¾ inch (1.9 cm) apart. Glue or staple ends of tape onto blocks at both ends (sketch a).
* ★ Place remaining blocks between end blocks. Alternate blocks over and under tape as shown in sketch b.
* ★ Weave the shorter length of tape through blocks as shown in sketch b. Glue or staple ends of tape onto inner sides of end blocks.

* ★ Hold Clatter Blocks vertically by the end block. Then grasp the second block and let the first block fall. This action should cause the other wood pieces to fall in succession.

Enrichment Idea: Stain or paint blocks with acrylic paint. Spray with clear acrylic spray before attaching twill tape.

Conversation:

Another name for these Clatter Blocks is "Jacob's Ladder." Why do you think it is called "Jacob's Ladder"? Your Clatter Blocks are like a puzzle that takes time to figure out. Some of the most important things in life take a while to understand. For instance, it's not always easy to understand why God lets bad things happen to us or our families, but if we keep reading the Bible and talking to Him we will grow to understand His ways more and more.

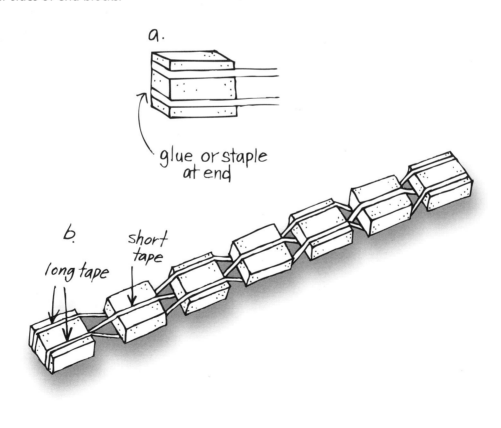

a.

glue or staple
at end

b.

short tape

long tape

Games and Toys

Materials: White construction paper, writing paper, photocopier, fine-tip felt pens, transparent tape, scissors, glue. For each child—one cylinder canister (such as an oatmeal or bread crumb container), six small glittery pom-poms, color-coded dot stickers (such as Avery®).

Preparation: Cut construction paper into rectangles large enough to wrap around container—one for each child. Type and print out suggested conversation starters. Photocopy one page for each child to cut into small strips and place in canisters.

Instruct each child in the following procedures:

★ Use felt pens to draw various faces on the dot stickers—happy, sad, afraid, surprised, angry (sketch a).

★ Letter "Communication Can" in center of construction paper. (Teacher helps as needed.)

★ Stick dots randomly onto construction paper.

★ Wrap construction paper around container and tape in place.

★ Glue pom-poms onto canister for decoration.

★ Cut apart and place conversation strips in Communication Can.

★ At mealtime, play the game by passing the Communication Can around the table. Each family member draws a conversation strip, reads it aloud (or chooses another family member to read it) and then answers the question on his or her strip.

Conversation Strips:

★ Tell about something funny that happened to you today.

★ What did you see that God created today?

★ How were you a helper today?

★ What kind words did someone say today?

★ What was the best part of your day?

★ Tell about something that you did in the morning.

★ Tell about something you did in the afternoon.

★ What did you learn today?

★ How did God take care of you today?

★ What can you thank God for today?

Enrichment Idea: Older children can create and write out their own conversation starters.

Conversation:

When is a good time for your whole family to get together each day and talk? Some families talk at mealtime! God planned for our families to listen and talk to each other. Playing the Communication Can game will be a fun way to start conversations.

Games and Toys

EARLY CHILDHOOD • YOUNGER ELEMENTARY • OLDER ELEMENTARY

Materials: Fabric scraps; crepe paper streamers or Mylar strips; rags or old socks; string, yarn or bias tape; scissors; measuring stick.

Preparation: Cut fabric scraps into 7-inch (17.5-cm) squares—one for each child. Cut streamers or Mylar strips into 1-yard (.9-m) lengths—two for each child. Cut yarn or string into 8-inch (20-cm) lengths—one for each child.

Instruct each child in the following procedures:

★ Place fabric square print side down. Lay middle of streamers or Mylar strips in the center of fabric square (sketch a).

★ Place a small pile of rags or an old sock on top of strips (sketch a).

★ Gather up edges of fabric and tie tightly with string, yarn or bias tape (sketch b).

★ Throw comet up in the air and catch it. Or throw it to a friend across from you.

Enrichment Idea: Older children may measure and cut their own fabric, yarn and streamers.

Conversation:

Have you ever looked up in the sky at night and seen a shooting star? A comet looks a lot like a shooting star, but it's larger. Today we're making a toy that looks like a comet. You can throw your comet in the air!

a. crepe paper
fabric
rags

b.

Games and Toys

Materials: Dried cornhusks (available at craft stores and some grocery stores), large plastic tub, cotton string, chenille wires, straight pins, Styrofoam cups, glue, scissors, warm water, paper towels, newspaper. For each child—¾-inch (1.9-cm) Styrofoam ball, toothpick.

Preparation: Fill plastic tub with warm water and soak cornhusks for 5 to 10 minutes; then drain on newspaper. Pat dry with paper towels. Husks should be damp while students work. Cut string into 5-inch (12.5-cm) lengths—10 for each child.

Instruct each child in the following procedures:

★ Gather four or five husks together. About 1 inch (2.5 cm) from end, wrap string around husks several times and tie a knot so that husks will not fall apart (sketch a). As you work, trim all knotted strings close to knots.

★ Stick a toothpick into Styrofoam ball. Then stick the other end of toothpick into the tied bundle of cornhusks (sketch b).

★ Fold long husks down over Styrofoam ball to form head (sketch c). Secure with string. Tie a narrow strip of cornhusk around string to make neck.

★ To make arms: Wrap a wide husk strip around length of chenille wire and secure in place with string at each end (sketch d).

★ For woman's sleeves: Cut one length of husk in half. Tie one half around end of arm (sketch e). Fold sleeve back over arm and tie near center of arm piece (sketch f). Repeat on other end to make other sleeve.

★ Place arm piece between layers of husk below doll's head. Roll up lengths of narrow husk strips into a cylinder and place between layers of husk, below arms, to form chest. Tie string around husks just below chest (sketch g).

★ Wrap a wide husk strip over each shoulder, crisscrossing strips in front and back. Tie string around waist to secure (sketch h).

★ Gather several wide husks around waist so that husks cover the head. Secure with string (sketch i).

★ For woman's skirt: Fold husks down over body, pin husks together and trim ends to desired length (sketch j). Tie a narrow strip of cornhusk around woman's waist.

★ For man's legs: Bend another chenille wire in half and bend each end to form feet (sketch k). Insert wire between husks below waist. Wrap equal portions of husks around each leg and tie at the bottom to secure in place. Wrap narrow strips around uncovered wire at feet and ankles (sketch l). Tie a narrow strip of husk around man's waist.

★ Allow figures to dry overnight. (For woman figure, place skirt over an inverted Styrofoam cup before drying. After figure is dry, remove pins. Glue may be used to secure husks in place.)

Enrichment Ideas: Add corn silk for hair. Use additional husk strips to make bonnets, hats and other accessories. Ahead of time, add color to cornhusks by soaking them in a mixture of fabric dye and boiling water. Remove pot from heat and soak overnight.

Conversation:

Until recently, people used what they had available to make items they needed. Corn is a common crop, so people would use the husks to make things like dolls, mats or trivets.

CORNHUSK PEOPLE

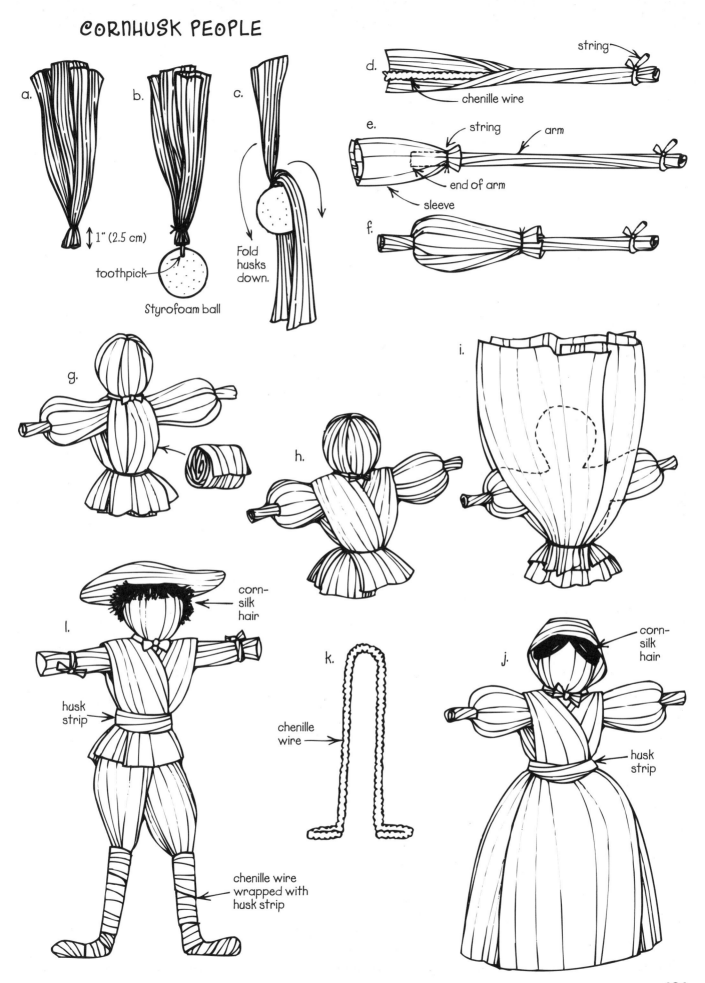

a.

↕ 1" (2.5 cm)

toothpick

Styrofoam ball

b.

c.

Fold husks down.

d.

string

chenille wire

e.

string

arm

end of arm

sleeve

f.

g.

h.

i.

l.

corn-silk hair

husk strip

chenille wire wrapped with husk strip

k.

chenille wire

j.

corn-silk hair

husk strip

Games and Toys

Materials: Faith Catcher Pattern, photocopier, white copier paper, scissors, colored felt pens.

Preparation: Photocopy pattern onto white paper—one for each child.

Instruct each child in the following procedures:

★ Cut out Faith Catcher on solid line.

★ Color each balloon with a different color felt pen.

★ Lay paper printed side down.

★ Fold Faith Catcher in half on dotted line. Open the paper.

★ Fold paper in half in the opposite direction. Open the paper (sketch a).

★ Fold paper corners to the middle of back side of paper on dotted lines (sketch b).

★ Turn folded paper over and fold paper corners into the middle of square on dotted lines (sketch c).

★ Fold paper in half. Open and fold in half in the opposite direction (sketch d).

★ Slip your thumbs and pointer fingers into the folded pockets of the game (sketch e).

★ Move your fingers back and forth and side to side to make the game open and close.

To play game with a partner:

1. Place Faith Catcher on fingers and ask partner to pick a colored balloon.

2. Spell the color name while moving the catcher open for each letter. The catcher should remain open.

3. Have partner choose one of four words of faith. Open and close the catcher to spell out the word.

4. Partner chooses another word of faith. Take the catcher off fingers and open to read the verse printed under the word.

5. Play the game again, this time letting your partner move the catcher.

6. After playing several times, see if you can say the verse under the flaps without looking at them!

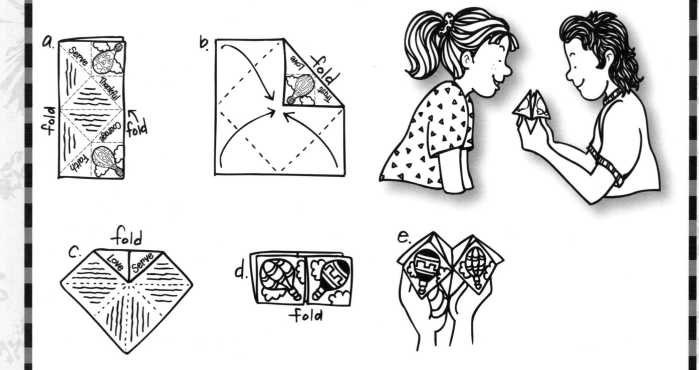

FAITH CATCHER PATTERN

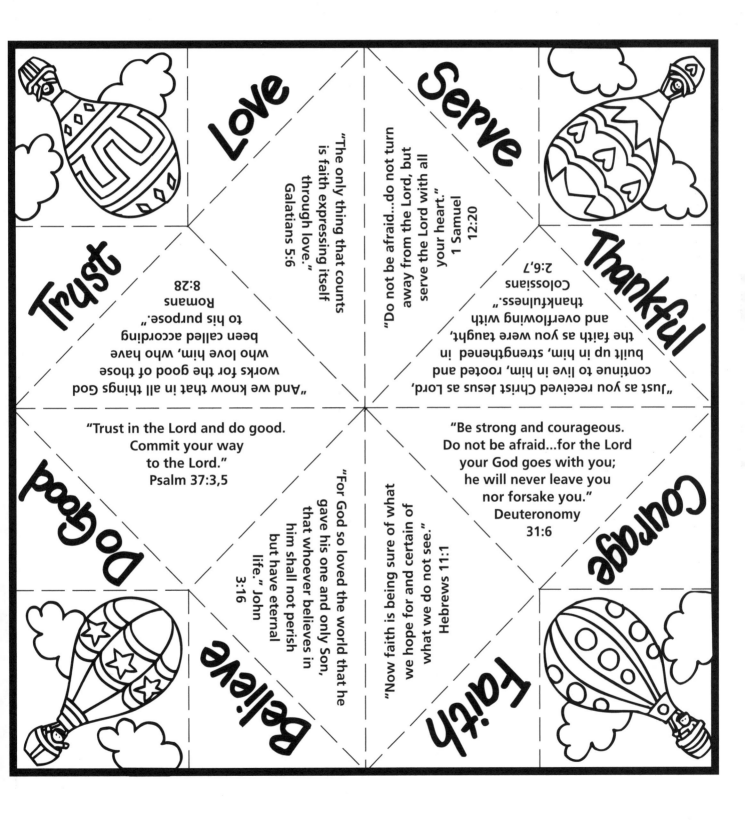

Love

Serve

"The only thing that counts is faith expressing itself through love."
Galatians 5:6

"Do not be afraid...do not turn away from the Lord, but serve the Lord with all your heart."
1 Samuel 12:20

Trust

Thankful

"And we know that in all things God works for the good of those who love him, who have been called according to his purpose."
Romans 8:28

"Just as you received Christ Jesus as Lord, continue to live in him, rooted and built up in him, strengthened in the faith as you were taught, and overflowing with thankfulness."
Colossians 2:6,7

"Trust in the Lord and do good. Commit your way to the Lord."
Psalm 37:3,5

"Be strong and courageous. Do not be afraid...for the Lord your God goes with you; he will never leave you nor forsake you."
Deuteronomy 31:6

Do Good

Courage

"For God so loved the world that he gave his one and only Son, that whoever believes in him shall not perish but have eternal life." John 3:16

"Now faith is being sure of what we hope for and certain of what we do not see."
Hebrews 11:1

Believe

Faith

Games and Toys

GO FISH GAME
(20-25 MINUTES)

Materials: Fish Pattern, lightweight cardboard, tempera paint in various colors, cotton string or narrow ribbon, colored electrical tape, silver and/or gold glitter in shaker container, pencil, glue in squeeze bottles, scissors, paintbrushes, measuring stick, shallow containers, newspaper. For each child—14- to 16-inch (35- to 40-cm) long sticks or dowels at least ¼ inch (.625 cm) in diameter, large metal paper clip, two round magnets.

Preparation: Trace Fish Pattern onto cardboard and cut out—two for each child. Glue two cardboard fish together to make one thick fish—one for each child. While glue is still drying, insert a paper clip between the two fish cutouts, near the mouth (sketch a). Cut string into 3-foot (.9-m) lengths—one for each child. Glue two magnets together—one glued pair for each child. Cover work area with newspaper. Pour paint into shallow containers.

Instruct each child in the following procedures:

★ Paint fish on both sides. Sprinkle glitter sparingly on wet paint. Allow paint to dry.

★ With teacher's help, tie and knot one end of string around end of stick (sketch b). Wrap a piece of tape around tied string to secure.

★ With teacher's help, tie magnet to other end of string. Squeeze a little glue on string and magnet to secure string.

★ To go fishing: Place fish on the floor and try to "catch" fish by placing magnet near the fish's mouth (sketch c).

Simplification Idea: Instead of using magnets, simply tie end of string to paper clip.

Conversation:

Have you ever gone fishing? Sometimes catching a fish can take a long time. What kinds of things can you do while you're waiting to catch a fish? Talking to God is a great thing to do while fishing. The Bible says, "The Lord will hear when I call to him" (Psalm 4:3). **We can pray anytime and anywhere!**

a.

paper clip

tape

b.

string

magnets

GO FISH GAME PATTERN

Materials: Wild grass 36 inches (90 cm) or more in length or loose straw (available at craft stores), green or brown yarn, $\frac{1}{16}$-inch (.15-cm) dowels, string, fine-tooth saw, plastic tub, scissors, measuring stick, warm water, paper towels.

Preparation: Cut yarn into 5-foot (1.5-m) lengths—four for each child. Saw dowels into 4-inch (10-cm) lengths—one for each child. Cut seed heads off grass and save. Gather 10 blades of grass into a bundle and tie a piece of string around the midpoint—three bundles for each child (sketch a). Put warm water in plastic tub. Soak bundles in water for one hour before use; then pat dry with paper towel.

Instruct each child in the following procedures:

★ Tap bundles of grass on flat surface so that ends are even. Trim long ends if needed.

★ Take one bundle and bend in three places to form head, neck and body (sketch b). Neck should be approximately 4 inches (10 cm) long.

★ Tightly wrap a length of yarn around horse's nose several times and tie a knot. Without cutting, move yarn to next wrapping point and repeat process (sketch c). After you have wrapped yarn in all designated places, knot yarn and trim excess.

★ Bend second bundle in thirds to form two legs and body. Body section should be the same length as body section of first bundle. Wrap yarn around one end of leg and tie in a knot. Continue to wrap and knot yarn as described previously, at five additional points along body and leg sections (sketch d). Trim excess yarn.

★ Repeat previous step with third bundle to make two more legs.

★ Attach two leg bundles to body bundle, firmly wrapping and knotting yarn at each end of body (sketch e). Trim excess yarn. Trim legs to equal lengths and appropriate size for horse.

★ Carefully insert dowel through neck portion of grass bundle to hold head upright.

★ Attach grass seed heads for mane and tail by wrapping with yarn (sketch f).

Enrichment Idea: Children make bridle and reins using colorful yarn, and make a saddle using leaves or felt. Attach saddle to horse using a needle and thread.

Conversation:

Have you ever gone horseback riding? Did you enjoy it? At one time, people rode and used horses for work, to travel and just for fun.

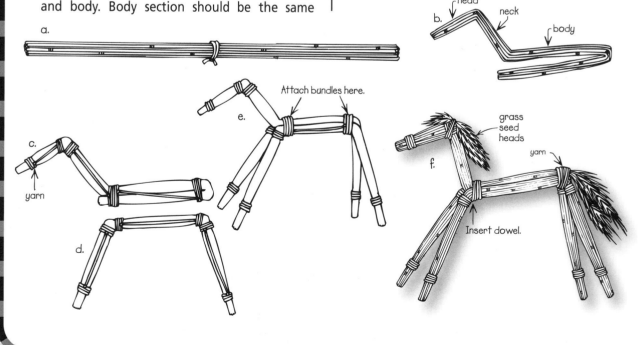

a.

b. head neck body

Attach bundles here.

e.

c. yarn

d.

f. grass seed heads yarn

Insert dowel.

Games and Toys

Materials: Sturdy wrapping paper in bold prints, kite string, 3/16-inch (1/5-cm) dowels, saw, white plastic trash bags, transparent or masking tape, pencils, rulers, scissors, measuring stick. For each child—one toilet paper tube or wood scrap. (Safety Note: Never use metal such as wire, tinsel or foil to make a kite.)

Preparation: Saw dowels into 18-inch (45-cm) lengths and 24-inch (60-cm) lengths—one of each length for each child. Cut wrapping paper into 18x24-inch (45x60-cm) rectangles—one for each child. Cut string into 30-foot (9-m) lengths—one for each child. Cut trash bags into 1x14-inch (2.5x35-cm) strips—three for each child.

Instruct each child in the following procedures:

★ Fold wrapping paper in half lengthwise.

★ Unfold wrapping paper. Make a light pencil mark on fold line, 8 inches (20 cm) from edge (sketch a). Crease at pencil mark as shown in sketch a.

★ Refold wrapping paper lengthwise. Cut paper as shown in sketch b to make a kite shape.

★ Open kite. Tape long dowel or "spine" lengthwise along center fold. Tape shorter dowel or "spar" along other fold, between "wing tips" (sketch c).

★ Use pencil to make four small holes near where dowels intersect (sketch d). Thread string through holes in crisscross manner and tie in a knot to secure (sketch d).

★ Wrap remaining string or "flying line" around toilet paper tube or wood scrap to make a kite reel.

★ Tie plastic bag strips together to make a long kite tail (sketch e). Tape tail to bottom of spine.

★ To fly kite: Take kite outside and hold it up. As wind begins to carry kite, slowly release string so kite rises with the wind.

Enrichment Idea: Decorate kite reel.

Conversation:

Flying kites is a fun activity to do with your family. You can fly big fancy kites or use this homemade one! What fun activities can your family do together? You can keep these activities in mind and suggest them to your parents this weekend.

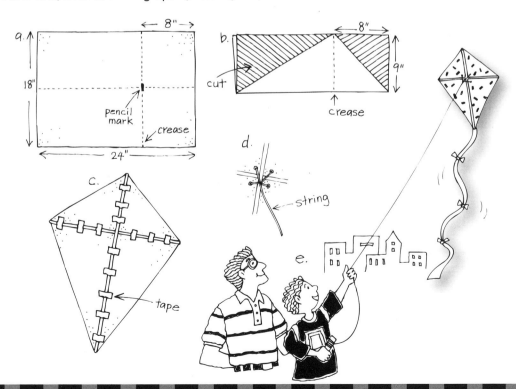

Games and Toys

Materials: Juggling Instructions, uncooked rice, funnels or small plastic water bottles, measuring cups, large bowl, photocopier and paper, sharp scissors, pencils. For each child—six 8-inch (20-cm) balloons in at least two different colors.

Preparation: Photocopy Juggling Instructions—one copy for each child. Pour rice into large bowl. If using water bottles for funnels, use scissors to cut off the bottom portions of bottles (sketch a).

Instruct each child in the following procedures:

★ With scissors, snip small circles, squares or diamonds out of three balloons. Then cut off the stems (sketch b).

★ Inflate the three remaining uncut balloons to stretch them out; then deflate.

★ Use funnel to fill one balloon with ⅓ cup rice. Use the eraser end of pencil to push rice into balloon.

★ Knot opening of the balloon and tightly roll the stem down. Push knot and stem into balloon (sketch c).

★ Carefully tuck the filled balloon into one of the cut balloons. Use opposite colors of balloons. Make sure the stem area of filled balloon is covered by the second balloon.

★ Repeat with the other balloons to make two more juggling balls (sketch d).

Conversation:

Jugglers entertain people around the world. Crowds gather to see the jugglers tossing knives, balls or cups. After the performance, a collection is usually taken.

a. funnel / cut

b. cut here / cut out shapes

c.

d.

JUGGLING BALLS INSTRUCTIONS

You can learn to juggle if you start out slowly and practice! As your skill grows, add more balls to your juggling routine. Have fun entertaining your family and friends with your talent. Maybe you can even teach someone your new skill!

START WITH ONE BALL:

★ Toss the ball from one hand to the other. Throw it up to arc over and fall into the other cupped hand.

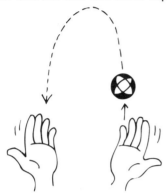

NOW JUGGLE WITH TWO BALLS:

★ Hold a ball in each hand.
★ Toss the ball in your right hand to a spot above your left hand. As the ball reaches the highest peak, toss the ball in your left hand a little higher above your right hand.

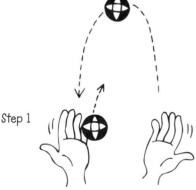

Step 1

★ Catch the first ball in your left hand. Catch the second ball in your right hand.

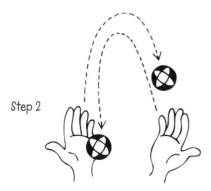

Step 2

(Note: Left-handed jugglers exchange left for right hands in all instructions.)

ADD ANOTHER BALL AND JUGGLE WITH THREE BALLS!

★ When juggling, keep your eyes on the balls at their peaks, not on your hands.
★ Hold two balls (balls A and C) in your right hand. Hold one ball (ball B) in your left hand.
★ Toss ball A to a point above your left hand. As it reaches the highest peak, toss ball B from your left hand to a point above your right hand.

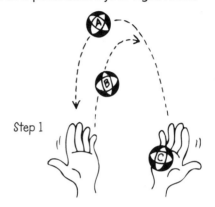

Step 1

★ Catch ball A with your left hand.
★ As ball B reaches its peak, throw ball C from your right hand to the point above your left hand.

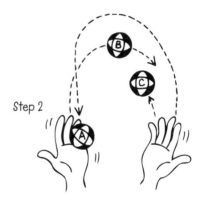

Step 2

★ Catch ball B with your right hand.
★ As ball C hits its peak, throw ball A from your left hand to the point above your right hand. Catch ball C in your left hand. Continue the pattern.

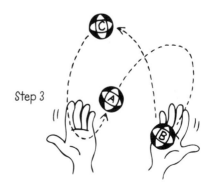

Step 3

HEY, GUESS WHAT? YOU'RE JUGGLING!

Games and Toys

Materials: Acrylic paints, clear acrylic spray paint, paintbrushes, shallow containers, rope, ¾-inch (1.9-cm) dowels, saw, ¾-inch (.32-cm) and ⅛-inch (.94-cm) drill bits, drill, sandpaper, masking tape, scissors, measuring stick, newspaper.

Preparation: Saw dowels into 5-inch (12.5-cm) pieces—two for each child. Use small drill bit to drill a small pilot hole about ¾ inch (1.9 cm) from end of each dowel piece (sketch a). Use large bit to drill final hole in each dowel piece (sketch b). Cut rope or cording into 3-yard (.9-m) lengths—one for each child. Cover work area with newspaper. Pour paint into shallow containers.

Instruct each child in the following procedures:

★ Use sandpaper to smooth any rough edges on dowel pieces.

★ Paint dowel pieces.

★ In well-ventilated area, spray dowel pieces with clear spray and allow to dry (about two minutes).

★ Wrap a piece of tape around ends of rope to prevent fraying.

★ Thread rope through holes in dowels and tie knots to secure (sketch c).

★ Your rope is ready for hopping, skipping and jumping!

Conversation:

Jump Rope is a popular game played by kids all over the world. How many times can you jump rope without missing? If you are good at jumping you might want to try the following: "Double Hopping" (add a second jump while the rope is over head); "Left, Right" (jump on one foot and then the other); "Rocking" (place one foot ahead of the other, jumping first on the front foot and then on the back foot). Show your friends and family the different ways you can jump rope!

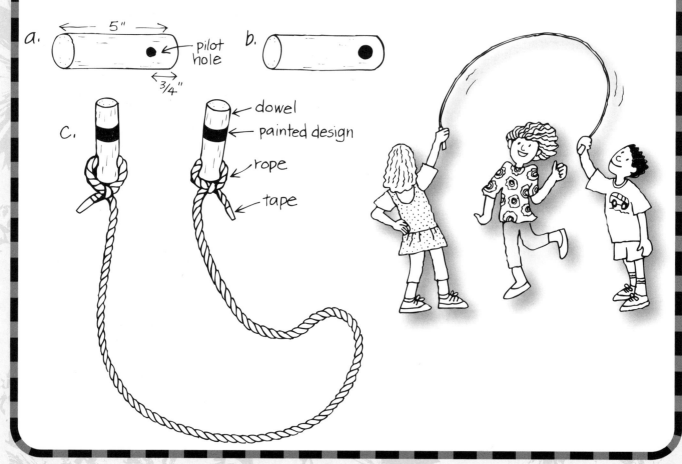

Games and Toys

Materials: Kite Pattern, sturdy, lightweight paper in a light color (wrapping paper, butcher paper, etc.), wide gift ribbon or crepe paper streamers (Safety Note: Never use metal such as wire, tinsel or foil to make a kite.), cotton string, photocopier, card stock, pencil, colored felt pens, transparent tape, scissors, hole punch, measuring stick. For each child—two drinking straws, toilet paper tube.

Preparation: Photocopy Kite Pattern onto card stock and cut out several patterns. Cut paper into 8x14-inch (20x35-cm) rectangles—one for each child. Cut ribbon or streamers into 30-inch (75-cm) lengths—two for each child. Cut string into 40-inch (1-m) lengths and 25-foot (7.5-m) lengths—one of each length for each child.

Instruct each child in the following procedures:

★ Fold paper in half the short way.
★ Place Kite Pattern on fold of paper as indicated on pattern (sketch a). Trace pattern and cut out kite.
★ Use colored pens to letter "LOOK UP!" on kite. Draw other decorations if desired.
★ Place a small strip of tape around each corner of kite to reinforce (sketch b).
★ Tape ends of straws on back side of kite as shown in sketch b.
★ Punch a hole in the two farthest corners (sketch b).
★ Tie a 1-inch (2.5-cm) loop at the midpoint of the shorter string (sketch c).
★ Tie each loose end of string through holes in corners of kite to make a bridle.

★ Tape ends of ribbon or crepe paper to bottom edge of kite to make kite tails (sketch d).
★ Reinforce bottom edge of kite with long strip of tape.
★ Flatten toilet paper tube and tie one end of long string around tube; tape to secure. Wrap remaining string, or flying line, around flattened tube to make a kite reel.
★ Tie other end of flying line to loop in bridle (sketch d).
★ To fly kite, take kite outside and hold it up; as wind begins to carry kite, slowly release string so that kite rises with the wind.

Enrichment Idea: Children may send their kites to friends by folding kites in half and mailing them in manila envelopes.

Conversation:

Your kites have the words "LOOK UP!" on them. It reminds us to look up to God in prayer. We don't have to really look up, though. We can pray with our eyes open or shut. We can pray wherever we are. Where are some places you can pray? When can you pray? What can you pray about? (Children respond.) Wherever you decide to fly your kite, you can always remember that God will always hear your prayers!

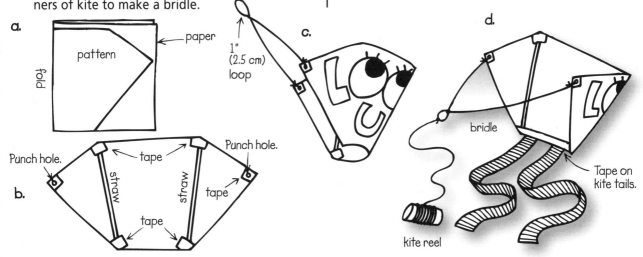

a. paper / pattern / fold
1" (2.5 cm) loop / c. / LOOK
b. Punch hole. / tape / straw / straw / tape / Punch hole. / tape / tape
d. bridle / Tape on kite tails. / kite reel

191

LOOK UP! KITE PATTERN

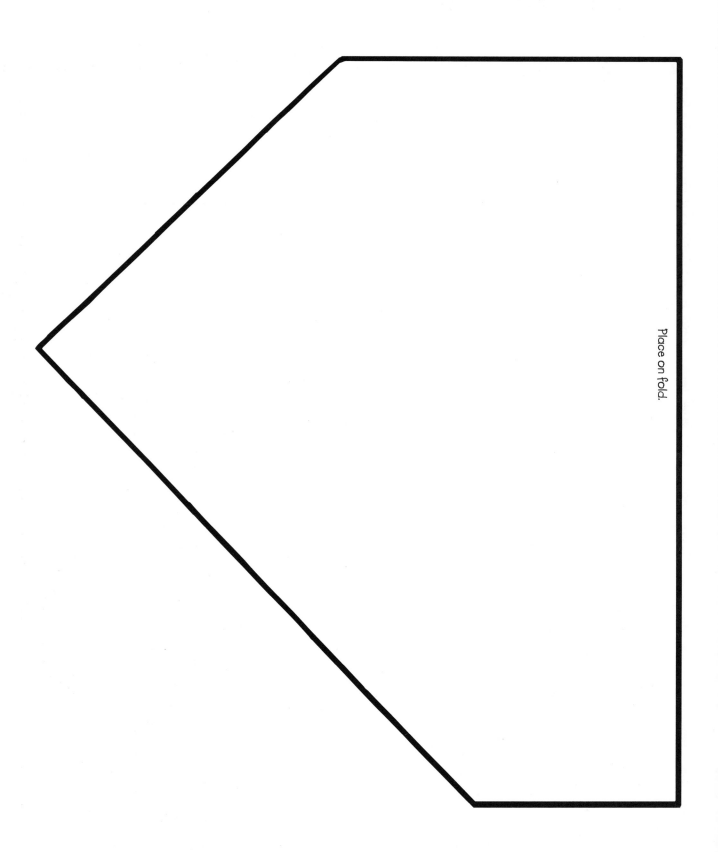

Place on fold.

Games and Toys

Materials: Parachute Figure Pattern, lightweight cardboard, pencil, colorful plastic shopping bags, ruler, poster board, yarn, felt pens in a variety of colors, scissors, hole punch, tape. For each child—one penny.

Preparation: Trace Parachute Figure Pattern onto lightweight cardboard and cut out several patterns. Cut plastic bags into 12x12-inch (30x30-cm) squares—one for each child. Cut poster board into 3x4-inch (7.5x10-cm) pieces–one for each child. Cut yarn into 20-inch (50-cm) lengths—four for each child.

Instruct each child in the following procedures:

✴ Punch a hole in each of the four corners of plastic bag square (sketch a).

✴ Thread a length of yarn through each hole and tie to secure (sketch b).

✴ Gather the four loose ends of yarn together and tie at end (sketch c).

✴ Use pencil to trace figure pattern onto poster board piece. Draw and color figure with felt pens.

✴ Cut out figure and tape a penny to back side.

✴ Use tape to secure figure to parachute where yarn is tied together (sketch d).

✴ Throw parachute in the air and watch it float to the ground!

Enrichment Idea: Use permanent felt pens to decorate plastic bags before assembling. Hand letter a Bible verse and child's name on bag.

Conversation:

What keeps the parachute floating in the air, instead of falling straight down? (The air is trapped inside the plastic bag and pushes back.) **We can't see the air, but we know it is there because we see what it does. What other things do you believe in even though you can't see them?** (The sun behind the clouds, electricity, wind, God, Jesus.) **When we believe in something, even though we can't see it, we have faith in it. When we believe in Jesus and have faith in Him, we can become God's children.**

Whee!

PARACHUTE FIGURE PATTERN

Games and Toys

Materials: Felt off the bolt, two or more colors of Fun Foam (available at craft stores), acrylic paints in a variety of colors, poster board, kitchen sponges, compressed sponges (available at craft stores), plastic disposable plates, yarn, straight pins, water, pencils, measuring stick, fabric scissors, scissors, rulers, newspaper. For each child—one crewel needle.

DAY ONE Preparation: Cut felt into 15x36-inch (37.5x90-cm) rectangles—one for each child. Cut yarn into 15-inch (37.5-cm) lengths—four for each child.

Instruct each child in the following procedures:

* Make a 6-inch (15-cm) fold on both ends of felt to make pockets (sketch a). Pin in place.
* Thread needle with a length of yarn and knot one end. Sew a running stitch 1 inch (2.5 cm) from corner edge of pocket, starting near the fold and ending where pocket ends. Knot yarn on back side of felt. Remove needle and tie another knot at end of yarn (sketch a).
* Sew all remaining pocket sides.

DAY TWO Preparation: Cut kitchen sponges into 1½-inch squares (3.75-cm)—two for each child. Cut compressed sponge into several 1-inch (2.5-cm) crowns and other shapes such as stars, hearts, etc. Dampen sponges. Cut poster board into several 1-foot (30-cm) squares. Trace 1¼-inch (3.125-cm) circles onto poster board and cut out—one circle pattern for each child. Cover work area with newspaper.

Instruct each child in the following procedures:

* Choose two different colors of Fun Foam for game pieces. Use circle pattern and trace 12 circles onto each color of foam. Cut out circle pieces.

* Squeeze a small amount of two colors of paint onto a plate and dip a crown-shaped sponge into one color. Print a crown on 12 foam playing pieces. Then print the other color on the remaining 12 pieces. Allow paint to dry.
* To make game board, center the square cardboard pattern in the middle of felt and trace with pencil.
* Use square sponges and the two colors of paint to stamp squares of game board. Begin at the corner of game board and stamp squares from left to right, alternating colors (sketch c). In the second row begin with the opposite color. Stamp squares in checkerboard design until there are eight rows of eight squares. Print small sponge shapes (star, heart, etc.) on pockets (sketch d).
* When paint has dried, store playing pieces in pockets. Fold each pocket toward the center (sketch e). Then fold once more, using yarn ties to close up game.

Conversation:

The game we now call Checkers was called Draughts (pronounced "drafts"). Many years ago, everyone played games, whether they were rich or poor, young or old. What games can children and adults enjoy playing together? When was a time an adult was surprised that you won the game?

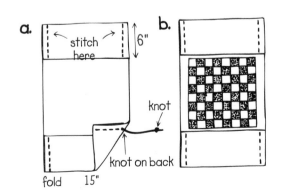

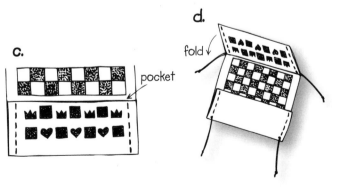

Games and Toys

Materials: Raindrop Toss Game Weather Patterns, pencil, acrylic paints in rainbow colors, paintbrushes, kitchen sponges, sharp scissors, glue, white heavy-weight poster board, wide-tip colored felt pens, shallow containers, clear acrylic spray, newspaper. For each child—one plastic gallon-sized milk jug.

Preparation: Using Raindrop Pattern, trace onto poster board and cut out 12 raindrops for each child. Cut a large opening in the top of each milk jug, leaving the handle intact (sketch a)—one for each child. Dampen sponges. Cut sponges into cloud shapes. Pour paint into containers. Cover work area with newspaper.

Instruct each child in the following procedures:

★ With paintbrush, paint a rainbow on the jug.

★ Paint a yellow sun.

★ Dip cloud-shaped sponge into blue paint and print several clouds on the jug (sketch b).

★ Let jug dry.

★ Use felt pens to color one set of six poster board raindrops one color.

★ Glue two raindrops together, colored sides facing out. Repeat to make three double-thick raindrops.

★ Color second set of six raindrops using a different color. Glue to make three double-thick raindrops.

★ In a well-ventilated area, teacher sprays milk jugs with clear acrylic spray. Let dry.

★ *To play with a friend:* Set jug on the floor. Each player stands the same distance from the jug holding one set of raindrops. Taking turns, they try to toss raindrops into the jug.

Enrichment Idea: Fill small balloons with a small amount of water or sand and tie. Make six filled balloons (three each of two different colors) for each child. Children use balloons as raindrop game pieces instead of poster board raindrops.

Conversation:

You can play your Raindrop Toss Game with a friend. Who is a friend you like to play with, (Jackie)? (Child responds.) **Jesus is your friend, too. He loves you. You can learn about Jesus when you listen to Bible stories. You can talk to Him when you pray. Jesus cares about you very much.**

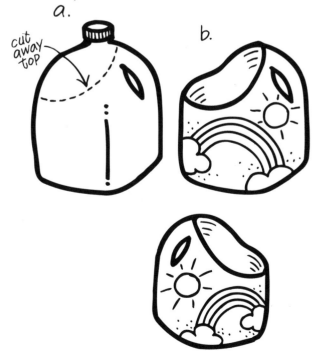

a.

cut away top

b.

RAINDROP TOSS GAME
WEATHER PATTERNS

Raindrop

Lightning Bolt

Cloud

Sun

House

Rainbow

Games and Toys

Materials: Horse Pattern, ¾-inch (1.9-cm) thick pine boards, jigsaw, drill with ⅛-inch (.3-cm) drill bit, jute twine, sandpaper, black permanent fine-tip pens, wood glue, pencil, transparent tape, scissors, ruler. For each child—two medium-sized wooden spools.

Preparation: Trace Horse Pattern onto wood—one horse for each child. Use jigsaw to cut out horses. For each horse, drill one shallow hole near edge where tail should be, drill four shallow holes near head where mane should be and drill two holes completely through wood near bottom of horse where legs should be (sketch a). Cut twine into 5-inch (12.5-cm) lengths—12 strands for each child.

Instruct each child in the following procedures:

★ Use sandpaper to smooth rough edges on wooden horse.

★ Gather two strands of twine together and tie a knot in the middle (sketch b). Repeat process to make a total of five bundles.

★ Fold one twine bundle in half and glue knot into shallow hole at rear of horse to make tail.

★ Fold remaining bundles in half and glue knots into holes on horse's neck and head for mane (sketch c). Allow glue to dry.

★ Use felt pen to draw "stitches" around edge of horse on both sides (sketch d). Then draw eye, mouth and nostril on each side of horse.

★ Wrap tape around the end of one remaining piece of twine and thread through hole in bottom of horse. Thread twine through hole in spool, tie ends together and trim excess (sketch e). Repeat process with remaining twine piece and spool.

★ For tail and mane, untwist twine, so ends are frayed. Trim excess twine on mane.

Enrichment Ideas: Before assembling, apply wood stain to horse and spools or paint with acrylic paints. Glue on length of twine to make reins.

Conversation:

Before trains were invented, the best way to travel long distances was by horse and wagon. As a result, horses were very valuable. What do you have that is valuable to you? Why? In God's eyes, you are the most valuable thing in the whole world. He sent Jesus to Earth to die on the cross because He loved us so much. Sharing the good news about Jesus with others is the most valuable thing we could ever give to someone.

HORSE PATTERN

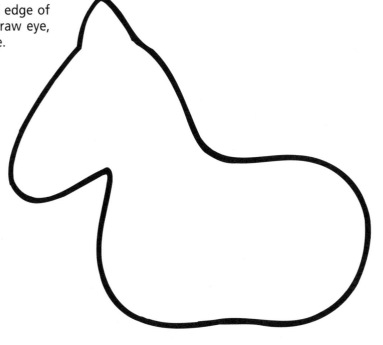

ROLLING HORSE PATTERN

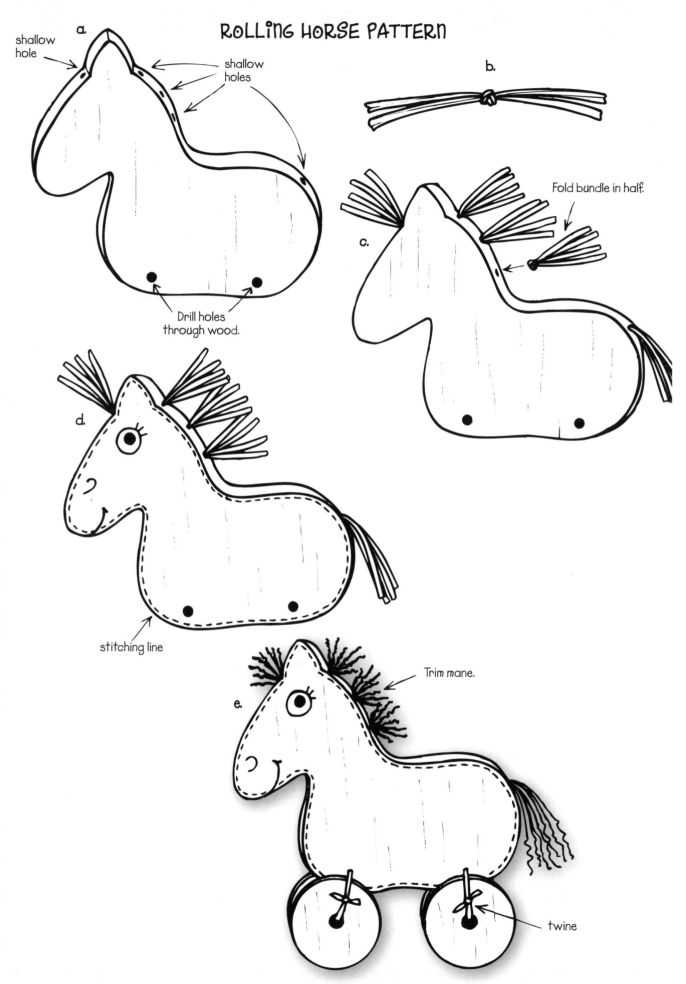

a. shallow hole

shallow holes

Drill holes through wood.

b.

c. Fold bundle in half.

d. stitching line

e. Trim mane.

twine

Games and Toys

Materials: Muslin or other light-colored fabric, printed calico fabric, narrow ribbon, polyester fiber-fill stuffing or cotton balls, pinking shears, permanent fine-tip felt pens, fabric scissors, measuring stick. For each child—one small rubber band, one cotton swab.

Preparation: Cut muslin into 8-inch (20-cm) circles—one for each child. Use pinking shears to cut calico fabric into 15-inch (37.5-cm) squares—one for each child. Cut ribbon into 16-inch (40-cm) lengths—one for each child.

Instruct each child in the following procedures:

★ Use felt pen to draw a face on muslin circle (sketch a).

★ Place stuffing or cotton balls in center of muslin circle. Gather fabric around cotton to form head and secure in place with rubber band (sketch b).

★ With wrong sides together, fold fabric square diagonally in half to form a triangle.

★ Lay head at top point of triangle (sketch c).

★ Place end of cotton swab at one point of triangle. Twist cotton swab to roll fabric toward center. Repeat with other side of fabric.

★ Have a friend hold rolled pieces in place while you tie ribbon around doll's neck to secure (sketch d).

Conversation:

Many years ago, there weren't toy stores like we have today. Most people had to make their own toys. Fabric dolls were a simple and inexpensive way to make a toy for someone. What will you do with your fabric doll? It's fun to give gifts, but the best gift you could ever give someone is to share the good news about Jesus!

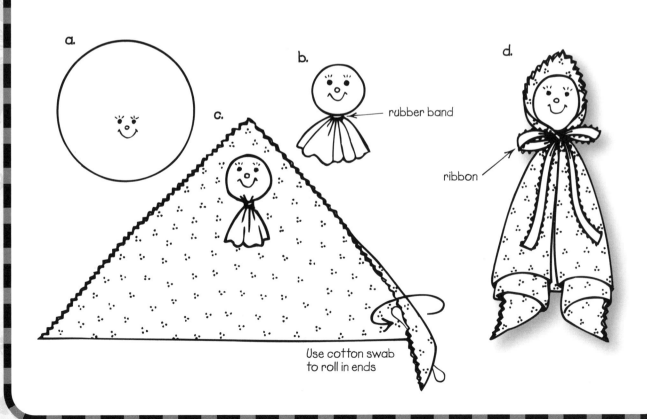

a.

b. rubber band

c. Use cotton swab to roll in ends

d. ribbon

Games and Toys

Materials: Plaster of paris, powdered tempera paint in a variety of colors, large bowl of water, wax paper, vegetable oil, napkins, measuring cups, tablespoons, newspaper. For each child—one 10-oz. plastic cup, one toilet paper tube, one craft stick.

Preparation: Place ½ cup of plaster of paris in each plastic cup. Tear off a piece of wax paper for each child to work on. Cover work area with newspaper.

Instruct each child in the following procedures:

DAY ONE:

★ Pour small amount of oil onto napkin and rub oil on the inside of cardboard tube.

★ Choose paint color. Add ½ cup of powdered tempera paint to plaster in cup.

★ Use craft stick to stir contents in cup.

★ Add one tablespoon of water to mixture and stir until it looks like thick pudding. (If mixture is too dry, add a little more water.)

★ Place end of cardboard tube on wax paper.

★ Pour mixture into tube, almost to the top (sketch a). Allow at least 4 to 5 hours for chalk to dry.

DAY TWO:

★ Tear tube away from chalk.

★ Use chalk to draw on pavement. Erase with water.

Conversation:

What message would you like to write or draw on the sidewalk in front of your house or apartment? On a street where lots of cars go by? What message do you think God might want to write on a busy street? God has written a message to all people; it's the Bible!

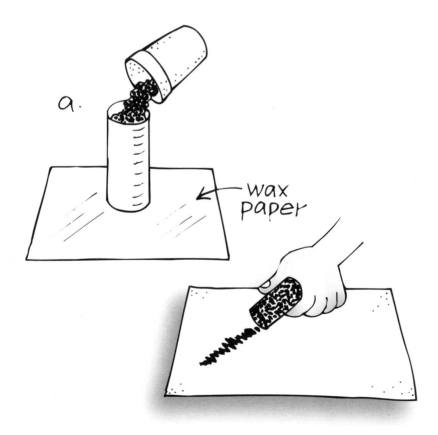

a.

wax paper

Games and Toys

Materials: Fine sandpaper in two colors, gold and silver metallic spray paint, jute twine, suede-like fabric, tag board, heavy-duty packing tape, several 8-inch (20-cm) paper plates, permanent felt pen, pencils, glue, paper cutter, scissors, ¼-inch (.626-cm) hole punch, sponge brushes, rulers, measuring stick, shallow containers, newspaper. For each child—24 small flat stones (available at garden or building supply stores).

Preparation: Set stones on newspaper in a well-ventilated area and spray-paint half of the stones silver and half of them gold. Allow to dry; then turn stones over and paint other side. Use paper cutter to cut sandpaper into 1½-inch (3.75-cm) squares—32 of each color per child. Cut tag board into 7x14-inch (17.5x35-cm) rectangles—two for each child. Cut jute twine into 20-inch (50-cm) lengths—one for each child. Cut suede-like fabric into 9-inch (22.5-cm) squares—one for each child. Pour glue into shallow containers.

Instruct each child in the following procedures:
To make game board:

★ Place two tag board rectangles together. Join the two boards with a strip of packing tape (sketch a). Turn game board over and fold in half to secure binding.

★ Unfold game board with taped-side facedown. Use ruler to find center of game board. Use pencil to draw a perpendicular line intersecting the fold (sketch b).

★ Beginning at center of game board, use sponge brush to spread an even layer of glue in small area.

★ Place sandpaper squares on glue, alternating the colors. Continue gluing squares on game board, working in small areas, using lines as guides (sketch c).

To make pouch for game pieces:

★ Place paper plate on fabric square. Trace around perimeter and cut out circle.

★ Use scissors to cut small slits at ½-inch (1.25-cm) intervals around edge of circle (sketch d).

★ Weave length of jute twine through slits.

★ Get 12 silver stones and 12 gold stones from teacher.

★ With pen, draw a symbol or your initial on one side of stone checkers to use as kings in game. Place stones in pouch and pull drawstring tight to close.

Simplification Idea: Use colored glass pebbles for game pieces instead of painting rocks.

Conversation:

What are some of your favorite games? With whom can you play checkers? Who do you know who might like to learn to play checkers?

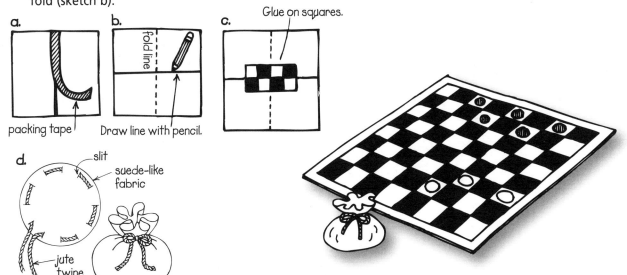

a.

packing tape

b.

fold line

Draw line with pencil.

c.

Glue on squares.

d.

slit

suede-like fabric

jute twine

Games and Toys

Materials: Brown butcher paper or grocery bags, tempera or acrylic paints in various colors, sponges, spring-type clothespins, pencil, glue, scissors, craft knife, paintbrushes, measuring stick, shallow containers, water, newspaper. For each child—one 42 oz. oatmeal container with lid.

Preparation: Glue lids to oatmeal containers. Cut brown paper into 9½x17-inch (23.75x42.5-cm) rectangles—one for each child. Glue a brown paper rectangle around each oatmeal container (sketch a). Trace lid onto brown paper and cut out—two circles for each child. Glue paper circles to top and bottom of oatmeal containers. Use craft knife to cut cradle as shown in sketch b. Cut sponges into several different shapes. Clip clothespins to sponge pieces to use as handles. Cover work area with newspaper. Pour paint into shallow containers. Fill several containers with water for rinsing paintbrushes and sponges.

Instruct each child in the following procedures:

★ Use sponge pieces and paintbrushes to paint a design on cradle (sketch c). Allow to dry.

Enrichment Idea:
Make a doll as instructed on p. 205. Use it with the cradle.

Conversation:

What kind of bed did you sleep in when you were a baby? In many parts of the world, parents make wooden cradles for their babies. They rock their babies in the cradles and sing as they rock their babies to sleep. Let's sing "Jesus Loves Me" as we rock our babies to sleep.

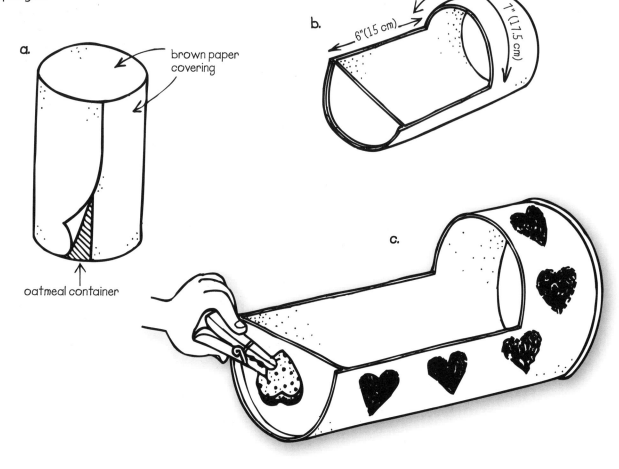

a. brown paper covering

oatmeal container

b. 6"(15 cm) 7" (17.5 cm)

c.

Games and Toys

Materials: Eye and Circle Patterns; discarded adult-sized denim jeans with back pockets; white, tan, and black felt; black or brown yarn; string; polyester fiberfill stuffing; saw; 1-inch (2.5-cm) dowels; pen; craft glue; fabric scissors; measuring stick.

Preparation: Saw dowels into 3-foot (.9-m) lengths—one for each child. Cut a 30-inch (75-cm) length from each pant leg—one leg section for each child. Turn leg section inside out. Tie leg bottom closed with a length of string (sketch a). Turn leg right side out. Cut two 1-inch (2.5-cm) ear slits about 10 inches (25 cm) from tied end of leg section (sketch b). Cut two rows of four ½-inch (1.25-cm) slits for mane as shown in sketch b. Cut pockets from jeans—one pocket for each child. Cut pockets in half diagonally (sketch c). Cut yarn into 9-inch (22.5-cm) lengths—at least 40 strands for each child. Bundle 10 strands of yarn together and tie at midsection with another length of yarn—four bundles for each child (sketch d). Cut string into 4-foot (1.2-m) and 2-foot (.6-m) lengths—one of each length for each child. Trace Eye Pattern onto white felt—two for each child. Trace Circle Pattern onto tan and black felt—two of each color for each child. Cut out all felt shapes.

Instruct each child in the following procedures:

★ Thread one bundle of yarn through each pair of slits for mane, with knots centered inside (sketch e).

★ Insert a generous amount of stuffing into jeans to make horse head.

★ Fold one pocket piece and insert corner into ear slit. Repeat process for second ear (sketch f).

★ Glue black felt circles onto white felt ovals. Glue onto horse's head for eyes.

★ Glue tan circles to horse's nose for nostrils.

★ Insert end of dowel inside horse's neck.

★ With teacher's help, wrap the shorter length of string several times around neck and then tie tightly and knot. Trim ends as needed.

★ Teacher wraps the long length of string around horse's nose and pulls down nose to bend head, tying the string ends to neck (sketch g).

Conversation:

How did you get here today? In the Old West, there were no cars. When people traveled, they rode horses or rode in wagons pulled by horses. In our Bible story, Paul traveled all around, telling people the good news about Jesus. You can tell other people that Jesus loves them, too!

EYE AND CIRCLE PATTERNS

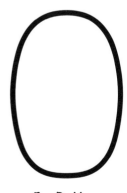

Circle Pattern   Eye Pattern

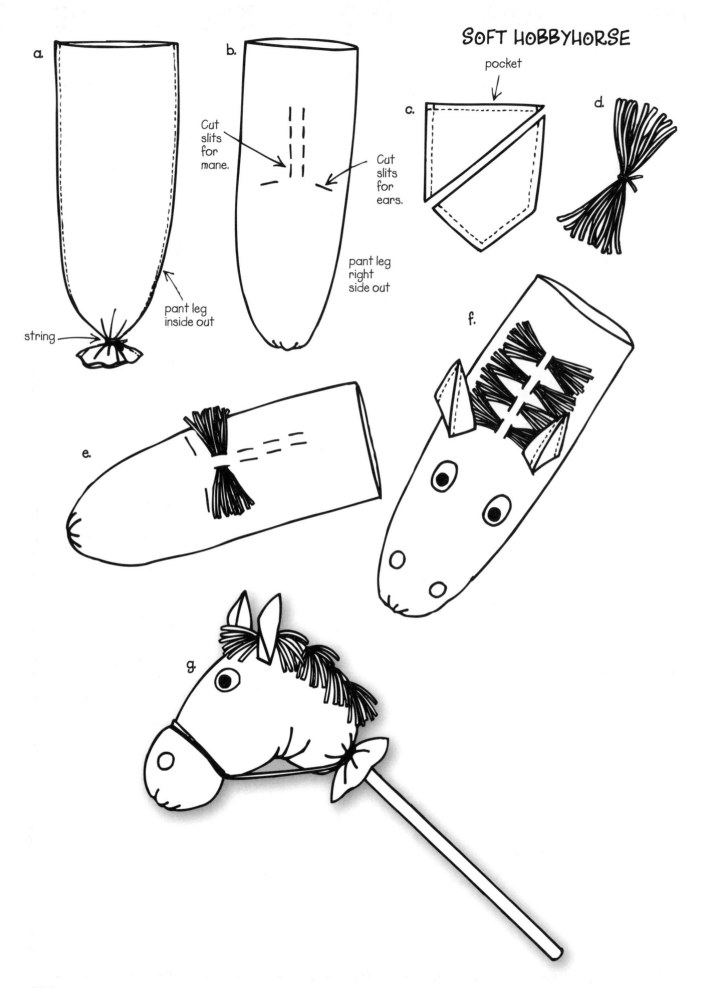

a.

string

pant leg inside out

b.

Cut slits for mane.

Cut slits for ears.

pant leg right side out

SOFT HOBBYHORSE

pocket

c.

d.

e.

f.

g.

Games and Toys

Materials: Tempera paint in skin-tone colors, calico or gingham fabric scraps, yarn and/or rickrack in various colors, buttons, felt pens, craft glue, fabric scissors, paint brushes, shallow containers, newspaper. For each child—wooden spoon with short handle, one child-sized solid-colored sock, empty plastic individual-sized water bottle.

Preparation: Cut rickrack and/or yarn into 1- to 3-inch (2.5- to 7.5-cm) pieces—several for each child. Cover work area with newspaper. Pour paint into shallow containers.

Instruct each child in the following procedures:

* Holding spoon by handle, paint the top portion of spoon. Allow paint to dry.
* Pull sock over bottle. With teacher's help, stuff top of sock into bottle neck (sketch a).
* Glue buttons, rickrack, yarn and fabric scraps onto sock to decorate.

* Use felt pens to draw eyes, nose and mouth on spoon to make face.
* Glue lengths of rickrack and yarn around face and back of spoon for hair (sketch b).
* Insert spoon into neck of bottle.
* With teacher's help, tie a scrap of fabric around neck for bandana (sketch c).

Simplification Idea: Do not paint spoons.

Conversation:

What is your favorite toy? Before the 1900s, there were no toy stores like we have today. Parents had to make toys, such as wooden dolls, for children to play with. Each doll was different, so they were very special. You are special, too. God made each of you different. He loves you very much.

a.

Stuff sock in bottle.

b.

yarn

rickrack

c.

Games and Toys

Materials: Muslin, fabric paint in various colors, various firm vegetables (carrots, potatoes, celery, etc.), paring knife, fabric scissors, ruler, disposable plastic plates, water, newspaper.

Preparation: Cut muslin into 9-inch (22.5-cm) squares—one for each child. (If making a quilt, wash and dry muslin to preshrink before cutting.) Wash and dry vegetables. Cut into pieces suitable to be held by small hands. Form stamps by carving a simple shape into flat edge of each fruit or vegetable piece, or use the shape of the vegetable itself. Cover work area with newspaper. Pour or squeeze paint onto plastic plates.

Instruct each child in the following procedures:

★ Dip vegetable stamp into paint and then press onto fabric. Repeat, dipping stamp in paint for each print.

★ Allow to dry for at least four hours.

★ Children may use squares as blankets for Simple Doll Cradle (p. 202).

Conversation:

How do you keep warm at night? People in the Old West kept warm by using blankets made from colored scraps of fabric. These warm blankets were called quilts. What colors did you stamp on your quilt square?

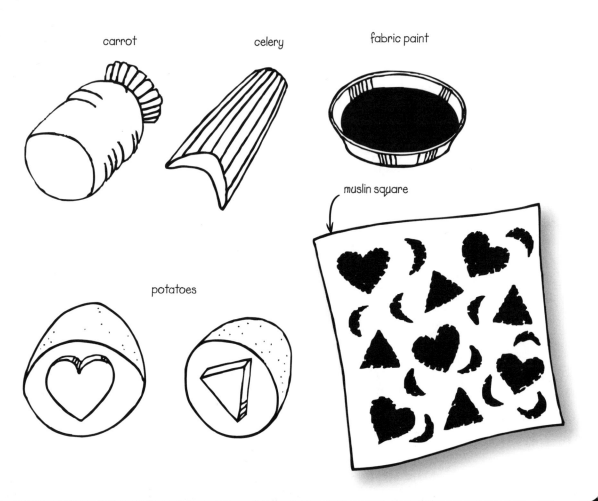

carrot

celery

fabric paint

muslin square

potatoes

Gifts

Here is an array of gift possibilities that will help your kids get excited about giving!

Gifts

Materials: ¾-inch gift wrap ribbon in a variety of bright colors, ¼-inch curling ribbon, measuring stick, scissors, transparent tape, permanent felt pens. For each child—one large balloon, one plastic berry basket, 5 chenille wires.

Preparation: Cut ¾-inch ribbon into 18-inch lengths—three or four lengths for each child.

Instruct each child in the following procedures:

★ Starting from the inside of the basket, weave one length of ribbon around the berry basket until ends meet. Trim ribbon ends and tape together inside the basket (sketch a).

★ Weave additional ribbons around basket in the same manner.

★ Cut lengths of curling ribbon about 8 inches (20-cm) long and tie to corners on the top rim of the basket.

★ With teacher's help, curl the ribbons with scissors (sketch b).

★ Bend one chenille wire into a circle and secure by twisting ends together.

★ Bend four remaining wires in half around the wire circle. Space the wires evenly around the circle (sketch c).

★ Lightly twist each wire together.

★ Attach each doubled-wire end around a corner rim of the basket, twisting wire ends to secure (sketch d).

★ Inflate balloon and tie.

★ Write a message or Bible verse on your balloon with permanent felt pens.

★ Set balloon on top of chenille wire circle and tape in place.

★ Fill the hot air balloon basket with candy or cookies and give to a friend or someone you love!

Conversation:

What are some things you could fill your balloon basket with, (Kendra)? (Child responds.) Who could you give your basket to? When you share what you have with others, you are doing what God wants you to do. You are serving God! The Bible says, "Serve the Lord with all your heart." (1 Samuel 12:20.)

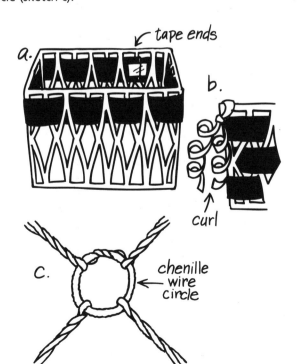

Materials: Fabric in a variety of bright colors, fabric scissors, fabric stiffener, hole punch, glue, ruler, shallow containers, newspaper. For each child—one 3-inch (7.5-cm) Styrofoam egg or ball, one bamboo skewer, two chenille wires, one paper nut cup.

Preparation: Pour fabric stiffener into shallow containers. Cut fabric into 1-inch (2.5-cm) squares, strips and triangles. Cover work area with newspaper.

Instruct each child in the following procedures:

* ✴ Dip one fabric piece into stiffener until saturated and smooth onto Styrofoam egg.
* ✴ Continue procedure, covering Styrofoam egg with fabric pieces.
* ✴ Punch four holes in nut cup (sketch a).
* ✴ With the pointed end of skewer, carefully poke a hole through the bottom of nut cup. Slide nut cup onto skewer.
* ✴ Glue skewer into narrow end of Styrofoam balloon (sketch a).
* ✴ Bend and glue two chenille wires onto balloon for ropes (sketch b).
* ✴ Poke chenille wire ends through nut cup holes and bend up wires. Adjust nut cup on skewer as needed (sketch b).

Conversation:

It takes some faith for a balloonist to launch his or her balloon. What are some things that a balloonist would need to have faith in before lift off? (The weather, the equipment, his training, God's protection, etc.) **The balloonist has to have faith before he or she will have the courage to act. When we have faith in God, He will give us the courage to act and do what is right. Who in your family takes care of your plants? You could give your plant stick to that person.**

BATIK QUILT HOT PAD

(TWO-DAY CRAFT/ 25-30 MINUTES EACH DAY)

Materials: Fabric scissors, measuring stick, water, paper towels, newspaper.

To make quilt square—Muslin, paraffin, fabric dye in one or two colors, large stainless steel pot for each color of dye, coffee can, double boiler, stove or hot plate, large stiff-bristle paintbrushes, iron.

To make hot pad—Fiberfill batting, seam binding, straight pins, one quilting needle for each child, thread.

DAY ONE Preparation: Wash and dry muslin to preshrink. Cut muslin into 9-inch (22.5-cm) squares—one for each child. Prepare fabric dye(s) in stainless steel pot(s), according to package directions. Heat water in double boiler on stove or hot plate. Place paraffin in coffee can; then place coffee can in double boiler to melt wax. Cover work area with newspaper.

Instruct each child in the following procedures:

To make quilt square:

✶ Paint hot wax design on muslin square using paintbrush (sketch a). Wax should penetrate cloth and look transparent in order to resist dye. Let cool.

✶ When wax has cooled, crumple up fabric square and then smooth out. Place fabric in dye bath.

✶ When fabric has reached desired shade, remove from dye and place on pad of newspaper. Cover with paper towels and a layer of newspaper. Iron until all wax has melted out of the fabric (sketch b).

DAY TWO Preparation: Cut an additional 9-inch (22.5-cm) muslin square for each child. Cut batting into 9-inch (22.5-cm) squares—one for each child. Cut seam binding into 40-inch (100-cm) lengths—one for each child.

Instruct each child in the following procedures:

To make hot pad:

✶ Place batik square facedown. Then place batting and a plain muslin square on top of the batik square. Secure with straight pins (sketch c).

✶ Pin seam binding around edges of square (sketch d) and stitch to secure.

Enrichment Idea: Stitch around design as shown in sketch e.

Conversation:

What would your quilt square look like if you had covered the whole square with wax? (Volunteers respond.) **The wax keeps the fabric from accepting the dye. That's what makes the pattern. Who do you think might enjoy receiving this hot pad?**

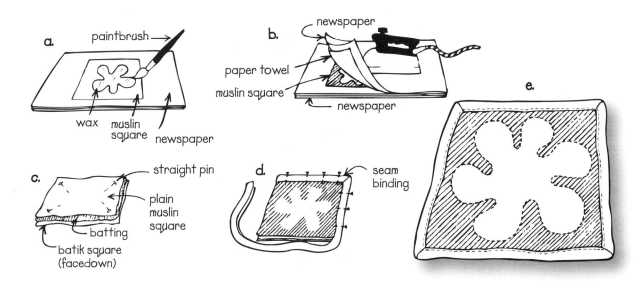

a. paintbrush
wax   muslin square   newspaper

b. newspaper
paper towel
muslin square
newspaper

c. straight pin
plain muslin square
batting
batik square (facedown)

d. seam binding

e.

Materials: Clear Con-Tact paper, ribbon in various colors, several different kinds of small leaves and small flowers, gold glitter in shaker container, scissors, ruler.

Preparation: Cut Con-Tact paper into 4x6-inch (10x15-cm) rectangles—two for each child. Cut ribbon into 6-inch (15-cm) lengths—one for each child.

Instruct each child in the following procedures:

★ Lay one Con-Tact paper rectangle with the backing face up. Peel off backing. Place end of ribbon on the adhesive side at bottom of rectangle (see sketch).

★ Arrange several leaves and/or flowers on adhesive side of paper, near the center.

★ Sprinkle a small amount of glitter onto Con-Tact paper.

★ With teacher's help, peel backing off second paper rectangle and lay adhesive side directly on top of other rectangle. Press firmly together.

★ Trim edges, if desired.

Enrichment Ideas: Letter Bible memory verse on piece of paper and place between papers. Use decorative-edged scissors to trim edges of paper and/or bookmark.

Conversation:

What is your favorite Bible story, (Alex)? Your family can use your bookmark to mark your favorite story in your Bible or Bible storybook.

Gifts

Materials: Tempera paint in a variety of colors, paintbrushes, shallow containers, glue, newspaper. For each child—one small bottle or jar, approximately six eggshells.

Preparation: Wash eggshells and allow to dry. Pour glue into shallow containers. Pour paint into additional shallow containers. Cover work area with newspaper.

Instruct each child in the following procedures:

★ On paved area, place eggshells between two sheets of newspaper and stomp on shells to crush them. (Note: Make sure children are wearing shoes.)

★ Use paintbrush to cover entire bottle or jar with glue.

★ Remove top sheet of newspaper and roll bottle or jar onto crushed eggshells (sketch a). Allow glue to dry.

★ Paint vase to decorate. Let dry.

Simplification Idea: Crush eggshells ahead of time.

Conversation:

We broke eggshells to make our vases. Have you ever broken something in your house and were afraid to tell your mom or dad? When you tell the truth about breaking something, what would you like your (mom) to say or do? We're glad when people love and forgive us. You can give your vase to someone you love.

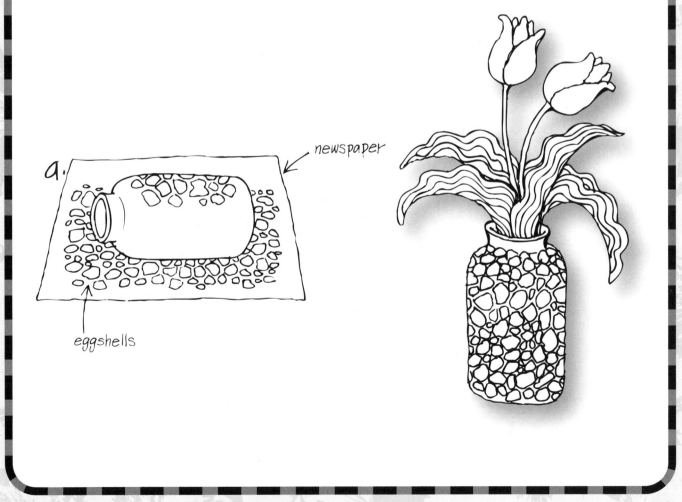

a. *newspaper*

eggshells

Gifts

Materials: ¼-inch (.625-cm) satin ribbon, straight pins, sequins, beads, fabric scissors, transparent tape, measuring stick, measuring spoon, small containers. For each child—one lemon or small orange, one paper plate, one tablespoon of whole cloves (Note: Cloves may be purchased economically in bulk at discount food stores.), one toothpick.

Preparation: Cut ribbon into 2-foot (60-cm) lengths—two lengths for each child. Pour sequins and beads into small containers. Place a tablespoon of cloves on each child's plate.

Instruct each child in the following procedures:

★ Place a length of tape around the lemon or orange, starting and ending at the top. Repeat with another length of tape to intersect the first taped line (sketch a).

★ Use a toothpick to poke holes into fruit along outside edges of tape (sketch b).

★ Insert pointed ends of cloves into holes in fruit (sketch b).

★ Fill in sections between tape lines with sequins and beads by inserting straight pins through holes and into citrus. Or insert more cloves into fruit.

★ Carefully remove tape.

★ Fold length of ribbon in half to find midpoint. Pin the midpoint of ribbon to bottom end of fruit. Following the empty space where the tape had been, bring ribbon ends up to the top and tie in a knot (sketch c).

★ Repeat with the second ribbon in the other empty space. Tie ends of ribbon in a bow on top of first ribbon knot (sketch d). Pin in place.

★ Make a loop hanger by tying the ends of the first ribbon in a knot (sketch d).

★ The fruit will shrink in the next few weeks as it dries. Untie ribbons and re-tie to make ribbon snug again.

Conversation:

We hang pomanders to perfume a room or closet. What will you do with your pomander?

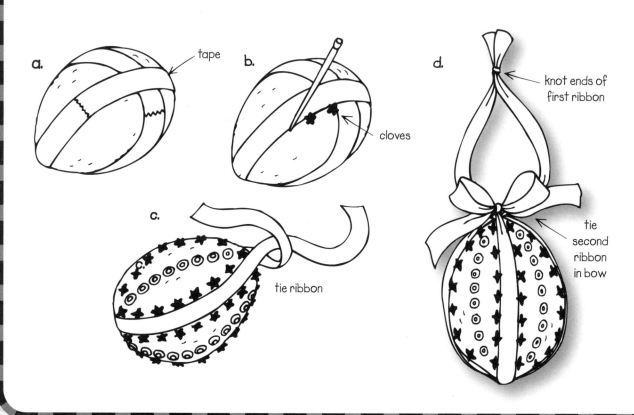

a. tape

b. cloves

c. tie ribbon

d. knot ends of first ribbon / tie second ribbon in bow

Materials: Yellow poster board, cardboard, ⅛-inch (.32-cm) black graphic tape (such as Formaline®, available at graphics supply stores), nail, black felt pens, pencils, craft knife, glue, scissors, rulers. For each child—one 1¾-inch (4.4-cm) suction cup with hook (available at craft stores).

Preparation: Cut poster board into 8-inch (20-cm) squares—one for each child. Cut a 3x4½-inch (7.5x11.25-cm) opening from the center of each poster board square as shown in sketch a. Cut cardboard into 8-inch (20-cm) squares—one for each child. Use craft knife to score one side and cut three sides of a 3½x5-inch (8.75x12.5-cm) opening from each cardboard square as shown in sketch b.

Instruct each child in the following procedures:

★ Glue poster board square onto cardboard square so that openings match up (sketch c).

★ Use pencil to sketch a ½-inch (1.25-cm) border around the edge of poster board square (sketch c).

★ Cut and place graphic tape on pencil lines.

★ Use a thick felt pen to letter "(Smith) Family on Board" on frame.

★ Use nail to poke a hole at top corner of frame (sketch d). Insert hook of suction cup through hole.

★ Take frame home. Open cardboard flap opening. Place photograph onto front of flap and close (sketch e). Press suction cup on window or mirror to hang picture frame.

Conversation:

What road signs have you seen that are the shape of your photo frame? What is the longest drive you and your family have taken? What games does your family play in the car? Road trips can be a great way to spend time talking and playing with your family. Who do you think would enjoy receiving this framed photo of your family?

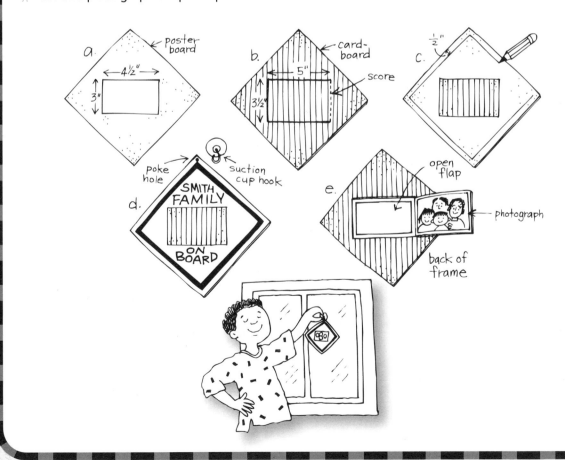

Gifts

Materials: Several magazines with a variety of pictures (showing animals, foods, sports, etc.), poster board in a variety of colors, clear self-adhesive paper, glue sticks, scissors, measuring stick.

Preparations: Cut poster board into 9x12-inch (22.5x30-cm) mats—two for each child. Cut self-adhesive paper into 10x13-inch (25x32.5-cm) rectangles—four for each child. Look through magazines and tear out appropriate pages.

Instruct each child in the following procedures:

★ Cut out magazine pictures of objects that tell about two family members (such as hobbies, interests, favorite animals, favorite food). Medium-sized pictures work best—8 to 12 for each family member.

★ Arrange cutouts for one family member on a poster board mat of his or her favorite color. Lightly glue cutouts in place. Repeat process for second family member.

★ With teacher's help, peel adhesive backing from clear paper and place on front of place mat. Then, peel adhesive backing from second piece of clear paper and place on back of place mat. Repeat process for second place mat.

★ With teacher's help, cut edges of self-adhesive paper as close as possible to edges of place mats.

★ At home, child places place mats on table where the family members sit.

Simplification Idea: On poster board, children draw pictures of objects representing family members.

Enrichment Ideas: Make place mats for additional family members as time allows. Use felt pens or cut out letters to spell out family member's name on place mat.

Conversation:

What is your (sister's) favorite color? What is your (dad's) favorite food? Each member of your family has different likes and dislikes—that's what makes us special! You can give your place mats to show how each family member is special.

Gifts

Materials: Cement; sand; 5-gallon bucket or large plastic tub; short sticks or dowels; a variety of mosaic materials, such as aquarium pebbles in a variety of colors, colored glass pebbles, small mosaic tiles, smooth pebbles, etc.; garden hoe; trowel; one pair of rubber gloves; water; soap; shallow containers. For each child—one round or square disposable aluminum baking pan.

Preparation: A half hour before beginning project, in an outside area, make concrete in bucket or tub. Wearing rubber gloves (concrete can damage skin), mix one part cement with two parts sand using a hoe. Then, a little at a time, mix in water to make a thick cement mixture. If mixture is too thin, it will require more time to set before children can use it. Use trowel to fill each baking pan with concrete and level the tops (sketch a). Pour mosaic materials into shallow containers.

Instruct each child in the following procedures:

★ Decide how you want to design your stepping stone.

★ Use a stick to draw an object or write your name, date or a short word in the concrete. You may want to use your hand to make a handprint (sketch b).

★ Press aquarium pebbles into the lines you have drawn, if desired.

★ Use mosaic materials to decorate stepping stone by pressing items into concrete. Make borders around the edges or create a mosaic picture using different colors of pebbles and tiles (sketch c).

★ Carefully transfer pans to a flat surface to dry overnight. Wash hands in soap and water.

★ Carry your stepping stone home in the pan. At home, pull sides of pan away from concrete and discard. Your stepping stone will take two or three days to dry completely.

Conversation:

Many beautiful works of art have been created using thousands of small stones to make a picture. They are called mosaics. Artists have made mosaics of Jesus and people of the Bible to decorate the walls and floors of churches. The mosaics you made on your stepping stones are each different and unique, too. Who might like to have your stone in their garden?

a.

concrete

b.

glass pebbles

aquarium pebbles

tile

c.

Gifts

Materials: Felt in a variety of colors including white, sewing machine and thread, yarn, tempera paint, squeeze bottles of fabric paint, straight pins, plastic-coated paper plates, scissors, measuring stick, water and soap for cleanup, paper towels, newspaper. For each child—one plastic drinking straw.

Preparation: Cut white felt into 7x9-inch (17.5x22.5-cm) rectangles—one for each child. Cut colored felt into 4½x6-inch (11.25x15-cm) rectangles—one for each child. Cut each colored rectangle into two triangles by cutting in half diagonally (sketch a). Lay short sides of triangles over bottom edge of white banner rectangle, overlapping in the center and making outer edges of triangle even with banner. Pin in place. Machine stitch triangles to banner (sketch b). Fold over 1 inch (2.5 cm) at the top of banner. Cut four equally spaced ⅛-inch (.3125-cm) slits in fold (sketch b). Cut yarn into one 28-inch (70-cm) length and four 12-inch (30-cm) lengths for each child. Pour paint onto paper plates. Cover work area with newspaper.

Instruct each child in the following procedures:

★ Weave the straw through slits in the banner (sketch c).

★ With teacher's help, tie an end of the long length of yarn onto each of the straw ends.

★ Tie two short lengths of yarn onto each end of straw for tassels.

★ Dip hand into the paint on paper plate. Print your hand in the center of felt banner.

★ Wash and dry hands.

★ Teacher writes child's name on banner with fabric paint. Allow to dry overnight.

Simplification Idea: Use hot glue or craft glue to assemble banner instead of sewing.

Enrichment Idea: Children decorate triangle flags with fabric paint or glue on small felt shapes, acrylic jewels or sequins.

Conversation:

(Julia), your banner is different from everyone else's because it has your own handprint on it. God made everyone special. (Emily) has (brown) hair. Who has hair that is a different color? Whose hair is the same color? Who will you give your bannner to?

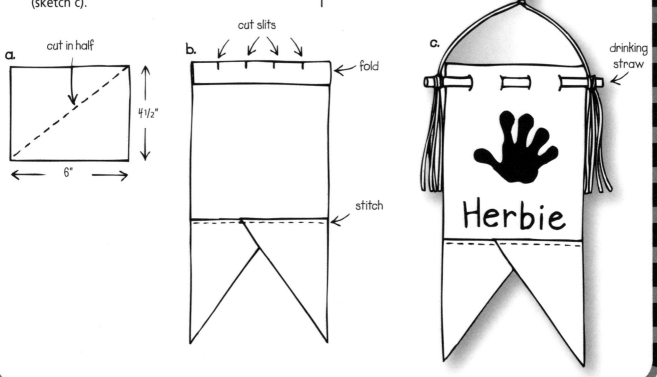

a. cut in half

4 1/2"

6"

b. cut slits

fold

stitch

c. drinking straw

Herbie

Gifts

Materials: Kitchen sponges, scissors, spring-type clothespins, glue gun, glue sticks, ruler, acrylic paints, unlined index cards, rubber stamps in hot air balloon shapes, ink pads, acrylic spray finish, shallow containers, newspaper. For each child—one white 3-inch (7.5-cm) ceramic tile, one spring-type wooden clothespin. Optional—permanent felt pens.

Preparation: Dampen sponges and cut into 2-inch (5-cm) squares. Clip clothespins to sponges to use as handles for sponge painting (sketch a). Pour paint into containers. Cover work area with newspaper.

Instruct each child in the following procedures:

★ Dip sponge into paint and dab gently onto tile a few times.

★ Repeat sponging with one or two different colors. Let dry.

★ Using the rubber stamps and the ink pads, stamp a balloon image in the upper left corner of several index cards.

★ With glue gun, teacher glues the wooden clothespin onto the center back of tile (sketch b). Tile will stand upright.

★ In well-ventilated area, teacher sprays tile with acrylic spray finish.

★ Place index cards in clothespin.

Enrichment Idea: With permanent felt pen, teacher letters "(Mom's, Dad's, Grandpa's) Memos" or "(Mom's, Dad's, Grandma's) Recipes" on tile before spraying with acrylic. Older children may letter a simple word such as "Mom" or "Memos" on the tile themselves.

Conversation:

Who are you making your tile for, (Shestin)? (Child responds.) **Your (grandma) can use the tile to hold notes or recipes. Your tile will also remind her of how much you love her!**

Gifts

Materials: Dried, fresh or artificial flowers—a small bunch for each child, water-based colored felt pens, masking tape, paper towels. For each child—one empty glass bottle (such as salad dressing or soda bottle).

Preparation: For younger children, tear masking tape into pieces about 1 to 3 inches (2.5 to 7.5 cm) long and place pieces on table edges or other place where children can easily access them. Older children may tear their own tape. (Cutting tape pieces with scissors does not produce the same effect.)

Instruct each child in the following procedures:

★ Place pieces of tape on surface of bottle. Overlap pieces of tape until entire bottle is covered.

★ Use felt pens to color a small section of bottle.

★ Rub colored section with paper towel to give an old, faded look.

★ Repeat process with various colors until entire bottle is colored.

★ Place flowers inside vase.

Conversation:

You made a colorful old-fashioned vase for flowers. Flowers are nice to give to people. Who would you like to give flowers to? Giving gifts is a way of showing love. Our Bible says, "Love each other as I have loved you" (John 15:12). **God loves us so much! He wants us to share His love with other people, too.**

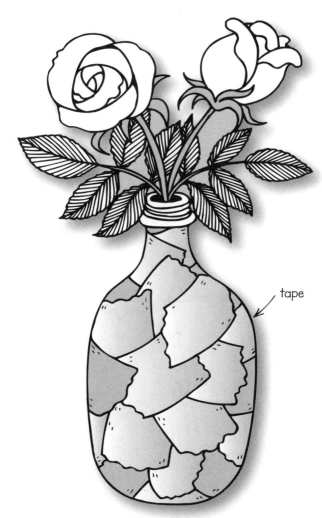

tape

Gifts

Materials: Fabric scraps in various colors and patterns, heavyweight cardboard or mat board, narrow ribbon in various colors, pencil, glue, masking tape, fabric scissors, craft knife, foam paintbrushes, ruler, shallow containers, water, newspaper. For each child—one large paper clip, several small buttons.

Preparation: Cut fabric into 1½-inch (3.75-cm) squares—15 to 20 squares for each child. Cut cardboard or mat board into 7-inch (17.5-cm) squares—one for each child. Cut a 3-inch (7.5-cm) square from the center of each frame (see sketch). Cut ribbon into 2- to 6-inch (5- to 15-cm) lengths—several for each child. Cover work area with newspaper. Dilute portion of glue with a small amount of water in shallow containers.

Instruct each child in the following procedures:

★ Use foam paintbrush to spread glue mixture onto front of frame and stick on different colors of fabric squares. Cover entire front of frame with squares.

★ Spread another coat of glue mixture on top of fabric.

★ Glue buttons and lengths of ribbon onto frame to decorate.

★ Tape paper clip securely to back of frame to make a hanger.

★ Allow frame to dry. Take frame home and tape a photograph to back of frame.

Simplification Idea: Instead of fabric, use construction paper or tissue paper squares or have children tear paper into small pieces to use.

Conversation:

Your frames are beautiful. What will you do with them? (Volunteers respond.) **You could give them to people you love. God loves you, (Margaret). Our Bible says, "God . . . loved us and sent his Son"** (1 John 4:10).

paper clip

3"(7.5 cm)

7" (17.5 cm)

button

ribbon

Gifts

Materials: Balloon Frame Pattern, camera, film, scissors, craft knife, sturdy poster board, small aquarium pebbles in a variety of bright colors, bottles of glue, hole punch, shallow containers, transparent tape.

Preparation: Before craft, take a horizontal photo of each child standing in front of a blue or sky background. Photograph child from the waist up. Develop film. Trace Balloon Frame Pattern onto poster board and cut out—one for each child. With craft knife, cut out opening for photo on each balloon. Punch a hole at the top of poster board balloons. Pour colored pebbles into shallow containers—one container for each color.

Instruct each child in the following procedures:

✶ With teacher's help, squeeze thick lines of glue from the top of balloon to the bottom to make balloon stripes (sketch a).

✶ Place colored pebbles on glue lines to fill in stripes. Make each stripe a different color.

✶ With teacher's help, squeeze glue on balloon basket (sketch b).

✶ Place pebbles on glued basket. Let dry.

✶ With teacher's help, tape photo to the back of poster board at opening, trimming photo edges where needed.

Enrichment Idea: Older children may make their own designs with glue on the balloon and basket, then cover with pebbles.

Conversation:

(Tony,) does your balloon frame feel heavy or light with all the pebbles on it? (Heavy.) **A real hot air balloon is very light. Who will you give your picture to?**

PEBBLED BALLOON FRAME PATTERN

Materials: Pop-Up Balloon Card Patterns, photocopier, white and brightly colored copier paper, pencils, 9x12-inch (22.5x30-cm) blue and yellow construction paper, ruler, scissors, colored felt pens, glue sticks.

Preparation: Fold blue construction paper in half to make cards—one for each child. Use pencil and ruler to mark a 3-inch (7.5-cm) square in the upper right corner of back and front pages of cards (sketch a). Cut away squares. Photocopy Cloud Patterns onto white paper and Balloon Pattern onto colored paper—one set of photocopied patterns for each child.

Instruct each child in the following procedures:

* With pencil, draw a curved line diagonally from the top of the card to the corner of the square (sketch b). Cut on line.
* Cut out colored balloon pattern.
* Open card and glue paper balloon onto the curved section of card (sketch c).
* Fold card again with the inside facing out. Then fold the curved portion down diagonally. Turn card over and fold diagonally again (sketch d).
* Open card and fold in the original position. With teacher's help, fold the pop-up part of the card to the inside on the pre-folded lines (sketch e).
* Cut out a yellow circle for the sun. Glue to fold in the front of card (sketch f).
* Cut out large cloud patterns and glue onto front of card.
* With felt pens, write message on the clouds.
* Open card to the inside. Decorate balloon with felt pens and write message.
* Cut balloon basket out of yellow construction paper and glue in place.
* Cut out small cloud patterns. Write words on clouds for an additional message, if desired.
* Cut blue construction paper into narrow strips, about 1 inch (2.5 cm) long. Fold strips accordion-style (sketch g).
* Glue one end of folded paper strips onto clouds, then glue opposite end to the inside of card (sketch g).
* Close your card, then open to see your message pop-up!
* Cards may be used in a variety of ways: invitations, get-well cards for hospital patients, encouragement cards for missionaries and thank-you cards.

Simplification Idea: Handletter card messages onto Balloon and Cloud Patterns before photocopying.

Conversation:

Your pop-up balloon card can show someone how much you love and care for him or her. When we tell people that we love or appreciate them, we are treating them the way Jesus would treat them. We can show Jesus' love to other people by doing and saying kind things to them. When has someone done something for you that was loving and kind?

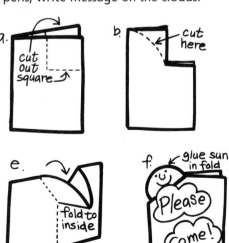

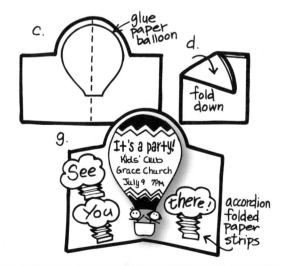

POP-UP BALLOON CARD PATTERNS

Balloon Pattern

Cloud Patterns

"PUNCHED-TIN" WINDOW ORNAMENT
(20-25 MINUTES)

Materials: Heavy-duty aluminum foil, ribbon, permanent felt pen, scissors, glue, measuring stick, newspaper. For each child—medium-sized wooden embroidery hoop, large metal paper clip.

Preparation: Tear a length of foil slightly larger than embroidery hoop—one for each child. Use felt pen to draw a simple design or shape on foil pieces. Cut ribbon into 24-inch (60-cm) lengths—one for each child. Bend one end of each paper clip to make a poker (sketch a). Take apart embroidery hoop to make an inner hoop and outer hoop. Cover work area with a thick layer of newspaper.

Instruct each child in the following procedures:

★ Lay foil piece flat on newspaper. Use end of paper clip to carefully punch small holes along lines of design.

★ With teacher's help, lay foil on inner hoop and fold edges around hoop; carefully place outer hoop over foil and tighten screw securely.

★ Glue ribbon around outside of embroidery hoop, leaving an excess of at least 5 inches (12.5 cm) on either side of metal closure (sketch b). Allow to dry.

★ With teacher's help, tie ends of ribbon into a bow at top of hoop.

★ Take ornament home and hang in front of a window to see light shine through the design.

Enrichment Idea: Older children may draw simple designs on foil themselves.

Conversation:

Your hoop pictures are beautiful! You listened and followed my directions. Thank you. Who might like to get this as a gift from you? That's a way to show love to (your grandma).

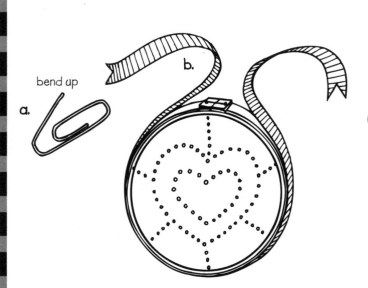

bend up

a.

b.

Gifts

Materials: Acrylic spray paint in a variety of bright colors, poster board, ribbon, stapler and staples, pencil, masking tape, craft glue, scissors, ruler, newspaper. For each child—20 small jigsaw puzzle pieces (they don't need to fit together).

Preparation: In well-ventilated area, cover ground with newspaper and spray paint front of puzzle pieces in a variety of colors. Cut poster board into 4x5-inch (10x12.5-cm) rectangles—two for each child. Cut a 2x3-inch (5x7.5-cm) opening from the center of one rectangle to make a frame (sketch a)—one for each child. Use pencil to draw a line along sides and bottom of frame border as a guide for gluing. Cut ribbon into 12-inch (30-cm) lengths—one for each child.

Instruct each child in the following procedures:

★ With teacher's help, staple one end of ribbon onto corner of uncut poster board piece. Staple other end of ribbon onto opposite corner to make a hanger (sketch b).

★ Spread glue along pencil lines around frame (sketch c).

★ With teacher's help, place uncut poster board piece on top of frame with staples facing in (sketch c).

★ Overlap and glue puzzle pieces around frame to decorate. Allow glue to dry.

★ Take frame home. With parent's help, slide a family photograph through top of frame. Hang picture frame.

Simplification Ideas: Omit painting puzzle pieces. Use pasta boxes (the kind with plastic windows) to make front of frame.

Enrichment Ideas: Children use felt pens instead of spray paint to color the back sides of puzzle pieces. Glue a frame stand to back of picture instead of hanging.

Conversation:

Families are like puzzles—each person is a separate piece—but when they are joined together, they make one whole family. God created our families to stick together, even when times are tough! Who in your family would like this picture frame?

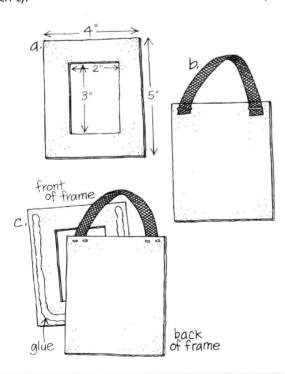

Gifts

Materials: Craft tissue paper in various colors, scissors, liquid starch, shallow containers, ruler, sponge brushes, clear acrylic spray, newspaper. For each child—one small glass soda or water bottle.

Preparation: Cut tissue paper into 1½-inch (3.75-cm) squares. Pour liquid starch into shallow containers. Cover work area with newspaper.

Instruct each child in the following procedures:

★ Paint starch onto the outside of the glass bottle.

★ Lay tissue paper squares on top of starch.

★ Gently paint more starch on top of tissue and smooth out any wrinkles.

★ Cover the bottle completely, overlapping tissue. Let dry.

★ In a well-ventilated area, teacher sprays vases with clear acrylic spray.

Conversation:

Your Rainbow Vase has many pretty colors on it, just like a rainbow! What colors are in a rainbow, (Justine)? God made the rainbow in the sky. You can give your vase to someone as a reminder of God's love.

Gifts

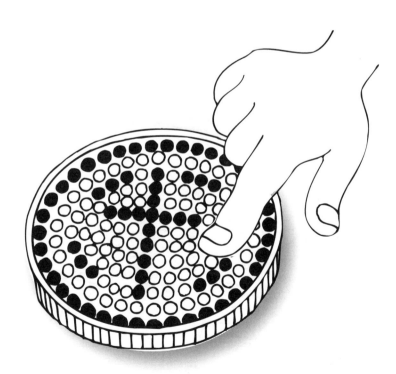

Materials: Pre-mixed tile grout adhesive (available at home hardware stores), various colors of aquarium rocks, large spoon, shallow containers. For each child—one wide-mouth canning jar ring and lid.

Instruct each child in the following procedures:

★ Push colored aquarium rocks into the grout to make a design (see sketch). Use several different colors.

★ Allow to dry overnight. You may give your mosaic to someone to use as a coaster or trivet.

Enrichment Idea: Older children may make a simple picture with rocks, such as a flower, cross, heart, tree, rainbow, etc.

Conversation:

Artists make pictures called mosaics by using small pieces of rock and tile. Many ancient mosaics show stories from the Bible. (Roberto), who do you think you'll give your mosaic to?

Gifts

Materials: Felt in a variety of bright colors; brown, black, orange, white and yellow yarn; round stones in a variety of shapes and sizes; small wiggle eyes; craft glue; scissors; cotton balls. For each child—a small piece of driftwood.

Instruct each child in the following procedures:

★ Choose one stone and two wiggle eyes for each family member.

★ Glue two eyes onto each stone. Allow glue to dry.

★ With teacher's help, cut and glue yarn and felt on top of each stone to make hair or a hat for each family member.

★ Glue stones onto piece of driftwood, in nooks and crannies. To secure each stone in place, wedge pieces of cotton into gaps between driftwood and stone.

Simplification Idea: For younger children, glue eyes, yarn, etc. onto one large stone to make one family member.

Enrichment Ideas: Glue small seashells onto tops of stones for hats. Use white correction fluid and permanent black felt pen to draw eyes on pebbles. Glue pieces of moss onto driftwood for further decoration. Brush clear nail polish on pebbles to make them shiny.

Conversation:

How many people are in your family? We can give these as gifts to our families. Some families are small and some families are large. But God loves every family no matter what size it is. Let's thank God for giving each of us a family!

Gifts

Materials: Acrylic paints in various colors, shallow containers, large paintbrushes, thin paintbrushes, toothpicks, clear acrylic spray, newspaper. For each child—two smooth stones 3-4 inches (7.5-10 cm) in diameter.

Preparation: Pour paint into shallow containers. Cover work area with newspaper.

Instruct each child in the following procedures:

★ Use large paintbrush to paint one stone a solid color. Set aside.

★ Paint second stone a solid color. Set aside.

★ Use thin paintbrush to paint designs on first stone. Use toothpicks to make small dots. Let dry.

★ Paint designs on second stone. Let dry.

★ In a well-ventilated area, teacher sprays stones with clear acrylic finish.

★ Share one of your painted stones with someone you love!

Conversation:

You can share one of your painted stones with someone you love. Who will you give your stone to, (Abel)? (Child responds.) **Giving gifts to our friends or family is one way to show that we love them. God loved us so much that He gave us Jesus. Who is Jesus?** (God's Son.)

Gifts

Materials: White and black poster board, desk lamp or slide projector, chair, gold doilies, silver paint pen, pencils, glue, glue sticks, masking tape, scissors, measuring stick. For each child—12x18-inch (30x45-cm) black construction paper, self-adhesive picture hanger.

Preparation: Cut white poster board into 16x18-inch (40x45-cm) rectangles—one for each child. Cut black poster board into 2x16-inch (5x40-cm) and 2x18-inch (5x45-cm) strips—two of each length for each child. Place a chair, sideways, about 12 inches (30 cm) from wall. Place light source approximately 4 inches (10 cm) from chair. (Note: Each portrait takes about three minutes, so large classes may need additional helpers and more light sources.)

Instruct each child in the following procedures:

To make picture frame:

★ Make the picture frame while waiting to have your silhouette drawn.

★ Write your name on back of white poster board.

★ Glue four black poster-board strips to the white poster board to make a frame.

★ Decorate edges of frame with silver paint pen, and/or cut pieces of gold doilies and glue to black strips (sketch a).

To make silhouettes:

★ Teacher calls children one at a time to sit in chair. Teacher tapes black paper to wall directly behind child's head.

★ Child holds head sideways with shoulders against back of chair and tilts chin up slightly (raising chin a bit more than natural gives a better profile of chin and neck).

★ Teacher uses pencil to outline silhouette on black paper (sketch b).

★ Child carefully cuts out silhouette along pencil line.

★ Apply glue stick to all edges of portrait. Glue portrait to center of white poster board (sketch c).

★ Attach picture hanger to back of frame, near the top.

Simplification Idea: Eliminate black poster-board frame and use pens to draw a decorative border around edge of white poster board.

Enrichment Ideas: Teacher collects large silhouettes and photocopies onto card stock at 50 percent reduction. Teacher writes child's name on back of each photocopy and gives to child to take home (or child makes an additional smaller frame for photocopy). Trace outline of student praying and letter on picture: "Call to me and I will answer you. Jeremiah 33:3."

Conversation:

Before cameras were invented, people would get their portraits sketched. But that could be expensive. Silhouettes like these were much easier for average folks to make to remind them of their loved ones. Who will you give your silhouette to?

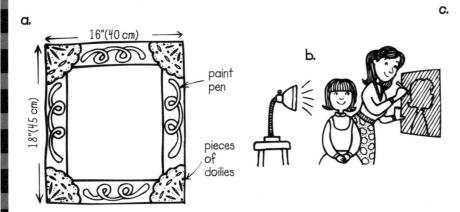

a.
16"(40 cm)
18"(45 cm)
paint pen
pieces of doilies

b.

c.

Materials: Window Design Patterns, tissue paper in a variety of colors, black permanent felt pens, photocopier, copier paper, glue, scissors, ruler, shallow containers. For each child—one overhead transparency sheet, thin paintbrush. *Optional*—simulated liquid lead (available at craft stores).

Preparation: Photocopy Window Design Patterns onto paper—one copy of each pattern for each child. Cut tissue paper into 1-inch (2.5-cm) squares. Pour glue into shallow containers.

Instruct each child in the following procedures:

★ Choose one of the Window Design Patterns and place it under transparency sheet. Use felt pen to trace the design onto transparency or create your own design. Remove pattern.

★ Brush glue on one section of transparency design.

★ Use paintbrush to pick up a piece of tissue paper and place it on the glued section (sketch a). Continue to add pieces of the same color of tissue paper to fill in section, trying to stay within the black lines.

★ Lightly brush more glue over completed tissue paper section. If tissue paper overlaps a black line, use the end of paintbrush to push paper back into section (sketch b).

★ Fill in each section of design with a different color of tissue paper. Allow to dry.

★ *Optional:* After tissue paper dries, turn transparency over and outline sections with liquid lead.

★ Tape your finished creation in a sunny window to display.

Conversation:

For hundreds of years, glassworkers have made beautiful windows with pieces of colored glass. They put the pieces together with liquid metal, which hardens to hold the window together. When the window is finished, the pieces form a beautiful picture. In churches, stained-glass windows show pictures of people from the Bible. Since most people in olden times couldn't read, they learned about Jesus and the Bible by looking at the windows. Who can you give your window picture to?

a.

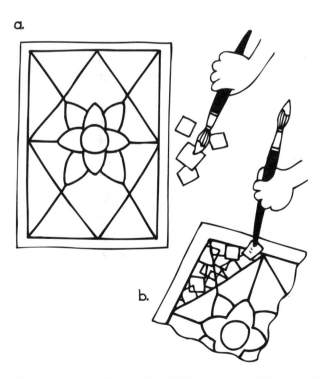

b.

STAINED-GLASS WINDOW DESIGN PATTERN 2

EARLY CHILDHOOD • YOUNGER ELEMENTARY • OLDER ELEMENTARY

Materials: Rainbow-colored candy sprinkles, flour, salt, water, measuring cup, large bowl, mixing spoon, cookie sheet, small cookie cutters, forks, oven, clear acrylic spray, medium-width ribbon, glue, scissors, measuring stick, newspaper. For each child—one small glass jar with metal lid, one plastic sandwich bag.

Preparation: Make dough. The following recipe will make enough dough for eight children: Mix 4 cups flour, 1 cup salt and 1¼ cups water until mixture clings together. Knead mixture on floured surface until smooth. Divide mixture into eight balls and place in individual sandwich bags. Make additional dough for decorations. Cut ribbon into 18-inch (45-cm) lengths—one for each child. Cover outside area with newspaper.

Instruct each child in the following procedures:

DAY ONE:

* Shape dough ball onto top of jar lid (sketch a).
* Flatten additional dough on flat surface. Press cookie cutter into dough to make a shape.
* Moisten bottom of dough shape with water and place on top of dough lid (sketch b).
* Use fork to poke several holes in dough to allow air to escape when baking.
* Place dough lids on cookie sheet. Teacher bakes dough at 250 degrees for two to three hours or until dough hardens.

DAY TWO:

* Glue candy sprinkles or other decorations onto lid.
* In well-ventilated area, spray jar lid with clear spray and allow to dry (about two minutes).
* With teacher's help, tie ribbon around rim of jar.
* Gently screw lid onto jar.
* Use jar for storage at home.

Enrichment Idea: Paint fun-shaped pasta and glue onto top of dough lid.

Conversation:

Who in your family cooks the most meals? Do you think you'll give your jar to that person? How do you help out in the kitchen? What will you do today to help someone in your family?

a.

b.

Materials: Acrylic paint in a variety of colors, clear acrylic spray, paintbrushes, shallow containers, permanent fine-tip felt pens, drill, ¹⁄₁₆-inch (.16-cm) drill bit, sandpaper, craft glue, scissors, ruler, newspaper. For each child—one precut wooden shape (available at craft stores), three ¾-inch (1.9-cm) cup hooks.

Preparation: Drill three holes in each wood shape at least 1½ inches (3.75 cm) apart (see sketch). Cut ribbon into 10-inch (25-cm) lengths—two for each child. Cover work area with newspaper. Pour paint into shallow containers.

Instruct each child in the following procedures:

★ Use sandpaper to smooth rough edges on wood.

★ Paint wooden shape and allow to dry.

★ Use felt pen to letter "Family Keys" at top of wooden shape.

★ In well-ventilated area, spray key holder with clear spray and allow to dry.

★ Glue ribbon onto each side of wood shape as shown in sketch.

★ Screw cup hooks into drilled holes.

Enrichment Idea: Use fine-tip permanent felt pens to letter the three keys to good communication (listed below) next to cup hooks.

Conversation:

What are the keys in your house used for? What happens when someone in your family loses their keys? We use keys to lock and unlock valuable items. We also use the word "key" to mean an "important point." For example, there are three keys to good communication. Do you know what they are? (Listen, be kind, tell the truth.) **Who do you plan to give your key holder to?**

ribbon

Family Keys

Gifts

Materials: Acrylic paints in white, black and denim blue; sheets of Fun Foam in various colors; raffia; variety of pony beads, buttons and charms; bandanna or gingham print ribbon; excelsior or straw; old toothbrushes; craft sticks; small disposable plastic plates; packing boxes; 18-gauge wire; wire cutters; flat-head nail; hammer; black permanent fine-tip felt pen; masking tape; scissors; foam paintbrushes; measuring stick; shallow containers; newspaper. For each child—large empty fruit or vegetable can (28 oz.), unsharpened pencil with eraser, two small jingle bells, two candy sticks. *Optional*—small pads of paper, sheets of stickers, church brochures or other publicity items.

DAY ONE Preparation: Use hammer and nail to punch holes on both sides of can, near the top (sketch a). Cut raffia into 18-inch (45-cm) lengths—one for each child. Cover work area with newspaper. Pour blue paint into shallow containers. Squeeze small amounts of white and black paint onto plastic plates.

Instruct each child in the following procedures:

★ Paint can with denim-blue paint.

★ Place can in box to splatter-paint. Dip toothbrush bristles into black and white paint. Hold brush downward over can and run craft stick over bristles to splatter paint (sketch b). Set aside to dry.

★ Tear off narrow strip of tape. Take one long strand of raffia and tape midpoint onto top of pencil, just below eraser (sketch c).

★ Tightly wrap each end of raffia several times around taped end of pencil. Tie ends.

★ Thread beads, buttons and charms onto ends of raffia. Split each strand of raffia in half and tie on bell (sketch d). Trim off any excess.

DAY TWO Preparation: Cut Fun Foam into 1x3-inch (2.5x7.5-cm) strips—one for each child. Cut wire into 12-inch (30-cm) lengths—one for each child. Cut raffia into 12-inch (30-cm) lengths—several strands for each child. Cut ribbon into 18-inch (45-cm) lengths—one for each child.

Instruct each child in the following procedures:

★ Use pen to letter the words "Howdy, Neighbor!" onto strip of Fun Foam. Trim one end to make points on flag.

★ Near untrimmed end of flag, poke wire in and out of foam. Then thread ends of wire through holes in can and twist to secure handle (sketch e).

★ Tie several strands of raffia around handle to make a bow. Trim excess.

★ Tie ribbon around can.

★ Use pen to make stitch lines around top and bottom of can (sketch f).

★ Place a handful of excelsior or straw inside can.

★ Fill can with decorated pencil and candy sticks. (*Optional:* Add pads of paper, sheets of stickers and publicity items to can.)

★ Deliver Welcome Can to a neighbor's doorstep.

Simplification Ideas: To make this a one-day project, paint cans blue ahead of time. Eliminate splatter-painting and follow remaining decorating instructions. Children may fill cans with water and fresh flowers instead of other items.

Enrichment Idea: Letter a memory verse on side of can.

Conversation:

Romans 15:7 says, "Accept one another, then, just as Christ accepted you, in order to bring praise to God." Being kind to others is what God calls us to do. To whom will you deliver your can? What is another way you can show you accept that person?

WELCOME CAN

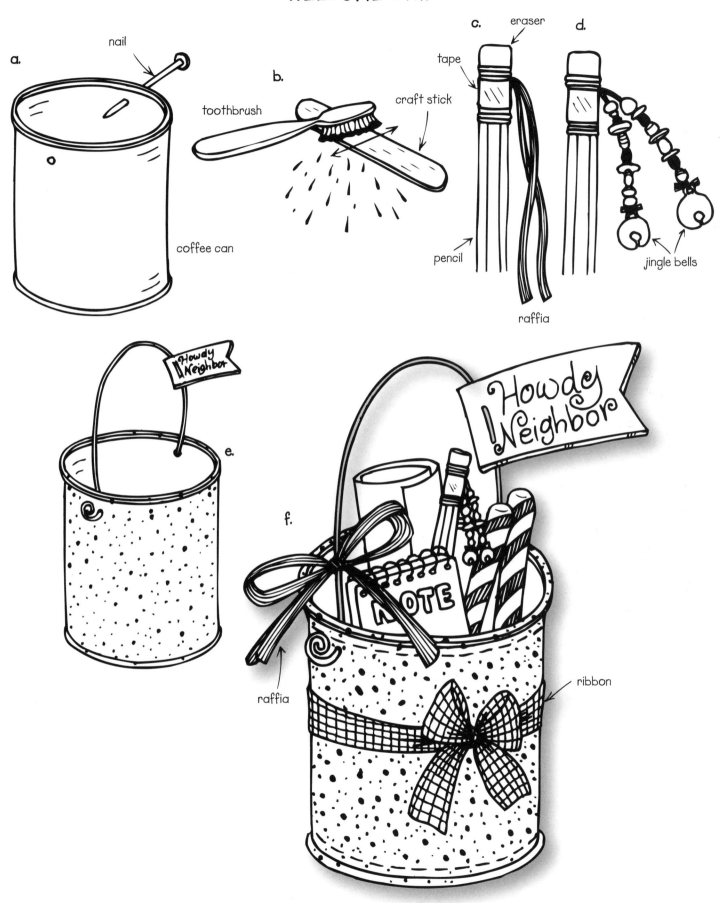

a. nail

coffee can

b. toothbrush

craft stick

c. eraser

tape

pencil

raffia

d. jingle bells

e. Howdy Neighbor

f. Howdy Neighbor

NOTE

raffia

ribbon

God's Kingdom

If royalty is your theme, here are ways for kids in God's Kingdom to have some fun!

God's Kingdom

Materials: Construction paper in a variety of colors, colored felt pens, glue, scissors, pencils, ruler, stapler and staples. For each child—one individual-sized milk carton or coffee creamer carton, one coffee stirrer, two 12-oz.-size frozen juice cans.

Preparation: Cut construction paper into 5x9-inch (12.5x22.5-cm) strips—two for each child. Cut a 3¾x9-inch (9.4x22.5-cm) rectangle—one for each child. Open top of each milk carton, rinse out and allow to dry. Cut away a portion of the carton top to make two triangle roofs (sketch a).

Instruct each child in the following procedures:

★ To make towers, glue a construction paper strip around each juice can so that excess paper is above can openings.

★ Use scissors to snip the excess paper at top of towers every ½ inch (1.25 cm) to make tabs. Bend every other tab down and glue to the inside of can to make parapets of tower (sketch b).

★ With felt pens, draw windows, bricks, ivy, etc. on tower walls.

★ Glue the construction paper rectangle around sides of milk carton.

★ Lay roof of milk carton on top of another piece of construction paper. Trace around roof triangle twice. Cut out both triangles and glue onto milk carton roofs (sketch c).

★ Use felt pens to draw a door, bricks, etc. on castle walls.

★ Cut out a flag from construction paper. Wrap and glue one edge of flag around coffee stirrer. Glue coffee stirrer to back of roof (sketch d).

★ Teacher staples juice can towers to sides of milk carton to make castle organizer.

Conversation:

You may use your castle to organize your pencils, pens, crayons and scissors. What activities do you like to do with pens, crayons or scissors? (Writing, drawing pictures, making projects, coloring, etc.) **How could you use those items to show kindness to someone? God wants the people in His Kingdom to use their abilities to show kindness to other people.**

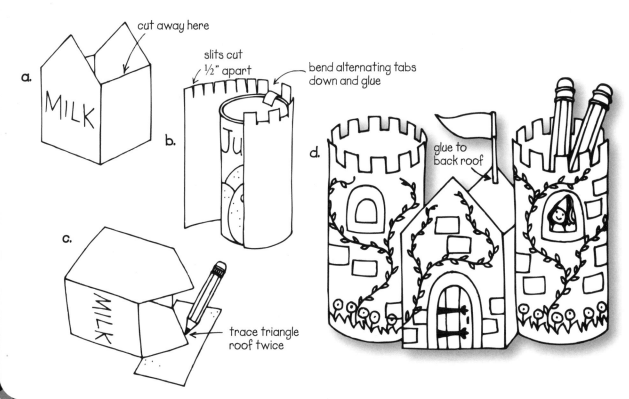

a. cut away here

b. slits cut ½" apart — bend alternating tabs down and glue

c. trace triangle roof twice

d. glue to back roof

God's Kingdom

Materials: Castle Patterns; brown, light gray and dark gray tempera paint; corrugated cardboard; cording; kitchen sponges; disposable paper or plastic plates; photocopier; colored copier paper; colored felt pens; pencil paintbrushes; shallow containers; glue; measuring stick; hole punch; craft knife; scissors; newspaper. For each child—two coffee stirrers.

DAY ONE Preparation: Cut cardboard into 9x12-inch (22.5x30-cm) rectangles—one for each child. Lay cardboard horizontally. Fold sides of cardboard 3½ inches (8.75 cm) toward the center. Trace Drawbridge Pattern onto center section of each cardboard piece, 1 inch (2.5 cm) above bottom edge. With craft knife, cut drawbridge on solid line only (sketch a). Punch two holes in drawbridge and four holes above door (sketch b).

Cut sponges into 1½-inch (3.75-cm) squares. Pour brown and light gray paints into shallow containers. Pour dark gray paint onto plates. Cover work area with newspaper.

Instruct each child in the following procedures:
★ Lay cardboard down with drawbridge bent up.
★ Paint cardboard castle wall with light gray paint.
★ Paint front and back of drawbridge brown.
★ Press a square sponge into dark gray paint. Print over castle walls to make bricks (sketch c). Allow to dry.

DAY TWO Preparation: Cut cording into 18-inch (45-cm) lengths—one for each child. Photocopy Flag and Window Patterns onto colored paper and cut out—two flags and windows for each child.

Instruct each child in the following procedures:
★ Glue the short edge of each triangle to a coffee stirrer to make flags. Lay flat to dry.
★ With felt pens, draw a picture of a person (king, queen, jester, yourself, a friend) in each window.
★ Glue a window on each side of drawbridge.
★ With teacher's help, thread cord through holes in castle drawbridge and door frame. Knot ends (sketch d).
★ To close drawbridge, pull cord on the inside of castle. To open, pull down on drawbridge.
★ Glue flag poles inside corners of castle (sketch e).
★ Fold sides of castle back to allow castle to stand.

Enrichment Idea: Older children may cut out flags and windows themselves.

Conversation:

(Marta), who did you draw in your castle windows? (Child responds.) **God is the King over all the world. His family is special to Him. He says we are like princes and princesses!**

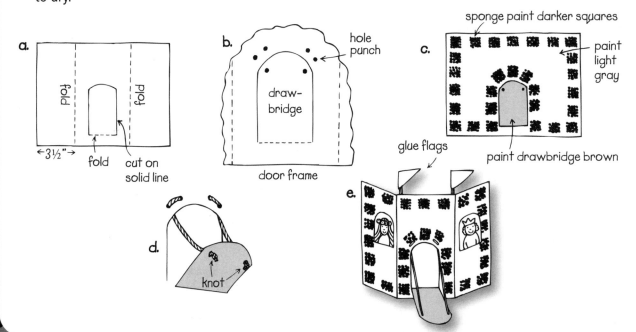

a. fold fold 3½" fold cut on solid line

b. hole punch draw-bridge door frame

c. sponge paint darker squares paint light gray paint drawbridge brown

d. knot

e. glue flags

CASTLE DRAWBRIDGE PATTERNS

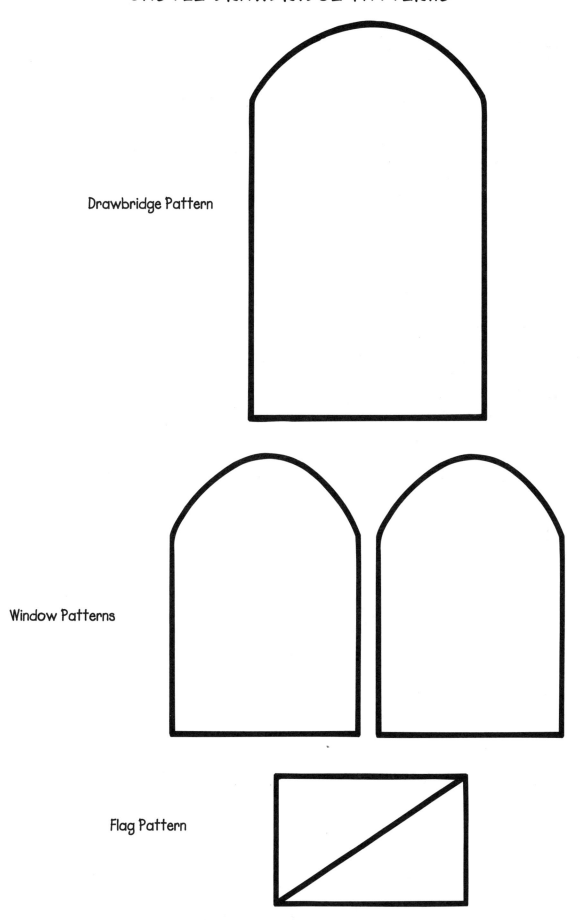

Drawbridge Pattern

Window Patterns

Flag Pattern

God's Kingdom

Materials: Castle Patterns, Fun Foam in a variety of colors (available at craft stores), poster board, corrugated cardboard, toothpicks, hot glue gun and glue sticks, paper clips, pencils, scissors, glue.

Preparation: Cut some of the Fun Foam into 6x7-inch (15x17.5-cm) rectangles—one for each child. Trace Castle Window Pattern about 1½ inches (3.75 cm) down from the top of each foam rectangle and cut out (sketch a). Cut additional Fun Foam into 5½-inch (13.75-cm) squares—one for each child. Cut cardboard into 6-inch (15-cm) squares. Trace Castle Roof Pattern several times onto poster board and cut out for children to use as patterns. Before beginning project, plug in hot glue gun out of reach of children.

Instruct each child in the following procedures:

★ Cut notches out of top of Fun Foam rectangle to make castle parapets (sketch b).

★ Cut Fun Foam scraps into small brick or stone shapes and glue to castle.

★ Trace Roof Pattern onto Fun Foam square and cut out roof. Glue bottom edge of roof to the back of tower near the top edge (sketch c).

★ Cut two small flags from Fun Foam. Glue a toothpick onto each flag.

★ Glue end of toothpick to top edge of cardboard square, one near each corner.

★ Squeeze a line of glue along the sides and bottom of cardboard square (sketch d). Press foam castle tower on top of cardboard.

★ Teacher attaches a paper clip "hanger" to the top center of frame backing with hot glue (sketch e). Allow frame to dry.

★ Slide your favorite photo through the top opening of frame.

Conversation:

Whose picture are you going to put in your frame? People who are part of God's family are royalty to God! Your royal frame can hold a photo of people in God's (the King's) royal family!

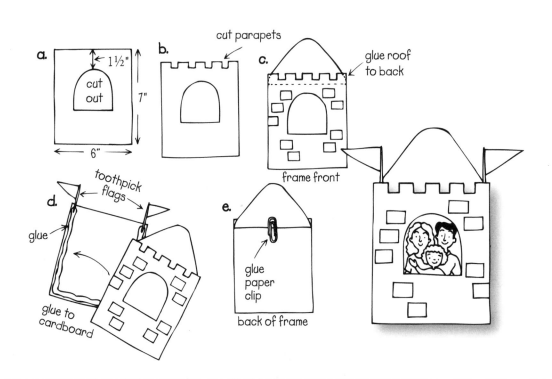

a. 1½" cut out 7" 6"

b. cut parapets

c. glue roof to back
frame front

d. toothpick flags
glue
glue to cardboard

e. glue paper clip
back of frame

CASTLE PiCTURE FRAME PATTERNS

Window Pattern

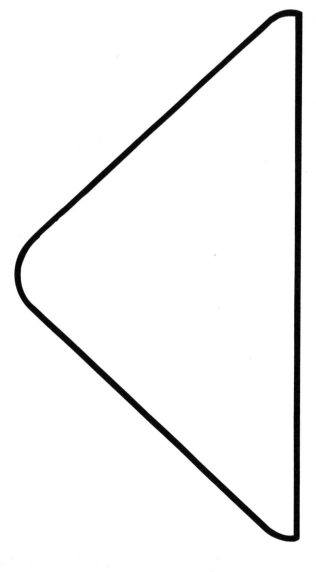

Roof Pattern

God's Kingdom

CROWN JEWELS BOX

(ONE- OR TWO-DAY CRAFT/ 50-60 MINUTES TOTAL TIME)

Materials: Crown Pattern, gold foil card stock (found in art stores, paper supply stores or in the photo album decorative supply section of craft stores), 1¼-inch (3.125-cm) wide satin ribbon, flat gold trim or rickrack, quilt batting, velvet fabric, acrylic jewels, gold pony beads, large paper clips, lightweight cardboard, craft glue, glue sticks, pencil, ruler, black felt pens, fabric scissors, scissors. For each child—two 6-oz. tuna or cat food cans.

DAY ONE Preparation: Cut ribbon into 11-inch (27.5-cm) lengths—one for each child. Cut gold foil card stock into 1¼x11-inch (3.125x27.5-cm) and 2½x11-inch (6.25x27.5-cm) strips—one strip of each size for each child. Trace several 4-inch (10-cm) circles onto lightweight cardboard and cut out to make circle patterns. Trace around a can on quilt batting and cut out circle—one batting circle for each child. Cut velvet into 5-inch (12.5-cm) squares—two for each child.

Instruct each child in the following procedures:

* Using a can as a pattern, trace a circle onto the back of a piece of velvet. Cut out velvet circle. Glue back of velvet to the inside bottom of one can. This is the inside of the box.

* Glue a length of wide ribbon around the insides of can (sketch a).

* Use glue stick to thoroughly cover the back of the narrower gold card-stock strip with glue. Wrap strip around outside of can. Overlap ends and press firmly to adhere. Use a large paper clip to hold ends together until dry, if needed. This completes the box part of the Crown Jewels Box.

* Use cardboard circle pattern and felt pen to trace a circle onto the back of the second velvet piece. Cut out velvet circle.

* Place the other can upside down. This can will be the box lid. Glue the batting circle to the bottom of can.

* Rub glue stick around the outside of can to cover only the top ½ inch (1.25 cm) of can (sketch b).

* Center the velvet circle on top of batting and smooth edges over sides of can. Press to adhere (sketch c).

DAY TWO Preparation: Trace Crown Pattern several times onto lightweight cardboard, extending crown lines to edge of page to make crown 11 inches (27.5 cm) in length. Cut out.

Instruct each child in the following procedures:

* Trace crown pattern onto the remaining gold foil card-stock strip. Cut out.

* Spread glue onto back of gold foil crown strip, leaving about ½ inch (1.25 cm) on the bottom unglued. Wrap strip around the velvet-topped can so that the straight edge extends about ½ inch (1.25 cm) below the edge of can and the scalloped edge of crown covers the edge of velvet (sketches d and e). Press firmly to adhere. If needed, paper clip ends to the can until glue dries.

* Use craft glue to glue a gold pony bead to the center of velvet top of crown.

* Glue gold trim around bottom edge of box lid and trim ends.

* Decorate your crown by gluing on jewels, beads, or shapes cut from gold foil card stock. Use craft glue sparingly.

* Allow the lid and bottom of box to dry separately. Then place the crown lid on top of your box (sketch f).

Conversation:

In castle times, the people of a kingdom served their king and queen. They promised to obey their king and the king promised them protection in return. God is our King. He loves and protects us. When we realize how much God cares for us, we want to serve Him, too. What are some ways in which we can serve God? Your Crown Jewels Box can remind you to serve your King. What will you keep in your box?

CROWN JEWELS BOX

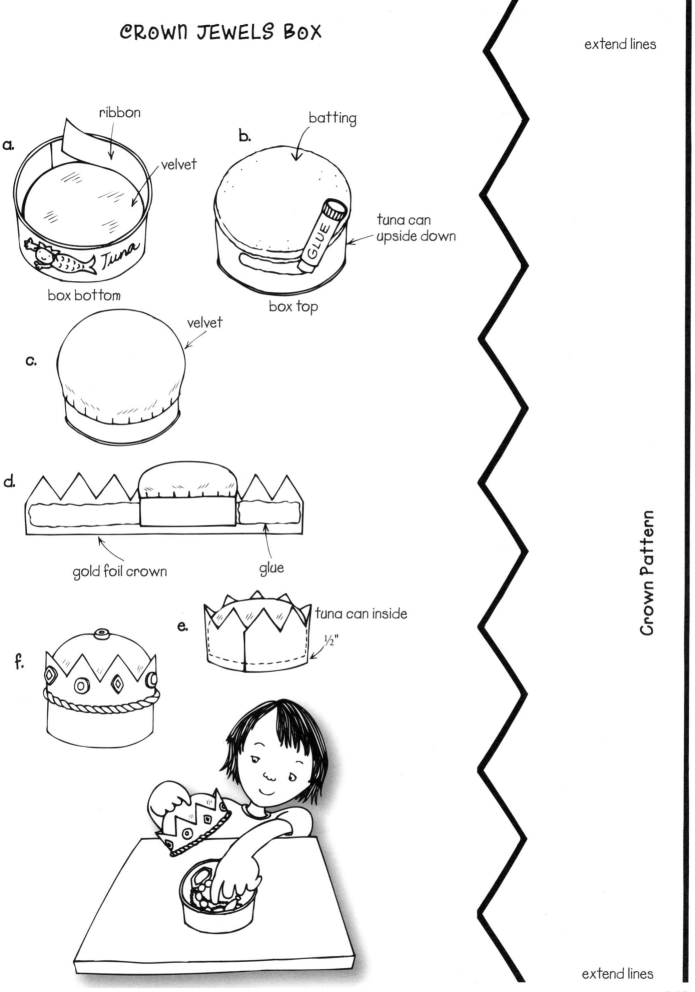

a. ribbon
velvet
box bottom

b. batting
GLUE
tuna can
upside down
box top

c. velvet

d. gold foil crown   glue

e. tuna can inside
½"

f.

Crown Pattern

extend lines

extend lines

God's Kingdom

Materials: Illumination Alphabet Patterns, colored pencils, fine-tip gold and silver paint pens, ribbon (velvet, satin, grosgrain) in a variety of colors and widths, clear gloss acrylic spray, photocopier, white card stock, craft glue, scissors, fabric scissors, pencils, rulers, newspaper.

Preparation: Photocopy several copies of Illumination Alphabet Patterns onto card stock. Cut alphabet apart into four or five sections. In an outside or well-ventilated area, spread newspaper to cover work area.

Instruct each child in the following procedures:

✶ Choose your initial from the Alphabet Patterns. Cut out your initial.

✶ Color the initial with colored pencils.

✶ Use a gold or silver paint pen to outline or accent your initial. (Press pen down on another sheet of paper to start ink flowing to pen tip.)

✶ Use the initial block as a pattern and trace a square onto a plain piece of card stock. Cut out the card stock square slightly smaller than tracing line. Set aside.

✶ Set colored initial on newspaper in a well-ventilated area and spray with a few coats of acrylic spray. Allow to dry.

✶ Cut a 10-inch (25-cm) piece of wide ribbon and a 9-inch (22.5-cm) piece of narrow ribbon.

✶ Cut a "v" in both ends of each ribbon (sketch a).

✶ Place a dot of glue about 3 inches (7.5 cm) down from top of wide ribbon. Glue narrow ribbon on top (sketch a).

✶ Glue colored initial square onto ribbons about 2 inches (5 cm) from the top. Glue smaller card stock square to back of initial square with ribbons in between (sketch b). Allow glue to dry.

Conversation:

In the Middle Ages, some men called monks devoted their lives to serving God. Many monks worked long hours making copies of the Bible. Since the printing press wasn't invented yet, they copied the Bible word-for-word by hand. They learned to write beautifully and often drew fancy letters and pictures around the margins of the page. These were called illuminations and they illustrated the Bible stories. Many people couldn't read, so the monks' pictures helped them learn about God and the stories in the Bible. What are some ways that people today learn about God and the Bible?

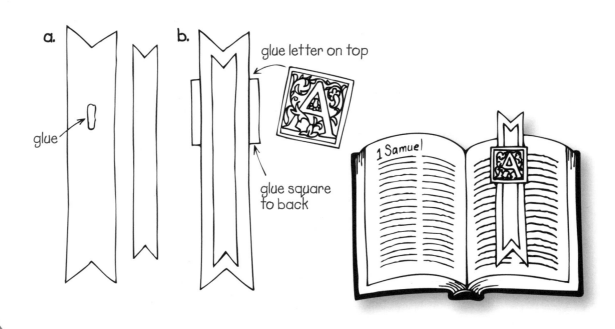

a.

glue

b.

glue letter on top

glue square to back

1 Samuel

Illumination Bookmark Alphabet Patterns

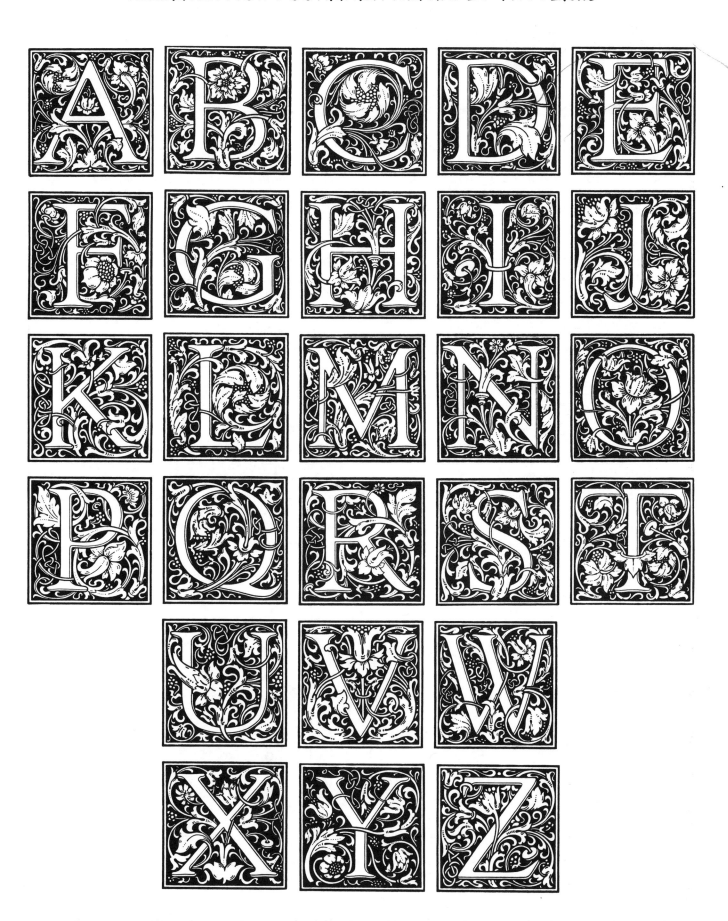

God's Kingdom

Materials: Keeper Patterns, felt in a variety of colors, construction paper in flesh-tone and hair colors, jewels, sequins, fake fur, lace, photocopier, bright yellow card stock, glue, measuring stick, red and black felt pens, pencils, scissors. For each child—one 18-oz. oatmeal canister with plastic lid, two large wiggle eyes.

Preparation: Photocopy Keeper Patterns onto yellow card stock—one copy for each child. Cut flesh-tone construction paper into 3x13-inch (7.5x32.5-cm) lengths—one for each child. Cut hair-colored construction paper into ½x3-inch (1.25x7.5-cm) strips—about eight for each child. Cut some of the felt into 4½x12-inch (11.25x30-cm) rectangles—one for each child. Cut remaining felt into 1½x4½-inch (3.75x11.25-cm) strips—one for each child

Instruct each child in the following procedures:

* Cut out crown and circle. Glue circle to top of canister lid.
* Glue jewels or sequins on crown to decorate. Set aside.
* Glue flesh-tone construction paper around top portion of canister (sketch a).
* Draw nose and mouth with felt pens to make face. Glue on wiggle eyes.

* Glue construction paper strips to top edge of canister on both sides of face for hair. To make curly hair, wrap the ends of strips around a pencil to make paper curl; then glue the top of strips to canister (sketch b). Glue a paper strip mustache above king's mouth.
* Glue the large felt rectangle piece around canister for clothing, placing the seam in front. Glue a contrasting-colored felt strip over seam (sketch c).
* Decorate clothes by gluing on jewels, lace, fur and/or sequins.
* With lid on, glue bottom edge of crown around the top ½ inch (1.25-cm) of canister. Allow to dry.
* Use your King or Queen Keeper as a decoration or use it to store crayons, felt pens or toys.

Conversation:

In the days of kings and queens, workers and servants served the king. The king and queen helped the workers as well. The royal castle provided a safe place for people to live. The king protected them. God is our King and He protects us, too. What are ways you can serve God, our King?

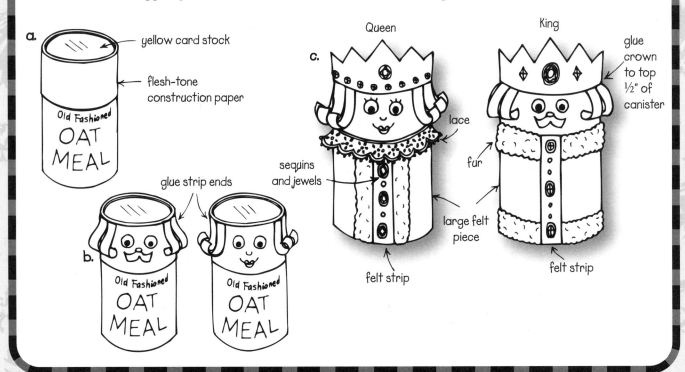

a. yellow card stock
flesh-tone construction paper
Old Fashioned OAT MEAL

glue strip ends
b. Old Fashioned OAT MEAL — Old Fashioned OAT MEAL

Queen
King
c.
glue crown to top ½" of canister
lace
sequins and jewels
fur
large felt piece
felt strip
felt strip

KING OR QUEEN KEEPER PATTERNS

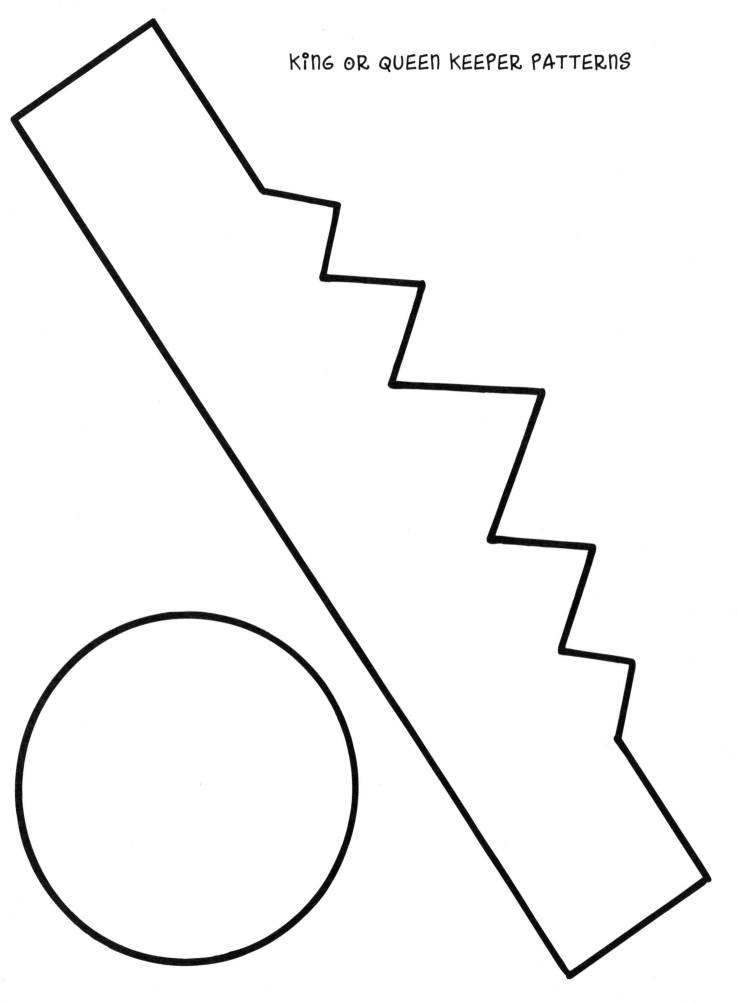

God's Praise

These crafts will help kids show their love for God by making the sounds of praise!

God's Praise

Materials: Thin metallic and iridescent gift-wrap ribbon, measuring stick, craft glue, scissors. For each child—one metallic or iridescent chenille wire, one plastic balloon stick (available at party supply stores).

Instruct each child in the following procedures:

★ Twist ends of chenille wire together and then bend to form a circle.

★ Shape wire circle into a heart (sketch a).

★ Squeeze glue onto twisted end of wire heart and insert into balloon stick.

★ Squeeze a dot of glue onto base of wire heart where it meets the stick (sketch b).

★ Tie and knot the middle of each ribbon over the glue. Tie one or more of the ribbons into a bow if you like. Allow glue to dry.

★ Wave your ribbon stick as you sing or listen to music. Run and make circles in the air with the beautiful ribbons. Be joyful!

Conversation:

What do you think it means when someone says, "Play the game with all your heart"? (Children respond.) **When we do something with all our heart, we are trying really hard to do our best. The Bible says, "I will praise you, O Lord, with all my heart"** (Psalm 9:1). **Praising God is telling God, and other people, how good God is and how much we love Him. How could you praise God with all your heart?** (Sing, dance, pray, thank God for His good gifts, tell others about Jesus' love, draw pictures, etc.) **You may use your Joyful Ribbon Stick to show praise to God when you sing to Him. Wave it with all your heart!**

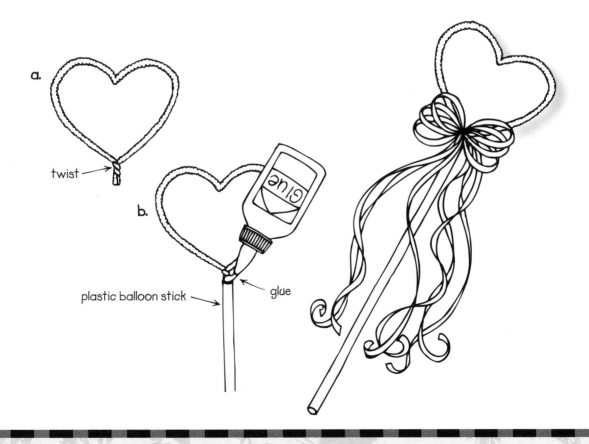

a.

twist

b.

plastic balloon stick

glue

God's Praise

Materials: Poster board, glitter glue pens, drinking straws, yarn, craft glue, hole punch, ruler, scissors, pencils.

Preparation: Cut poster board into 1x6-inch (2.5x15-cm) strips—two for each child. Cut straws into the following lengths: 7 inches (17.5-cm), 6 inches (15-cm), 5 inches (12.5-cm), 4 inches (10-cm), 3 inches (7.5-cm) and 2 inches (5-cm)—one length of each size for each child. Cut yarn into 2½-foot (75-cm) lenths—one for each child.

Instruct each child in the following procedures:

★ Punch holes on both ends of one poster board strip, near corners (sketch a).

★ Tie ends of yarn to punched holes.

★ Decorate one side of strip with glitter pens. Write your name, the word "Praise" and/or draw designs (sketch b). Set aside.

★ Squeeze a line of glue lengthwise down the center of the other poster board strip.

★ Evenly space the straws on the glued strip in graduating order. Make sure top ends of straws are even and extend about 1 inch (2.5 cm) above edge of strip (sketch c).

★ Squeeze another line of glue over the straws (sketch d).

★ Being careful not to smear glitter glue, place the decorated strip on top of straws. Align edges of top poster board piece with the bottom poster board piece. Allow to dry.

★ Play your Praise Pipes by placing your mouth about 1 inch (2.5 cm) above straws. Do not blow directly into straws. Blow air on the even ends of pipes to make different tones!

Conversation:

What instrument do you know how to play? What instrument would you like to learn to play? Let's blow across the tops of our pipes and make music to praise God!

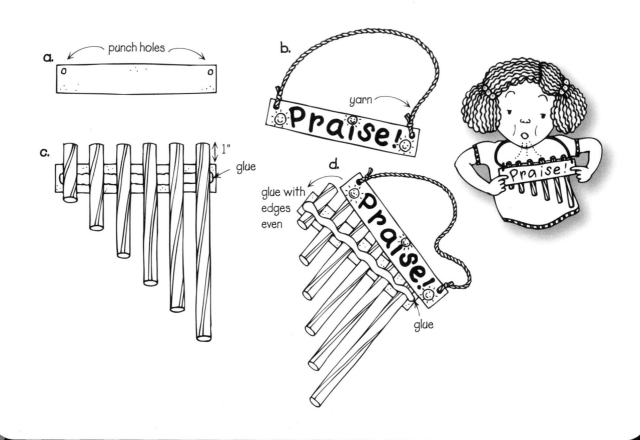

a. punch holes

b. yarn — Praise!

c. 1" glue

d. glue with edges even — glue — Praise!

God's Praise

Materials: Acrylic paint in a variety of colors, paintbrushes, shallow containers, dried beans, ¼-inch (.625-cm) dowels, saw, knife, glue, ruler, newspaper. For each child—one box from a bar of soap, one sheet of color-coded dot stickers (such as Avery®).

Preparation: Cut dowels into 6-inch (15-cm) lengths—one for each child. Use knife to poke a hole slightly smaller than ¼ inch (.625 cm) in bottom of each soap box (sketch a). Cover work area with newspaper. Pour paint into shallow containers.

Instruct each child in the following procedures:

* Insert end of dowel into hole at bottom of box. Glue around hole to secure dowel in place (sketch b).
* Place several dried beans inside box through top flap. Close flap and seal with glue.
* Paint box and allow to dry.
* Use dot stickers to decorate box.
* Hold dowel and shake maracas to create your own rhythm.

Simplification Idea: Cover soap box with white paper and use felt pens to decorate.

Enrichment Ideas: Bring in actual maracas to show to children. Play a recording in which maracas are used and have children play along.

Conversation:

Maracas are a popular rhythm instrument. What is your favorite musical instrument? What instruments do your family members play? Some instruments take a lot of practice to learn how to play. And some are easy to play—like our maracas. Let's shake our maracas and make up our own song to praise God!

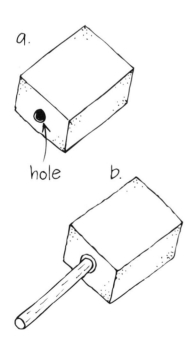

a.

hole

b.

God's Praise

Materials: Acrylic paint in a variety of bright colors, paintbrushes, shallow containers, dried beans, masking tape, permanent felt pens, water, glue, newspaper. For each child—one large round wooden clothespin (nonspring-type), one medium-size balloon, two paper towels.

Preparation: Mix two parts glue to one part water in containers. Cover work area with newspaper. Pour paint into shallow containers.

Instruct each child in the following procedures:

DAY ONE:

★ Place several beans inside balloon.

★ With teacher's help, blow the balloon up to a medium size. Tie a knot about 1 inch (2.5 cm) from lip of balloon.

★ Insert end of clothespin into lip of balloon and secure with tape (sketch a).

★ Wrap tape around clothespin to make a handle.

★ Tear pieces of paper towel or newspaper into thin strips. Dip strips into glue mixture and use to cover balloon (sketch b).

★ Let dry overnight.

DAY TWO:

★ Paint rattle and allow to dry.

★ Use permanent felt pens to draw a design on rattle.

★ Shake rattle to create a rhythm.

Enrichment Idea: Use dried gourds instead of balloons and clothespins. Make a small opening in gourd and add beans. Cover hole with masking tape and paint with acrylic paint.

Conversation:

In many parts of the world, people make rattles out of gourds. What is a gourd? (A vegetable that looks like a cross between a squash and a pumpkin.) **People also use gourds to make bottles, bowls, dishes and toys. Let's use our rattles to praise God here and at home!**

a.

tape

b.

God's Praise

Materials: ⅜-inch (.9-cm) wooden dowels, ¾-inch (1.9-cm) PVC pipe, 3x5-inch (7.5x12.5-cm) index cards, elastic cording, light-brown flat spray paint, colored electrical tape, drill with ⅜-inch (.9-cm) drill bit, PVC pipe cutter, saw, black permanent felt pens, craft glue, scissors, craft knife, measuring stick, newspaper. For each child—an empty laundry detergent box approximately 8½x9x4½ inches (21.25x22.5x11.25 cm).

Preparation: Use pipe cutter to cut PVC pipes into 3-foot (.9-m) lengths—one for each child. Drill holes through both sides of PVC pipe 1 inch (2.5 cm) from top, 10 inches (25 cm) from bottom and 1 inch (2.5 cm) from bottom (sketch a). Saw dowels into 3-inch (7.5-cm) lengths—three for each child. Cut elastic into 5-foot (1.5-m) lengths—one for each child. Use craft knife to cut a 3-inch (7.5-cm) circle from the center front of each laundry box. Cut ¾-inch (1.9-cm) holes in center of top and bottom of each laundry box (sketch b). Set laundry boxes on newspaper in a well-ventilated area and spray-paint brown. Cut index cards in half. Fold index-card halves into fourths and overlap ends to make triangular bridges for strings (sketch c).

Instruct each child in the following procedures:

★ Decorate laundry box with felt pens to make wood grain or other designs.

★ Attach a long strip of colored tape over length of PVC pipe to cover manufacturer's lettering.

★ Insert PVC pipe through holes in top and bottom of box.

★ Insert dowel pieces through holes in PVC pipe (sketch d).

★ Tie ends of elastic together and loop behind pipe above top dowel. Stretch elastic down front of instrument and hook around pipe below bottom dowel (sketch e).

★ Wrap colored tape around cardboard triangle to cover and secure. Glue just below large hole to make a bridge for strings to rest on (sketch e).

★ Rest box on the ground at a slight angle and strum the strings with your fingers.

Enrichment Idea: Instead of painting boxes, cover with wood-grained Con-Tact paper.

Conversation:

Who do you know that plays a real bass? What can you do to change the tone of the bass strings? Let's use our basses as we sing to God!

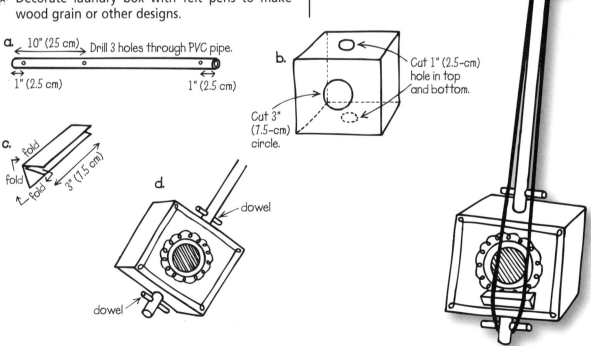

a. 10" (25 cm) Drill 3 holes through PVC pipe.
1" (2.5 cm)   1" (2.5 cm)

b. Cut 1" (2.5-cm) hole in top and bottom.
Cut 3" (7.5-cm) circle.

c. fold, fold, fold, 3" (7.5 cm)

d. dowel, dowel

God's World

Here are crafts that explore the wonders of God's creation in a variety of ways!

God's World

Materials: Animal crackers, acrylic paint in a variety of colors, paintbrushes, shallow containers, clear nail polish, narrow magnet strips, craft glue, scissors, ruler, newspaper.

Preparation: Cut magnet strips into ½-inch (1.25-cm) lengths—two for each child. Cover work area with newspaper. Pour paint into shallow containers.

Instruct each child in the following procedures:

★ Choose two unbroken crackers. (Note: Have extra crackers available, as they break easily.)

★ Paint fronts of crackers and allow to dry.

★ In well-ventilated area, brush clear nail polish on fronts and backs of crackers. Let dry.

★ Glue magnet piece onto back of each cracker (sketch a). Allow glue to dry.

Simplification Idea: Omit painting and just use clear nail polish. Or use clear acrylic spray instead of nail polish.

Enrichment Ideas: Make a jewelry pin by gluing a piece of poster board onto back of painted cracker. Glue pin back onto poster board (sketch b). Or glue painted cracker onto a barrette clip.

Conversation:

What animals can we find in our animal crackers today? Let's name them all! Have you ever been to the zoo? What is your favorite animal God made?

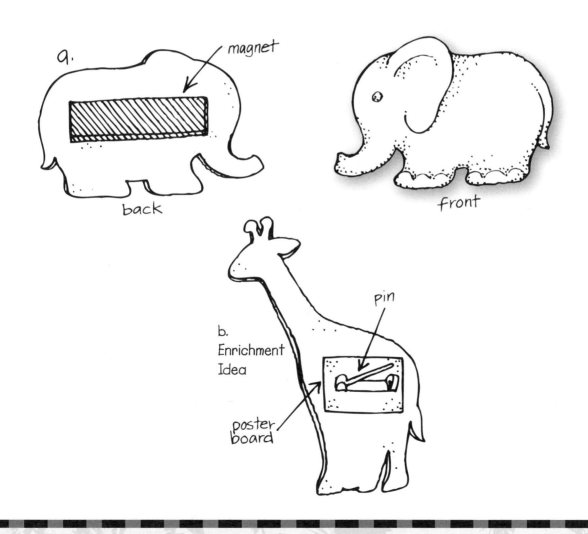

a.   magnet

back

front

b.
Enrichment
Idea

pin

poster
board

Materials: White burlap, ¼-inch (.625-cm) wood dowels, saw, measuring stick, craft glue, assorted bright-colored felt or small print fabrics, fusible webbing (such as Wonder-Under®), irons, old towels, pens, black crochet thread, straight pins, scissors, crewel needles, ⅛-inch (.31-cm) satin ribbon.

DAY ONE Preparation: Cut burlap into 15x20-inch (37.5x50-cm) pieces—one for each child. Following directions included with fusible webbing, iron webbing to the back of felt pieces. Leave the paper backing on the felt.

Instruct each child in the following procedures:

★ Remove enough burlap threads to allow for a 1-inch (2.5-cm) fringed border on all sides. Fold top 2 inches (5 cm) forward and pin (sketch a).

★ Thread needle with black thread and knot. Stitch across top, ½ inch (1.25 cm) from folded edge, using a simple running stitch (sketch a). Knot and cut thread to complete.

★ Draw shapes depicting the outdoors on the paper backing on the felt pieces. Be sure to include hot air balloon and basket shapes.

★ Cut out felt shapes.

DAY TWO Preparation: Cut dowels into 16-inch (40-cm) lengths—one for each child. Cut ribbon into 24-inch (.6-m) lengths—one for each child. Lay towels on a table for ironing. Plug in irons.

Instruct each child in the following procedures:

★ Peel away paper backing from felt shapes. Pin in place on burlap banner.

★ With teacher's help, iron felt pieces onto banner, following fusible webbing instructions.

★ Cut three lengths of satin ribbon to reach from the midpoint of the balloon to the top half of the basket.

★ Knot ribbon ends and glue in place (sketch b).

★ Slide dowel through casing at top of banner.

★ Tie 24-inch (.6-m) length of ribbon to ends of the dowel for hanger. Add a drop of glue to secure knots at each end of dowel.

Enrichment Idea: Using crochet thread and needle, sew ¼ inch (.625 cm) overcast stitches along felt edges. Sew stitches unevenly and at different angles to look haphazard (sketch c).

Conversation:

When riding in a hot air balloon, first-time travelers are surprised to notice that they do not feel any wind. Why do you think they don't feel the wind? (Students respond.) **Balloonists don't feel the wind because the balloon travels at the same speed as the wind. There is no air friction. Other vehicles of flight, such as hang gliders and airplanes often fly against the wind currents.**

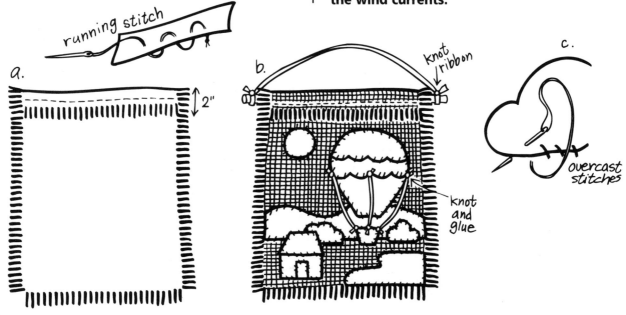

a. running stitch 2"

b. knot ribbon / knot and glue

c. overcast stitches

God's World

Materials: Colored tissue paper, liquid starch, sponge brushes, pencil, ruler, burlap, yarn, cotton balls, scissors, glue, transparent tape, shallow containers, newspaper. For each child—one clear overhead transparency, one large sheet of blue construction paper.

Preparation: Draw a large balloon pattern onto each sheet of construction paper and cut out interior of balloon, leaving the rest of the paper intact (sketch a). Cut yarn into 3-inch (7.5-cm) lengths—four for each child. Cut tissue paper into 1½-inch (3.75-cm) squares. Cut burlap into 3-inch (7.5-cm) squares—one for each child. Pour liquid starch into shallow containers. Cover work area with newspaper.

Instruct each child in the following procedures:

★ Use sponge brush to paint liquid starch over a section of the transparency.

★ Put squares of colored tissue onto starched area, then gently paint over tissue with more starch, smoothing down any wrinkles.

★ Continue covering the transparency with tissue and starch, overlapping squares. Leave an uncovered border of about 1 inch (2.5 cm). Let dry.

★ On the front of picture, glue yarn hanging from balloon for ropes.

★ Glue burlap square to ropes for basket.

★ Gently pull cotton balls apart to make clouds and glue to picture for clouds.

★ With teacher's help, carefully tape transparency to construction paper, with the tissue side of transparency showing through the balloon cutout (sketch b).

★ Tape your picture in a window to see your colorful hot air balloon glow.

Enrichment Ideas: Take a photo of each child, develop film and cut out child's image. Glue child's photo in balloon basket. Add hot air balloon stickers in the sky.

Conversation:

What colors are on your balloon, (Rachel)? What is your favorite color? What has God made that is (yellow)? God has made beautiful things for us to see in so many different colors!

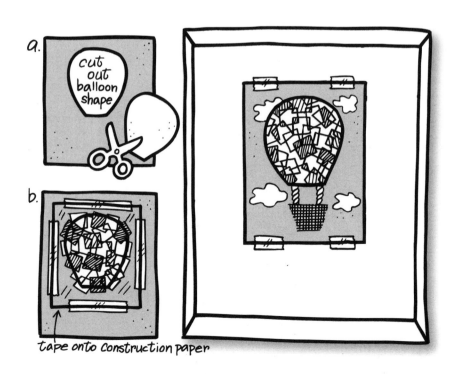

a. cut out balloon shape

b. tape onto construction paper

God's World

Materials: Bug Pattern, toilet paper tubes, poster board, construction paper, felt pens, pencils, craft glue, scissors, ruler. For each child—one small marble, two small wiggle eyes.

Preparation: Cut poster board into 1x2-inch (2.5x5-cm) rectangles—two for each child. Trace Bug Pattern onto remaining poster board and cut out several patterns. Cut tubes into ¾-inch (1.9-cm) hoops—one for each child. Cut construction paper into ¼x2-inch (.625x5-cm) strips—four for each child.

Instruct each child in the following procedures:

⭑ Bend hoops into oval shapes.

⭑ Trace Bug Pattern onto each poster board rectangle and cut out to make two side pieces.

⭑ Glue one side piece onto edge of hoop (sketch a). Let dry.

⭑ Place marble inside hoop.

⭑ Glue second side piece onto other edge of hoop. Let dry.

⭑ Glue wiggle eyes on front of bug (sketch b). Use felt pens to draw a face.

⭑ Glue three construction paper strips underneath bug for legs. Fold additional strip into a V and glue above eyes for antennae.

⭑ Place bug on a gentle slope and watch it boogie!

Enrichment Idea: Children can use felt pens to give their bugs stripes or spots.

Conversation:

What kinds of bugs have you found around your home? In some countries, people keep bugs for pets. In Japan many people have pet crickets and fireflies. Where have you seen a cricket? A firefly? God made many wonderful bugs!

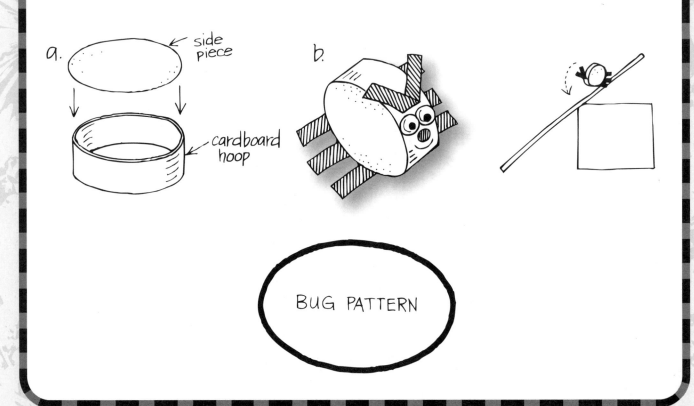

a. side piece

cardboard hoop

b.

BUG PATTERN

God's World

Materials: Sun Pattern, yellow construction paper, white butcher paper, lightweight cardboard, measuring stick, pencil, blue chalk, paper towels, crepe paper streamers in red, orange, yellow, green, blue, and purple, scissors, white glue or glue sticks, hole punch, aerosol hair spray, yarn. Optional—stapler and staples.

Preparation: Trace Sun Pattern onto yellow construction paper and cut out—one sun for each child. Draw a large pattern of a cloud, approximately 14x17 inches (35x42.5 cm), onto lightweight cardboard and cut out. Using cardboard pattern, trace and cut out two butcher paper clouds for each child. Cut crepe paper streamers into 18-inch (45-cm) lengths—one length of each color for each child. Cut yarn into 16-inch (40-cm) lengths—one for each child.

Instruct each child in the following procedures:

★ Color paper clouds with blue chalk.

★ In well-ventilated area, with teacher's help, spray the clouds with hair spray to set chalk.

★ Lay one paper cloud with colored side down.

★ Glue one end of each crepe paper streamer across the bottom of cloud in rainbow-color order (red, orange, yellow, green, blue, and purple—sketch a.

★ Lay the second cloud with the colored side down and apply glue around the edge of the cloud, leaving a 6-inch (15-cm) opening near the top (sketch b).

★ Place the glued cloud on top of the cloud with streamers, colored side up. Making sure edges are even, press glued edges together firmly (sketch b).

★ Scrunch up 3 or 4 paper towels and gently stuff into the opening near the top of cloud.

★ Glue opening closed.

★ Glue paper sun onto top corner of cloud.

★ Punch two holes near the top of the cloud, about 4 inches (10 cm) apart. Thread with yarn for hanging and tie a knot at ends (sketch c).

Simplification Idea: Teacher uses stapler to staple edges of clouds together for children.

Conversation:

You can hang your Breeze Catcher near an open window to see the streamers flutter in the wind. Many things float or fly in the wind. What can you name that floats or flies in the wind? (Hot air balloons, birds, airplanes, leaves, balloons, etc.)

BREEZE CATCHER SUN PATTERN

EARLY CHILDHOOD • YOUNGER ELEMENTARY • OLDER ELEMENTARY

Materials: Powdered tempera paint in a variety of colors, 8½x11-inch (21.5x27.5-cm) white paper, water, dish soap, newspaper. For each child—a drinking straw, one pie tin.

Preparation: Cut paper in half—several sheets for each child. Pour a small amount of dish soap and water into each pie tin. Cover work area with newspaper.

Instruct each child in the following procedures:

★ Choose paint color. Use end of straw to mix a small amount of powdered tempera paint into water mixture.

★ Place end of straw into paint mixture and blow into straw until bubbles appear on surface (sketch a). (Note: Have younger children practice blowing into straw—not sucking.)

★ Gently lay paper on top of bubbles only. Bubbles will stick to paper, then collapse, leaving a colorful print. Allow paper to dry.

★ Trade pie tins with other children to make additional colors on paper. Wash end of straw before using other colors.

Conversation:

What makes the bubbles? What is inside each bubble? How many colors have you tried? Let's thank God for the air we breathe and the colors we see!

a.

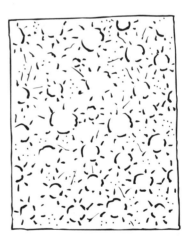

Materials: Bee Wing Pattern, yellow card stock, pencil, hole punch, transparent tape, wide-tip black permanent felt pens, black chenille wires, black yarn, scissors, measuring stick. For each child—one round yellow balloon.

Preparation: Use Bee Wing Pattern to trace onto card stock—two wings for each child. Cut out wings. Cut chenille wires in half—one half for each child. Cut yarn into 1-yard (90-cm) lengths—one for each child. Inflate balloons to approximately 5 inches (12.5 cm) in diameter.

Instruct each child in the following procedures:

★ With felt pen, draw a large circle on the top of balloon for the bee's face (sketch a).

★ Draw eyes, eyebrows, nose and mouth in the circle.

★ Draw wide stripes around the balloon to make the bee's body.

★ With hole punch, punch a hole in the round end of each wing.

★ Fold the straight edge of each wing down ½ inch (1.25 cm).

★ With teacher's help, tape the wings to the sides of the bee body. Tape underneath the wing and then on top of the wing to secure (sketch b).

★ With teacher's help, thread the yarn through hole in wing and tie in a knot. Repeat with the opposite end of yarn. Tie a knot in the middle of yarn to make loop for holding or hanging (sketch c).

★ Bend chenille wire into a U shape. Bend the tips of wire to make antennae. Tape the antennae to the top of the bee's face (sketch c).

Enrichment Ideas: Older children may cut out their own bee wings. Children may glue gold, clear or yellow sequins to the wings.

Conversation:

What sound does a bee make, (Kyle)? Where do you see bees? Bees keep busy outside in gardens where there are lots of flowers. They gather their food from the flowers and take it back to the beehive, where they make it into honey. God made the flowers so that the bees have food to eat. He made the bees so people and animals have honey to eat. What other good things has God made that you like to eat?

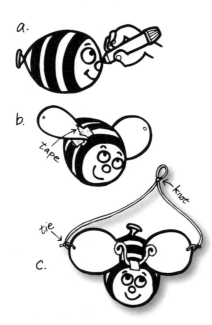

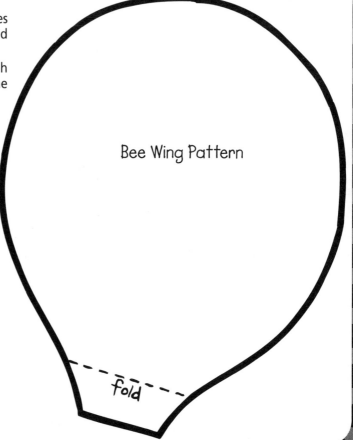

Bee Wing Pattern

fold

God's World

Materials: Dragonfly Wing Pattern, tagboard, pencil, window screen, clear or iridescent glitter, acrylic paint in a variety of colors (including iridescent or pearlized colors), thin paintbrushes, craft glue, ½-inch (1.25-cm) wide magnet tape, pens, scissors, ruler, shallow containers, newspaper. For each child—two wooden spring-type clothespins, two small wiggle eyes.

Preparation: Trace Wing Pattern on tagboard and cut out to make several patterns. Cut window screen into 5-inch (12.5-cm) squares—one for each child. Cut magnet tape into ¾-inch (1.9-cm) strips—one for each child. Remove springs from only half the clothespins. Cover work area with newspaper. Pour paint into shallow containers.

Instruct each child in the following procedures:

★ Paint two halves of separated wooden clothespin a solid color and allow to dry.

★ Use paintbrush handle tip (not brush end) to decorate painted clothespins by dotting with contrasting paint.

★ With a pen, trace pattern twice on screen (sketch a).

★ Cut out two pairs of wings.

★ Paint wings. While wet, sprinkle with glitter. Let dry.

★ Lay one clothespin piece with flat side facing up. Center both pairs of wings and glue 1 inch (2.5 cm) from rounded end of clothespin (sketch b).

★ Glue remaining clothespin piece on top of wings, flat side down. Use a second clothespin to hold together until dry.

★ Glue magnet to bottom of body.

★ Glue wiggle eyes on top of head (sketch c).

Conversation:

Where have you seen a dragonfly? (Students respond.) **Dragonflies live close to quiet water. During the first part of their lives, they are called nymphs and live underwater in ponds and swamps. When the nymphs mature, they crawl out and attach to a reed. Inside the nymph's body, the dragonfly forms. When the nymph skin splits, a beautiful dragonfly emerges. Soon the dragonfly gracefully flies over the water and darts among the reeds.**

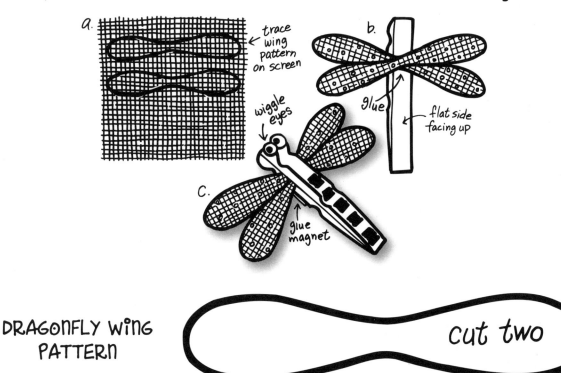

a. ← trace wing pattern on screen

b. glue ← flat side facing up

wiggle eyes

c. glue magnet

DRAGONFLY WING PATTERN

cut two

God's World

Materials: Sturdy wrapping paper in a variety of colors and patterns, discarded denim jeans, fabric paint, hole punches, transparent tape, glue, scissors, scribble pads or brown paper bags. For each child— one large cereal box, one 38-inch (95-cm) shoelace.

Preparation: Cut top, bottom and one side out of each cereal box (sketch a). Cut entire back pockets out of blue jeans (sketch b)—one pocket for each child.

Instruct each child in the following procedures:

★ Lay cereal box flat. Glue wrapping paper onto cereal box as you would a gift (sketch c).

★ Crease box into original shape. Punch two holes in front and back covers (sketch d).

★ Glue back of pocket onto front cover (sketch e).

★ Use fabric paints to decorate or write name on pocket. Allow to dry.

★ Tie shoelace through back and front holes (sketch e).

★ Cut scribble pads or brown paper bags into 12x19-inch (30x47.5-cm) sheets for scrapbook pages.

Conversation:

Who in your family do you look most like? Who do you act most like? Our scrapbooks are made from blue jeans but there is another kind of genes. Genes are tiny particles in your body that determine your looks and personality. Your genes are a mixture of your mother's and father's genes. It's fun to look at yourself in the mirror and see what parts of you look like your mother and what parts look like your father!

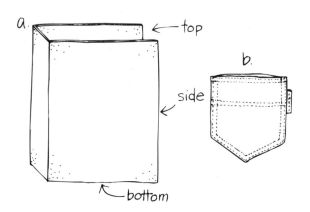

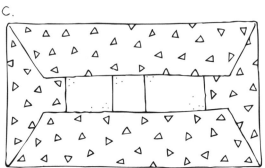

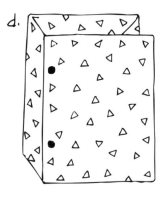

God's World

Materials: Yarn in a variety of colors, poster board, pencil, felt scraps, craft glue, scissors, measuring stick. For each child—two medium-size wiggle eyes, one small black pom-pom.

Preparations: Cut poster board into 3-inch (7.5-cm) squares—one for each child. Draw an X in the center of each square. Cut a slit on opposite sides of X as shown in sketch a. Cut yarn into 3-yard (.9-m) lengths—two for each child. Cut remaining yarn into 8-inch (20-cm) lengths—one for each child.

Instruct each child in the following procedures:

★ Choose two colors of long yarn lengths. Wrap both pieces of yarn around poster board square, perpendicular to slits (sketch b).

★ Slide smaller piece of yarn through slits. With teacher's help, pull ends together tightly and tie a knot (sketch c).

★ Slide scissors through top edge of wrapped yarn and cut (sketch d). Repeat for bottom edge of wrapped yarn.

★ Tear poster board away from yarn. Fluff yarn to make large pom-pom.

★ Glue wiggle eyes onto pom-pom "cat." Glue black pom-pom for nose and felt scraps for ears and tongue.

Enrichment Idea: Make a family of cats or other animals using smaller (or larger) squares of poster board.

Conversation:

Does your family have any pets? How can you help take good care of your pets? God made animals for us to take care of and enjoy. What are some other animals God made? Let's thank God for the animals He created!

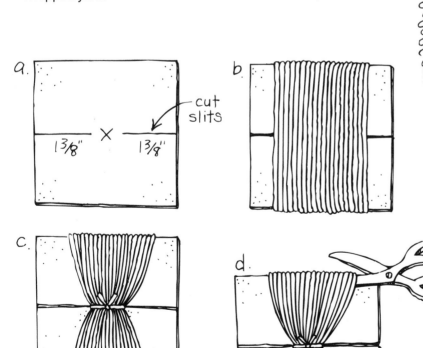

Materials: Fish Pattern, paper, lightweight clear vinyl (found at fabric stores), tape, permanent felt pens, measuring stick, scissors, squeeze-bottle fabric paints in a variety of colors including blue and green, paint shirts to protect clothing, straight pins, plastic lanyard lacing, several hole punches, iridescent cellophane or iridescent shredded gift filler, newspaper.

DAY ONE Preparation: Use felt pens to trace fish pattern onto two sheets of paper. Draw dots from pattern onto fish. Cut out fish outlines and tape together at top (sketch a). Cut vinyl into 12x36-inch (30x90-cm) pieces—one for each child. Lay the taped double fish pattern under the vinyl piece near the top. With a permanent felt pen, trace the fish pattern onto the vinyl. Mark dots on the underside of fish that indicate where streamers begin. Use measuring stick and felt pen to draw a straight line from each dot to the end of vinyl piece (sketch a). Repeat process to make vinyl fish for each child. Cover work area with newspaper.

Instruct each child in the following procedures:

* Cut out vinyl piece, following marked lines. Do not cut top of fish apart.
* Lay vinyl on a flat surface.
* With felt pen, draw eyes and fins on top and bottom of fish, following example on Fish Pattern.
* Apply fabric paints to eyes and fins over the felt pen lines (sketch b).
* Decorate fish with fabric paint, using small repeated patterns such as wavy lines, small circles, dots, etc.
* On streamer section, paint blue and green squiggles to look like seaweed. Paint dots or circles to look like bubbles.

* Allow to dry flat overnight.

DAY TWO Preparation: Cut lanyard lacing into 40-inch (1-m) lengths—one for each student.

Instruct each child in the following procedures:

* Fold double fish in half, matching edges to form one fish outline. Pin if necessary. Punch holes all around fish, spacing holes 1 inch (2.5 cm) apart and ¼ inch (.625 cm) from the edge.
* Beginning at the top of the fish, thread lacing through one hole. Leave 6 inches (15 cm) of lanyard extending from top of fish to use as a hanger.
* Continue lacing fish, but stop several inches before completing. Remove pins.
* Insert cellophane or filler to stuff fish.
* Finish lacing the fish closed. Lace ends of lanyard across each other and through two holes at the center top of fish (sketch c). Tie to make a hanging loop. Trim ends if necessary.
* Cut long vinyl piece into streamers approximately 1½ inches (3.75 cm) wide (sketch d).

Conversation:

The Bible says that Jonah was swallowed by a great fish, which might have been a kind of whale. What do you think it would be like in the belly of a whale? (Students respond.) **In 1891, a sailor working on a whaling ship fell into the sea. Three days later the sailors on the ship were cutting up a whale they caught. To their surprise they found their crewmate inside the whale's belly—alive!**

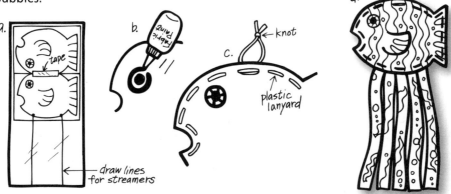

a. tape / draw lines for streamers

b. Fabric Paint

c. knot / plastic lanyard

d.

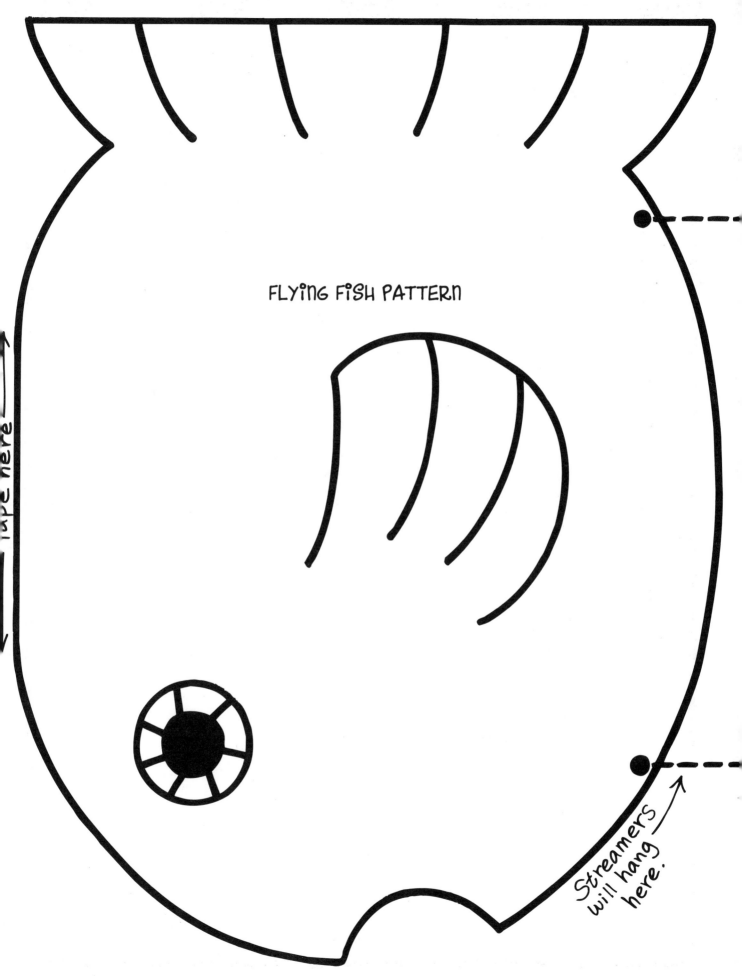

FLYING FISH PATTERN

Tape here

Streamers will hang here.

God's World

Materials: Balloon and Cloud Mobile Patterns, Sun Pattern, white poster board, old sponges, acrylic paint in a variety of colors (including light blue, yellow and orange), pencil, ruler, scissors, hole punch, string, newspaper, shallow containers. For each child—one wire or plastic clothes hanger.

Preparation: Trace Balloon and Sun Patterns onto poster board and cut out—one for each child. Trace Cloud Pattern onto poster board and cut out—two for each child. Cut a set of four lengths of string in various sizes from 3 inches to 12 inches (7.5 cm to 30 cm)—one set for each child. Cover work area with newspaper. Pour paint into shallow containers. Dampen sponges and cut into 2-inch (5-cm) squares.

Instruct each child in the following procedures:

★ Use light blue paint to sponge paint one side of clouds. Let dry.

★ Use yellow and orange paint to sponge paint one side of sun. Let dry.

★ Use a variety of colors to sponge paint one side of hot air balloon. Let dry.

★ When dry to touch, turn poster board pieces over and sponge paint the opposite sides of clouds, sun and hot air balloon in the same manner. Let dry.

★ With hole punch, punch a hole at the top center of each poster board piece.

★ Slip string through holes in poster board pieces and tie to hanger to secure, as shown in sketch.

★ Hang your hot air balloon mobile in your room as a breezy decoration!

Conversation:

If you were on a hot air balloon ride, would you like to fly above the clouds, in the clouds or below the clouds? What do you think you would see when you are in a cloud? When you are above the clouds? Some experienced balloon pilots say that flying inside the clouds and flying above the clouds is fun to do at first. But they enjoy flying *below* the clouds the most because then they can see how the land below them looks.

Cloud Mobile Pattern

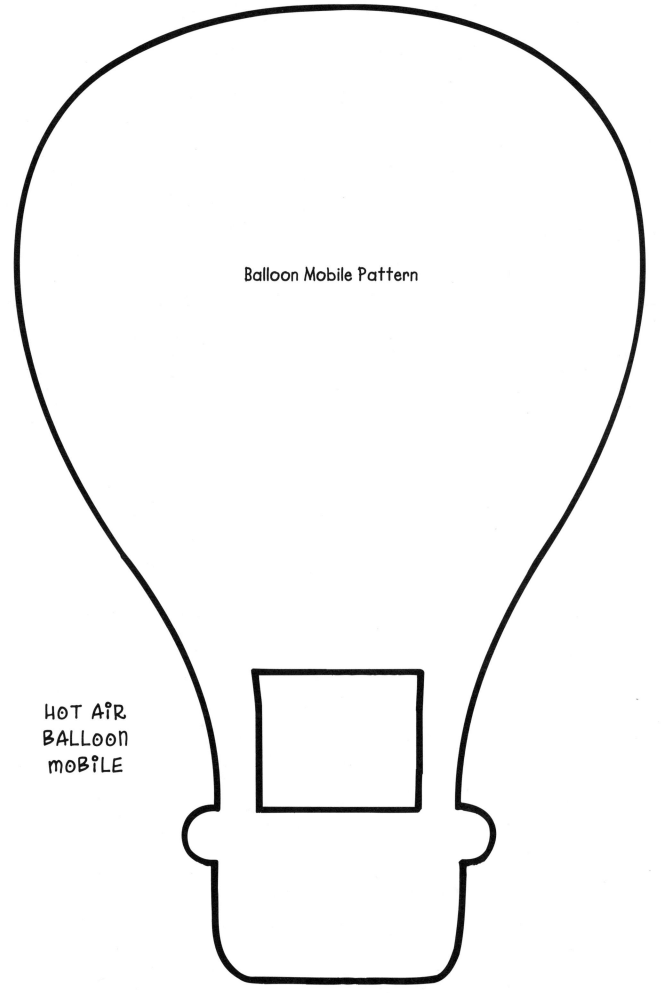

Balloon Mobile Pattern

HOT AIR
BALLOON
MOBILE

Sun Pattern

Materials: Panty hose in a variety of shades; fabric, felt and paper scraps; brown, black, orange and yellow yarn; buttons; ribbon; sequins; pliers; several mirrors; glue; scissors. For each child—one wire coat hanger.

Preparation: Cut legs off of panty hose—one stocking for each child. Use pliers to bend each coat hanger into an oval shape (sketch a).

Instruct each child in the following procedures:

★ Look in mirror and notice the shape of your face. With teacher's help, bend coat hanger to resemble shape of your face.

★ Choose a stocking that resembles your skin color. Pull foot of stocking over wire shape. Tie end of stocking in a knot near hook and cut off excess (sketch b).

★ Look in mirror and notice the color and shape of your eyes, mouth, nose and hair. Cut and glue materials onto stocking to make a mask that looks like you (sketch c).

Enrichment Idea: Children write several positive sentences describing themselves. They hold masks in front of their faces as they say their descriptions aloud.

Conversation:

There is no one exactly like you! God made you to be a unique combination of size, shape, color, personality, strengths and weaknesses! On a chalkboard, draw different shapes as you say, **Some people's faces are oval-shaped. Others are round or more like a triangle. What shape is your face? What color are your eyes? Your hair? What shape is your nose? God loves you and created you just the way you are!**

a.

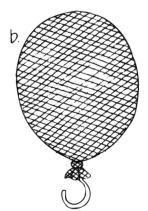

b.

c.

Materials: Dry beans; narrow red ribbon; polyester fiberfill stuffing; several long, narrow items (wooden rulers, dowels, knitting needles, etc.); needles; thread; craft glue; fabric scissors; ruler. For each child—man's tie, two 8-mm wiggle eyes, empty plastic film canister with lid.

Preparation: Check back side of ties to be sure they are sewn securely enough to be stuffed (sketch a). If necessary, stitch to secure. Cut ribbon into 3-inch (7.5-cm) lengths—one for each child. Cut a small V notch from one end of each ribbon piece to make a snake tongue.

Instruct each child in the following procedures:

★ Use narrow item to stuff fiberfill into tie. Stuff from both ends toward middle. At narrow end of tie, leave about 5 inches (12.5 cm) unstuffed. On wide end, stuff to the end.

★ Place several beans in film canister and snap on lid to make a rattle. Place rattle in narrow end of tie.

★ Tie a knot at narrow end of tie to secure film canister inside snake (sketch b).

★ With teacher's help, use needle and thread to stitch wide end of snake closed on underside (sketch c).

★ Glue ribbon tongue to underside of head.

★ Glue wiggle eyes to top side of head. Allow to dry (sketch d).

Conversation:

Have you ever seen a rattlesnake in the wild? What did you do? Snakes usually leave you alone if you leave them alone. What can you do when you're afraid? The Bible tells us we can talk to God and He will hear our call for help (see Psalm 145:18).

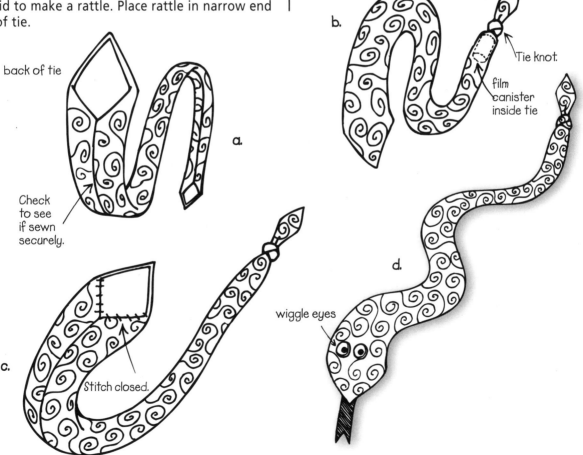

back of tie

Check to see if sewn securely.

b.

Tie knot.

film canister inside tie

c.

Stitch closed.

d.

wiggle eyes

Materials: Newspaper, white glue, water, scissors, large paintbrushes, shallow containers, white acrylic spray paint, craft-weight tissue paper in various bright colors, pearl cotton floss, hole punch, ruler. For each child—one medium-sized balloon, one solid-colored paper cup, one yogurt container or small bowl. *Optional*—clear acrylic spray.

DAY ONE Preparation: Tear newspaper vertically into 1-inch (2.5-cm) strips. Cut into 4-inch (10-cm) lengths. Inflate balloons to approximately 9 inches (22.5 cm) in length. In shallow containers, mix equal amounts of glue and water. Mix more as needed. Cover work area with newspaper.

Instruct each child in the following procedures:

* Set balloon in yogurt container or bowl to hold it upright while working.
* Immerse a single strip of newspaper in the glue and remove excess by pulling the strip between fingers. Apply strip to balloon. Smooth out wrinkles or bubbles.
* Cover entire balloon with two or three layers of newspaper strips.
* Set balloon on yogurt container to dry for 1 or 2 days (sketch a).

DAY TWO Preparation: Paint balloons with white acrylic spray paint. Cut colored tissue paper into 1-inch (2.5-cm) squares. Trim paper cups to 2 inches (5 cm) tall. Cut pearl cotton floss into 16-inch (40-cm) lengths—seven strands for each child. Cover work area with newspaper.

Instruct each child in the following procedures:

* Cut a few large simple shapes (such as hearts, stars, moon, etc.) from tissue paper. Brush glue on balloon and glue on shapes. Then brush with more glue.
* Apply the tissue squares to the rest of the balloon surface in the same manner (sketch b). Allow to dry.
* With hole punch, make six evenly-spaced holes around rim of paper cup.
* Glue tissue paper shapes and squares onto cup to decorate balloon gondola (sketch c).
* Tie a strand of cotton floss through each of the holes in cup.
* Loop remaining length of floss with strands and tie the loose ends of all strands in a single overhand knot (sketch d).
* Slip balloon between strands of floss and glue knot securely to the top of the balloon, keeping the loop free from the balloon for hanging.
* Arrange the six gondola strands evenly around the balloon.
* Put a drop of glue where each floss strand rests on the balloon's midpoint (sketch e).

Enrichment Idea: Spray papier mâché balloon with clear acrylic spray and allow to dry before assembling hot air balloon.

Conversation:

Why do balloonist use hot air in their balloons? (It is lighter than cold air.) **What is another gas that is lighter than air?** (Helium.) **Some kinds of balloons use helium to stay up in the air.**

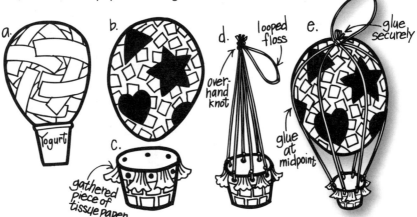

a. yogurt
b.
c. gathered piece of tissue paper
d. looped floss / overhand knot
e. glue securely / glue at midpoint

Materials: Colored poster board, hole punch, colored felt pens, small stickers (stars, hearts, circles or other shapes), glue, scissors, ruler, ribbon or rickrack scraps, ⅛-inch (.3125-cm) ribbon. For each child—two large sturdy white paper plates.

Preparation: For each child, glue the rims of two paper plates together with the front of plates facing to the inside (sketch a). With hole punch, punch a hole in the rim of glued paper plates at the top center. Punch two holes on the bottom rim, 3 inches (7.5 cm) apart (sketch b). Cut poster board into 3x3-inch (7.5x7.5-cm) squares—one square for each child. Punch two holes on one edge of each poster board square. Cut ⅛-inch (.3125-cm) ribbon into 12-inch (30-cm) and 6-inch (15-cm) lengths—one length of each size for each child.

Instruct each child in the following procedures:

★ Color both sides of paper plate balloon with felt pens.

★ Glue on ribbon scraps for balloon stripes.

★ Decorate balloon with stickers.

★ Use ribbon, stickers or felt pens to decorate poster board square as the balloon basket.

★ Thread longer length of ⅛-inch (.3125-cm) ribbon through holes at the bottom of balloon plate, then thread through holes in poster board square. With teachers help, tie ribbon ends together (sketch c).

★ Thread shorter length of ⅛-inch (.3125-cm) ribbon through hole at the top of plate. Tie the ends together to form a hanging loop.

Conversation:

A hot air balloon floats in the sky because it has hot air inside it. Hot air rises so it lifts up the balloon. The balloon pilot heats up the air inside the balloon with blasts of flames from a burner. What can you name that is hot? What things are really cold? God made us so that we can feel hot and cold things.

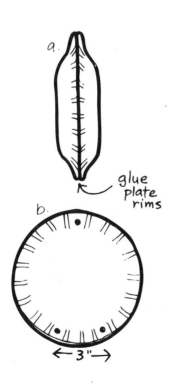

a.

glue plate rims

b.

← 3" →

c.

tie

tie

God's World

WEATHER HAT
(ONE- OR TWO-DAY CRAFT/35-40 MINUTES TOTAL TIME)

Materials: Weather Patterns; poster board in white, blue, and yellow; scissors; colored felt pens; silver glitter; glue; measuring stick; pencil; craft knife; tempera paint in light blue, green, purple and yellow; shallow containers; wide and thin paintbrushes; newspaper; blue curling ribbon; ¼-inch silver mylar ribbon (found with gift wrapping supplies); stapler and staples; cotton balls; snowflake confetti or sequins. For each child—one sturdy white 10-inch (25-cm) paper plate.

DAY ONE Preparation: Use ruler and pencil to divide the bottom of paper plates into eight even wedges (sketch a). With craft knife, cut wedges apart on pencil lines leaving a 1- to 2-inch (2.5- to 5-cm) uncut rim (sketch a). Pour paint into shallow containers. Cover work area with newspaper.

Instruct each child in the following procedures:

★ Lay paper plate upside down. Paint the cut portion of the plate blue for sky.

★ Use wide paintbrush to paint the rim of the plate green for grassy hills (sketch b).

★ With thin paintbrush, dot purple and yellow flowers on grass. Let paint dry.

DAY TWO Preparation: Trace Weather Patterns onto poster board. Cut out one yellow sun, one white lightning bolt, one white rainbow and four blue raindrops for each child. Cut curling ribbon and mylar ribbon into 18-inch (45-cm) lengths—four lengths of blue ribbon and five lengths of mylar ribbon for each child.

Instruct each child in the following procedures:

★ Glue a blue raindrop to one end of each blue ribbon.

★ Glue silver glitter onto white lightning bolt.

★ Color rainbow with felt pens.

★ Lay paper plate with paint side up. Bend blue sky wedges up (sketch c).

★ On bent up wedges, glue the colored rainbow, lightning bolt and yellow sun.

★ Glue cotton balls on sky for clouds.

★ Glue snowflake confetti or sequins on the sky.

★ With teacher's help, staple the free ends of blue ribbon and mylar ribbon onto one half of the hat rim. Alternate blue and mylar ribbons and space evenly (sketch d).

★ Try on your weather hat!

Enrichment Idea: Make a weather mobile by attaching four 2-foot (.6-cm) strings evenly around the plate and tying together to make a hanger.

Conversation:

Our world needs all kinds of weather. Why do we need rain? (It gives people, animals and plants water to drink. Rain fills our lakes and oceans.) **Why do we need sun?** (It keeps us warm, gives us light, makes plants grow.) **Who made the rain and sun?** (God.) **What other things do you see on your weather hat that God has made?**

a. cut here

b. green, blue

purple and yellow flowers

c. bend up wedges

d.

WEATHER HAT PATTERNS

Raindrop

Lightning Bolt

Cloud

Sun

House

Rainbow

Materials: Weather Wheel Patterns, old sponges, tempera paint in a variety of colors including blue and green, felt pens, shallow containers, spring-type clothespins, old blunt pencils with eraser tops, felt in a variety of colors including white, grey, light blue and yellow, yarn, craft knife, ruler, hole punch, glue, scissors, newspaper. For each child—two large, sturdy white paper plates, 1-inch (2.5-cm) paper fastener, one pony bead.

DAY ONE Preparation: With the pointed tip of craft knife, poke a small hole in the center of each paper plate. In half of the plates, use craft knife to cut out a pie-shaped window 1 inch (2.5 cm) above hole (sketch a). With pencil, draw a line for horizon (sketch a). Dampen and cut sponges into 1-inch (2.5-cm) pieces. Clip a clothespin to each sponge to use as a handle. Pour paint into shallow containers. Cover work area with newspaper.

Instruct each child in the following procedures:

★ Sponge paint the entire front of uncut plate with blue paint. Set aside and let dry.

★ On the front of the other plate, sponge paint the window portion blue for sky (sketch b).

★ Sponge paint the bottom portion of plate green for grass.

★ Sponge paint the rim of plate any color.

★ Dip eraser end of pencil into paint and press on grass several times to make flowers. Repeat with desired colors.

DAY TWO Preparation: Trace Weather Patterns onto felt and cut out blue raindrops, yellow suns, grey lightning bolts, white clouds and any color house—one of each shape for each child.

Instruct each child in the following procedures:

★ Glue felt weather cut-outs onto solid blue plate. Space evenly around plate (sketch c).

★ Glue felt house onto window plate and decorate with felt pens or felt scraps.

★ Punch hole in top of window plate. With teacher's help, cut and tie yarn through hole.

★ With teacher's help, assemble plates. Poke paper fastener through the center front of window plate. Thread a pony bead on the shank of fastener, then poke fastener into center front of second plate and bend fastener to secure in back (sketch d). Bead will keep plates spaced apart.

★ Turn bottom plate to view the four weather shapes.

Simplification: Use paper instead of felt for weather cutouts.

Conversation:

(Eric), what do you like to do when it is (sunny, rainy, cloudy, etc.)? You can turn your Weather Wheel to show the (sun). God gives us rain, snow and sun. God knows what our world needs to make plants, animals and people grow.

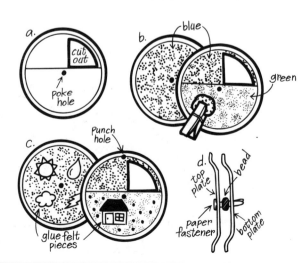

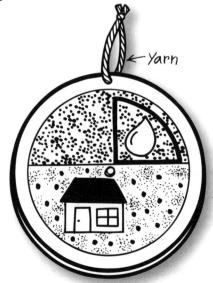

WEATHER WHEEL PATTERNS

Raindrop

Lightning Bolt

Cloud

Sun

House

Rainbow

God's World

Materials: Tempera paint in a variety of colors, paintbrushes, shallow containers, clear acrylic spray, hammer, nail, heavy string, scissors, measuring stick, newspaper. For each child—one medium-size jingle bell, two tin cans (one with a larger circumference than the other, height may vary).

Preparation: Use hammer and nail to make a hole in the center of each tin can bottom. Cut string into 2-foot (.6-m) lengths—one for each child. Cover work area with newspaper. Pour paint into shallow containers.

Instruct each child in the following procedures:

★ Paint a colorful design on bottoms and sides of cans (sketch a). Let dry.

★ In well-ventilated area, spray cans with clear spray and allow to dry.

★ Thread string through hole in can with smaller circumference (sketch b).

★ Tie jingle bell to end of string. Tie a large knot several inches from bell to secure bell inside of can (sketch b).

★ Tie another large knot in string outside top of can (sketch c).

★ Thread loose end of string through other can.

★ Make a large loop at end of string to hang Wind Clanger (sketch d).

★ Hang Wind Clanger in a tree. Listen to the sounds it makes when the wind blows.

Simplification Ideas: Omit jingle bell and use clanging of cans for noisemaker. Or, omit smaller can and use only the jingle bell for a noisemaker.

Conversation:

What noises do you hear on your street? What noises do you hear when the wind blows? God made the wind, but we cannot see it. But our wind clangers will tell us when it is windy by making sounds!

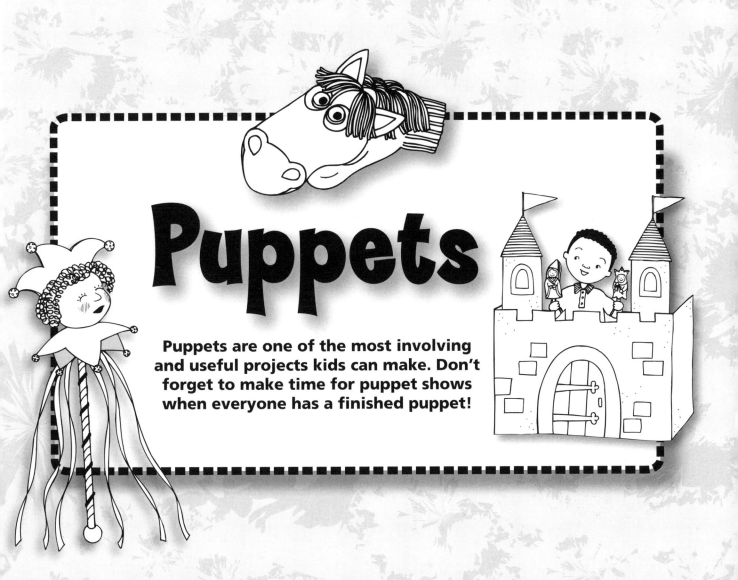

Puppets

Puppets are one of the most involving and useful projects kids can make. Don't forget to make time for puppet shows when everyone has a finished puppet!

Puppets

Materials: Green paint, cardboard egg cartons, stapler and staples, paintbrushes, shallow containers, newspaper, yellow construction paper, ruler, black felt pens, white poster board or card stock, scissors, glue. For each child—two paper fasteners, one empty food box (from crackers, cookies, croutons, cereal, etc.).

DAY ONE Preparation: Cut off top flaps of each box (sketch a) and save cardboard flaps. Cut boxes in half lengthwise as shown (sketch b). Cut egg carton sections apart into two-section pieces. Pour paint into containers. Cover work area with newspaper.

Instruct each child in the following procedures:

* With teacher's help, staple a cardboard flap inside each box half, for hand grips (sketch c).
* Glue egg carton section to top of one box half (sketch d).
* Paint outside of box halves green. Let dry.

DAY TWO Preparation: Cut white poster board into 1½-inch (3.75-cm) strips.

Instruct each child in the following procedures:

* Cut two white poster board strips to fit length of the box and two strips to fit the width.
* Cut a zig-zag pattern along one edge of all poster board strips to make teeth.
* Glue teeth to sides and front of box half that has egg carton section, teeth pointing down.
* Glue teeth to the front of the other box half, teeth pointing up (sketch e).
* Cut two semi-circles from white poster board for eyes. Draw two black circles inside each semi-circle. Glue eyes to front of green egg carton piece for eyes.
* Cut small rectangles from yellow construction paper and glue to top of alligator for scales.
* With teacher's help, join the two box halves together at back corners using paper fasteners (sketch e).
* Place thumb in bottom grip and other fingers in top grip to move alligator's mouth.

Conversation:

Alligators live in swamps, lakes and bayous. Is an alligator a mammal, fish or reptile? (Reptile.) **Alligators are unusual reptiles because they care for their babies like a bird or mammal might care for its young. When baby alligators hatch from their eggs, the mother alligator cares for them and keeps them safe by carrying them in her huge mouth. How would *you* feel in the mouth of an alligator?**

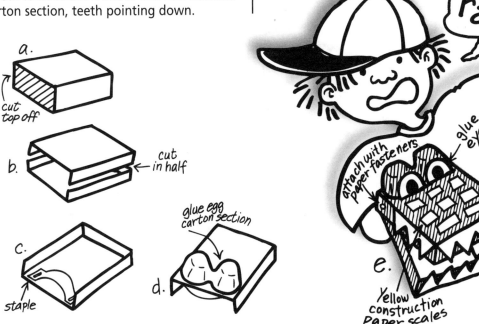

a. cut top off

b. cut in half

c. staple

d. glue egg carton section

e. rawr — attach with paper fasteners — glue eyes — teeth — Yellow construction paper scales

Puppets

Materials: A lunch-size paper bag, Bird Patterns, yellow and white card stock, photocopier, colored feathers, felt pens or crayons, glue, scissors.

Procedure: Photocopy Head, Claws, Tail and Wing Patterns onto white card stock. Photocopy Beak Pattern onto yellow card stock. Cut out. Use felt pens or crayons to color cutouts. Glue feathers onto head, wings and tail as desired. Glue head to flap of paper bag. Bend Beak pattern into a cone shape and glue to secure (sketch a). Fold tabs on beak to the inside of cone and glue to the head. Glue claws to the bottom edge of bag. Glue wings to the inside fold of the bag sides (see sketch). Fold tab on tail and glue to back of paper bag. *Optional*—Glue feathers to cover paper bag.

Conversation:

What kinds of birds live in your yard? What's the largest bird you've ever seen? The smallest bird? Let's thank God for all the birds we've seen!

BIRD BAG PUPPET PATTERNS

Bird Head Pattern

Glue beak here.

Bottom Beak Pattern

Top Beak Pattern

Claw Patterns

BIRD BAG PUPPET PATTERNS

Wing Patterns

fold

Tail Pattern

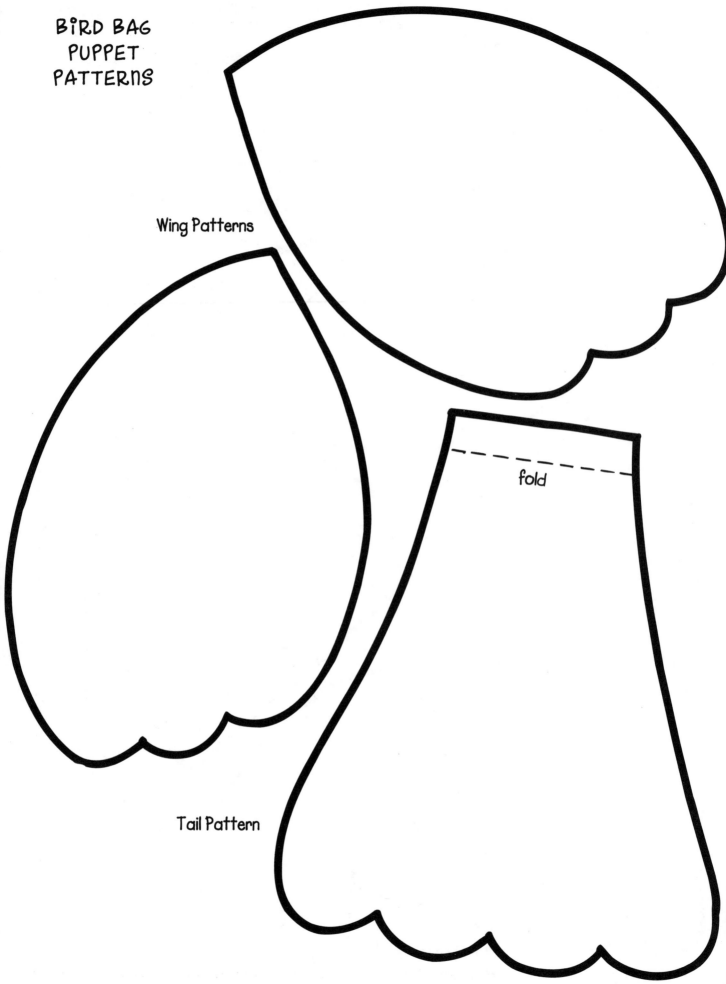

Puppets

Materials: Castle Stick Puppet Patterns, glitter glue pens, tongue depressors, photocopier, white card stock, crayons or felt pens, glue, scissors.

Preparation: Photocopy Castle Stick Puppet Patterns onto card stock—one copy for each child. Cut out.

Instruct each child in the following procedures:

* ⭐ With crayons or felt pens, color each puppet.
* ⭐ Use glitter glue to add details, like gold bells on the jester's hat and jewels on the king's crown.
* ⭐ Glue a tongue depressor to the back of each puppet. Allow glue to dry.
* ⭐ Have fun playing with your Castle Puppets!

Conversation:

God made us to laugh and have fun. What funny story can we make up for our puppets to act out? What makes you smile and laugh, (Angelo)?

Glitterglue

tongue depressor glued to back

CASTLE STICK PUPPET PATTERNS

Lady

King

Jester

Puppets

COWPOKE SPOOL PUPPET
(30-35 MINUTES)

Materials: Gingham fabric, denim fabric, fabric scraps, jute twine, string, scissors, glue, measuring stick, colored pencils. For each child—one large wooden bead, four small wooden beads, eight ¾x1-inch (1.9x2.5-cm) wooden spools, one unsharpened pencil.

Preparation: Cut gingham and denim fabrics into ¾x12-inch (1.9x30-cm) strips—one of each fabric for each child. Cut fabric scraps into 4-inch (10-cm) triangles—one for each child. Cut jute twine into 8-inch (20-cm) and 24-inch (60-cm) lengths—one of each length for each child. Cut string into 12-inch lengths—three for each child.

Instruct each child in the following procedures:

★ Glue the gingham fabric strip around middle portion of one spool and cut off excess (sketch a). Repeat to wrap three more spools with fabric.

★ Cut and glue the denim strip around remaining four spools in the same manner.

★ Use colored pencils to draw face on large bead.

★ To make puppet head: Fold longer length of jute in half. Thread folded end through large bead and tie knot at top of bead to make small loop (sketch b).

★ To make puppet's chest: Place center of one gingham-covered spool between strands of jute at puppet's neck. Tie firmly in place with a knot below spool (sketch c).

★ To make body: Thread both ends of jute through another gingham-covered spool.

★ To make legs: Thread one strand of jute through two denim-covered spools and one wooden bead. Tie end in knot (sketch d). Repeat with second strand.

★ To make arms: Thread shorter length of jute through one small bead, one gingham-covered spool, the chest spool, another gingham-covered spool and remaining small bead (sketch e). Tie each end in a knot.

★ Tie fabric triangle around puppet's neck to make bandana.

★ Tie lengths of string to the knots at ends of arms and top of head (sketch f).

★ Tie other end of each string around pencil to make puppet strings. Trim excess.

★ Move pencil up and down and side to side to make puppet dance.

Simplification Ideas: Instead of using fabric, color spools with felt pens or wrap in yarn. Omit puppet strings to make simple spool doll.

Enrichment Idea: Make a puppet theater out of empty cereal box. Cover box with self-adhesive paper and cut a large window out of front.

Conversation:

Puppets on strings are called marionettes. Have you ever heard the expression, "Someone's pulling your strings"? What do you think this expression means? (Volunteers respond.) **God wants us to obey Him. He knows what is best for us and wants us to follow His directions, instead of allowing our friends to control us.**

Puppets

Materials: Bible, yellow, red and orange construction paper, craft glue, small-sized rubber bands, scissors, thin black felt pens, ruler, fabric scraps. For each child—one half-gallon milk carton, one tongue depressor, four wooden craft spoons, six small wiggle eyes.

Preparation: Cut milk cartons to stand 4 inches (10 cm) high (sketch a). Cut a 1-inch (2.5-cm) slit in the bottom center of each milk carton. Cut construction paper into 5x12-inch (12.5x30-cm) rectangles—one of each color for each child. Cut fabric scraps into 2x3-inch (5x7.5-cm) rectangles—three for each child.

Instruct each child in the following procedures:

★ Wrap and glue fabric scraps onto three wooden spoons for headpieces. Secure onto spoon with small rubber bands as headbands (sketch b).

★ Glue two wiggle eyes onto each of the three wooden spoons.

★ Use felt pens to draw nose and mouth on each spoon.

★ Glue tongue depressor and wooden spoons together as shown (sketch c). Let dry.

★ Cut construction paper rectangles into 5-inch (12.5-cm) flames approximately 1-inch (2.5-cm) wide (sketch d).

★ Fold some flames (sketch e) and glue around top inside milk carton (sketch f).

★ Glue six to eight flames around all four sides of milk carton (sketch g).

★ Place tongue depressor through slot in bottom of milk carton. Shadrach, Meshach and Abednego are inside the fiery furnace! Say, as Nebuchadnezzar did, "Shadrach, Meshach and Abednego, servants of the Most High God, come out! Come here!" (Daniel 3:26) and move the tongue depressor up to make the men come out of the fire unharmed!

Enrichment Idea: Letter Daniel 3:26 on construction paper and glue to front of fiery furnace.

Conversation:

Why were Shadrach, Meshach and Abednego thrown into the fiery furnace? (They would not bow down and worship King Nebuchadnezzar's statue.) **Shadrach, Meshach and Abednego knew that they should only worship the one true God. They loved God and wanted to obey Him, even if they faced danger!**

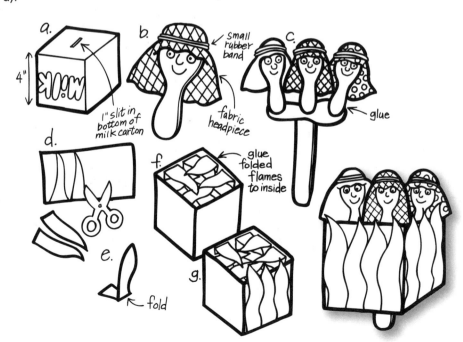

a. 4" milk 1" slit in bottom of milk carton

b. small rubber band / fabric headpiece

c. glue

d.

e. fold

f. glue folded flames to inside

g.

Puppets

EARLY CHILDHOOD • YOUNGER ELEMENTARY • OLDER ELEMENTARY

Materials: Horse Sock Puppet Patterns, one clean white or brown sock, brown and black felt, two safety pins or needle and thread, brown or tan yarn, two large wiggle eyes, pen, craft glue, scissors, ruler.

Instructions:

★ Trace Outer Ear and Muzzle Patterns onto brown felt and trace Inner Ear, Eye and Nostril Patterns onto black felt. Cut out.

★ Glue inner ear felt pieces to outer ear pieces to make puppet's ears (sketch a).

★ Place hand inside sock with fingers in toe and thumb in heel. Smooth sock over fingers and fold extra material at knuckles (sketch b).

★ Glue muzzle, eye and nostril felt pieces onto sock in the appropriate places (sketch c).

★ Mark positions for ears behind fold of sock at knuckles.

★ Remove sock from hand. Use safety pins to attach ears in marked positions or attach ears by sewing with needle and thread.

★ Cut yarn into 6-inch (15-cm) lengths. Use one strand to tie eight strands together to make a bundle. Make four yarn bundles (sketch d).

★ Glue or sew one yarn bundle between puppet's ears for pony's forelock.

★ Glue or sew remaining bundles down length of sock for the horse's mane (sketch e).

★ Glue wiggle eyes to felt eye pieces.

★ To make puppet "talk," slide hand inside sock with fingers in toe and thumb in heel. Open and close hand.

Conversation:

When have you seen or ridden a horse? What did the horse look like? What do you like best about horses? Thank you, God, for horses!

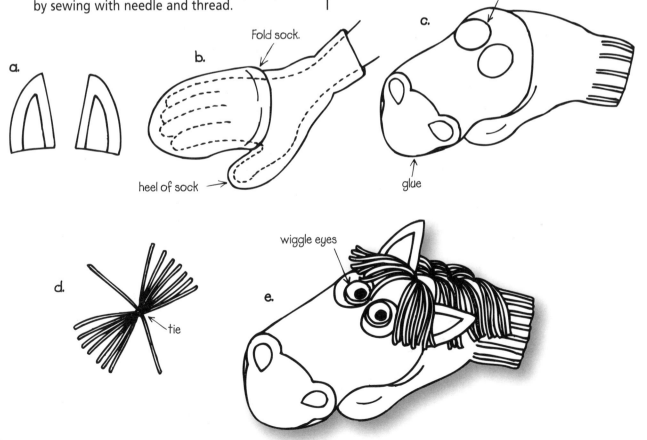

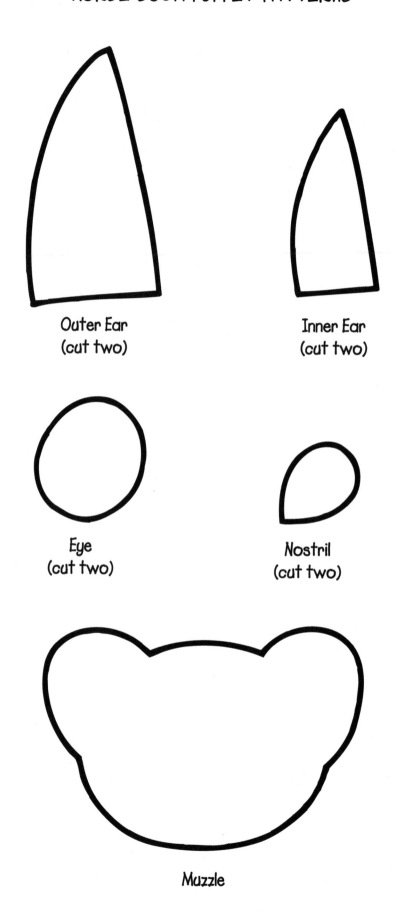

Outer Ear
(cut two)

Inner Ear
(cut two)

Eye
(cut two)

Nostril
(cut two)

Muzzle

Puppets

Materials: Jester Puppet Patterns, small jingle bells or pom-poms, one solid-colored lunch bag, photocopier, white card stock, colored paper or card stock, glue stick, colored felt pens, scissors, ruler. *Optional*—two large wiggle eyes, yarn for hair.

Instructions:

★ Photocopy Jester Puppet Patterns onto white card stock.

★ Color patterns with felt pens. Cut out.

★ Cut the top of bag in a zigzag border (sketch a).

★ With bag folded, glue jester's head to flap of bag (sketch b).

★ Glue the collar under the flap of bag bottom.

★ Cut colored paper into four 2x11-inch (5x27.5-cm) strips and accordion-fold each strip.

★ Glue a hand or shoe onto one end of each strip to make arms and legs.

★ Glue the arms on each side of the paper bag, in the folds (sketch c).

★ Glue the legs to the inside of bag at the front bottom opening.

★ Glue a bell or pom-pom onto each pointed end of hat, collar and shoes (sketch d).

★ *Optional*: Glue on yarn for hair. Glue on wiggle eyes.

★ To make puppet talk, slide hand inside paper bag. Open and close hand in flap of bag.

Conversation:

What could your puppet say or do to make someone smile? Try it today!

top of bag

a.

b. glue head to bottom of bag

glue collar under flap

c. glue arms to fold

d. bells or pom-poms

bells or pom-poms

Collar Pattern

JESTER BAG PUPPET PATTERNS

Shoe Patterns

Head Pattern

Hand Pattern

Hand Pattern

Hand Pattern

Puppets

Materials: Jester Patterns, white muslin, solid-colored fabric in rich colors, felt in rich colors, ¼-inch (.625-cm) wooden dowels, saw, fine-tip permanent felt pens in red and black, yarn, masking tape, craft glue, fabric scissors, ruler, pen. For each child—one toilet paper tube, one 1½-inch (3.75-cm) Styrofoam ball, three small jingle bells.

DAY ONE Preparation: With pen, trace Jester Collar and Hat Patterns onto felt and cut out—two hat pieces and one collar piece for each child. Trace Neck Pattern onto solid-color fabric and cut out—one fabric neck piece for each child. Cut muslin into 5⅓-inch (13.75-cm) circles—one for each child. Saw dowels into 12-inch (30-cm) lengths—one for each child.

Instruct each child in the following procedures:

★ With right side out, overlap neck fabric piece edges ½ inch (1.25 cm) to form a cone shape and glue seam (sketch a). Set aside to dry.

★ Glue pointed edges of the two felt hat shapes together (sketch b).

★ Lay hat flat and then glue a small jingle bell to each hat point. Allow to dry.

★ Insert end of dowel into Styrofoam ball.

★ Cover ball with muslin circle to make puppet head. Twist bottom edges of muslin around dowel and secure in place with masking tape (sketch c).

★ Draw a face on the jester's head with felt pens.

★ Fold the jester's collar in half and cut a small slit in the middle of the fold. Push the dowel through the slit and slide the collar up the dowel, under the head.

DAY TWO Preparation: Cut felt into 4½x6-inch (11.25x15-cm) rectangles—one for each child.

Instruct each child in the following procedures:

★ With teacher's help, insert end of dowel through small opening of cone-shaped fabric piece and slide up under collar. Tape opening to base of head to secure (sketch d).

★ Glue inside bottom edge of fabric cone to outside edge of paper tube (sketch e).

★ Glue felt rectangle around paper tube, covering raw edge of fabric cone (sketch e).

★ Cut the bottom edge of felt in a jagged pattern or cut slits to make the jester's costume fringed (sketch f).

★ Cut small pieces of yarn for hair and glue onto head.

★ Place a line of glue inside the rim of hat and glue onto head. Allow puppet to dry thoroughly.

★ Hold the tube and gently pull down on the dowel to hide the jester inside. Then gently push up the dowel to make your puppet pop up!

Conversation:

A jester told stories, juggled and performed acrobatic tricks. He had a talent for making people laugh. Who do you know who can make people giggle and laugh? (Children respond.) **How could someone use that talent to help someone?** (Cheer up someone who is sad. Make someone who is shy feel comfortable. Send a funny note or card to someone who is lonely, sick or has had a bad day.) **God has given each of us special abilities or talents that we can use to help others. You can even use the puppet you made today to make someone laugh!**

JESTER POP-UP PUPPET

a.

glue, overlapping ½"

b.

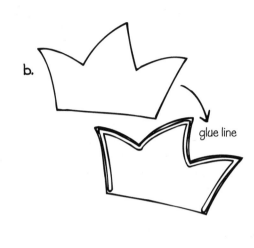

glue line

c.

muslin

tape

d.

collar

tape

fabric cone

e.

glue

glue

paper tube

f.

cut edge

JESTER POP-UP PUPPET PATTERNS

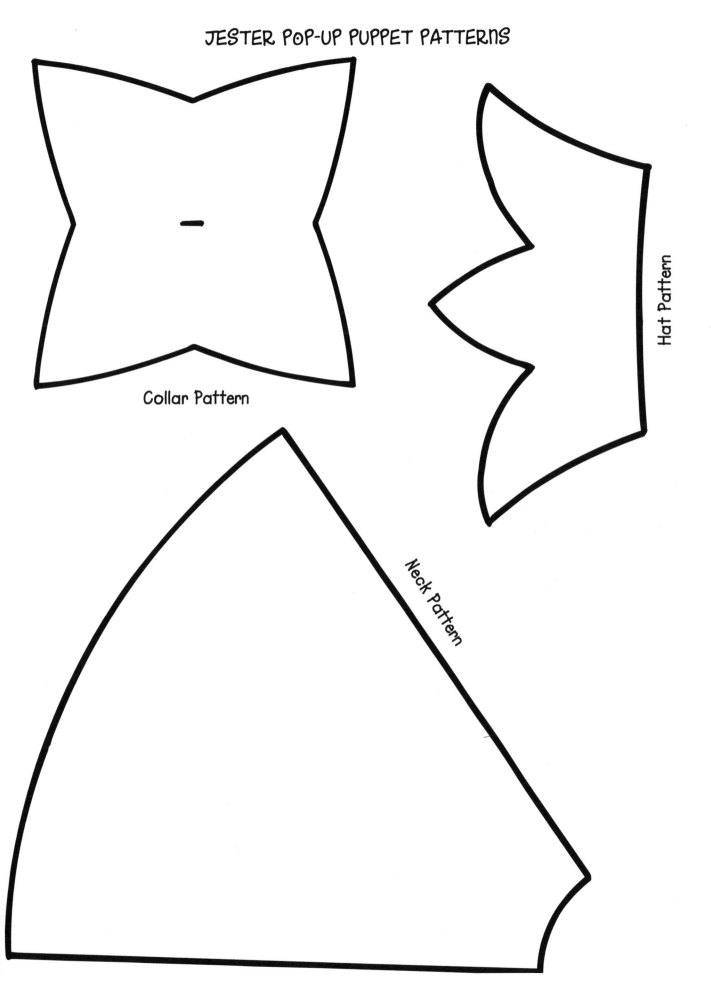

Collar Pattern

Hat Pattern

Neck Pattern

Puppets

JOLLY JESTER MAROTTE
(TWO-DAY CRAFT/30-35 MINUTES EACH DAY)

Materials: Jolly Jester Hat and Collar Patterns, felt in a variety of colors, ⅜-inch (.937-cm) dowels, saw, curly doll hair (available at craft stores), gesso (available at art supply stores), old pantyhose, small jingle bells, acrylic jewel beads, white bread slices, ¼-inch (.625-cm) satin ribbon in a variety of colors, acrylic paint in flesh-tone colors, straight pins, black and red fine-tip permanent felt pens, pencils, lightweight cardboard, glue, craft glue, shallow containers, sponge brushes, fabric scissors, pens, measuring stick. For each child—one 2½-inch (6.25-cm) Styrofoam ball, Styrofoam cup, craft stick.

DAY ONE Preparation: Trace Jolly Jester Hat and Collar Patterns onto lightweight cardboard and cut out to make several patterns. Pour glue into shallow containers. Mix gesso and flesh-tone paints together in a few shallow containers. Cut pantyhose into squares large enough to stretch over Styrofoam ball.

Instruct each child in the following procedures:

- To make cheeks of jester's face, roll one side of Styrofoam ball over the sharp edge of a table to make an indentation about 2 inches (5 cm) wide (sketch a). Press fingers above indentation to smooth down Styrofoam and slightly round off edges.
- About ¾ inch (1.9 cm) below the rise of cheeks, use a pencil to make a ¼-inch (.625-cm) round indentation for mouth (sketch b).
- Insert craft stick into Styrofoam ball where jester's neck would be (sketch c).
- Stretch pantyhose square over jester's head, gathering the ends near base of neck. Use straight pins to secure hose to the Styrofoam ball near the craft stick (sketch c).
- Insert three pins into mouth indentation to hold hose in mouth.
- Use sponge brush to paint white glue over pantyhose on Styrofoam head. Brush on several coats.
- Tear off a small piece of white bread and dip in white glue. Knead bread with your fingers to make a tiny ball of dough.
- Press ball of dough onto head above the mouth, in the middle of cheeks' rise, to make nose.

Smooth edges of dough onto Styrofoam head with fingers. Pinch end of dough to form nose (sketch d).

- Turn a Styrofoam cup upside down and push the craft stick through the bottom of cup to hold jester's head while drying.
- Choose two different colors of felt to make jester's hat. Use a pen to trace jester hat pattern onto each color of felt and cut out.
- Squeeze a line of craft glue along all edges, except the bottom, of one hat piece (sketch e). Press the two hat pieces together.
- Glue a bell or bead to each pointed tip of hat. Lay flat to dry.
- Paint a thick coat of gesso/paint mixture over the entire head, dabbing carefully around nose so it doesn't come off. Set jester's head back in Styrofoam cup to dry overnight.

DAY TWO Preparation: Saw dowels into 18-inch (45-cm) lengths—one for each child. Cut ribbon into 1-yard (.9-m) lengths—three for each child.

Instruct each child in the following procedures:

- Trace the jester collar pattern onto the same two colors of felt used for hat. Cut out both collars.
- Fold collars in half and cut a small slit in the center of each fold for dowel to slide through (sketch f).
- Glue jingle bells or beads to the points of one or both collars. Lay flat to dry.
- With red felt pen, color inside jester's mouth. Add turned-up corners of mouth, if desired. Outline mouth with black felt pen.
- Use black felt pen to draw eyes and eyelashes above cheeks (sketch g).
- Rub a little red felt pen on your finger and dab on cheeks lightly, if desired.
- Remove craft stick from ball. Trim off any pantyhose excess with scissors.
- Squeeze glue onto end of dowel and push dowel into the Styrofoam ball where the craft stick was before.

(See next page for further instructions.)

Puppets

★ Squeeze craft glue along inside rim of hat and glue to jester's head.

★ Glue a few curls of doll's hair to the head, all around the rim of hat.

★ Slide both collars onto dowel. Position them so their points alternate. Glue top collar to base of head (sketch g). Glue bottom collar to top collar.

★ Squeeze some glue on the dowel underneath the second collar. Tie three ribbons to the glued part of dowel.

Enrichment Idea: Glue and wrap ¾-inch (1.9-cm) ribbon and gold rickrack or braid around the length of the dowel. Glue the end of dowel into a drilled wooden bead or cap.

Conversation:

In medieval times, a court jester carried a wand that symbolized his job. It was called a "marotte," or a "fool's head." On the end was a miniature sculpture of the jester himself! The lord of a castle relied on his jester to entertain him and his guests, but jesters often did more than make people laugh. Some jesters risked great danger to protect their masters. A story is told of a jester named Gollet who overheard a group of men plotting to kill his master, the duke. He rushed to the duke's bedroom, pounded on the door and shouted a warning to him in rhyme! This jester served his master with all his heart!

God wants us to serve Him and others with all our hearts as well. When have you seen someone do something with all his or her heart?

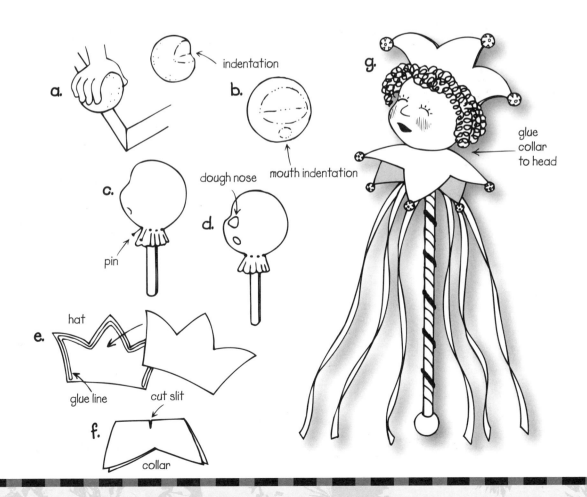

JOLLY JESTER MAROTTE PATTERNS

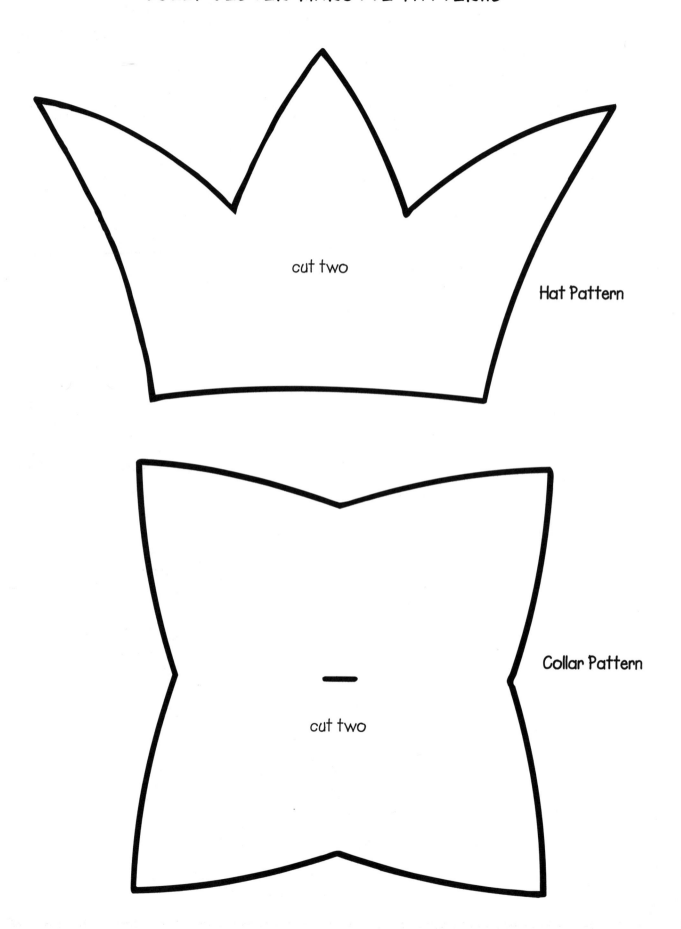

cut two

Hat Pattern

Collar Pattern

cut two

Puppets

Materials: Bible, Big Fish Pattern, poster board, blue or grey tempera paint, paintbrushes, black felt pens, pencils, ruler, fabric scraps, tissue paper scraps, construction paper, glue, glue gun and glue sticks, scissors, newspaper, shallow containers. For each child—one cookie, cracker or small cereal box; one wooden craft spoon; two small wiggle eyes.

Preparation: Enlarge Big Fish Pattern to cover boxes. Trace pattern onto poster board and cut out—one for each child. Cut out fin where indicated on pattern. Cut construction paper into 2x5-inch (5x12.5-cm) pieces—one for each child. Cut out an opening in the center of each box (sketch a). Pour paint into shallow containers. Cover area with newspaper. Plug in glue gun.

Instruct each child in the following procedures:

★ Paint big fish blue or grey. Let dry.

★ Imagine what Jonah saw inside the big fish. Inside opening of box, glue on tissue paper scraps to create a scene that looks like what Jonah saw (sketch a).

★ With felt pens, draw hair, beard and facial features on wooden spoon to make Jonah figure. Glue on wiggle eyes (sketch b).

★ Cut and glue fabric onto spoon for clothes.

★ Use construction paper and cut out a conversation balloon. Write what Jonah might have said while inside the big fish (sketch c).

★ With teacher's help, use glue gun to glue Jonah into the cutout opening of fish (sketch d).

★ Glue the conversation balloon to look like Jonah is talking (sketch d).

★ Use felt pen to draw eye and mouth onto big fish. Glue the painted fish onto box, with scene under fin.

★ Fold back fin to see Jonah.

Conversation:

Jonah didn't want to tell the people in Nineveh God's message. So he ran away from God and ended up in the belly of a big fish! What do you think it was like inside the fish's belly? (Children respond.) **What do you think Jonah thought while he was inside the fish?** (Read Jonah 2:1-3,7,9.)

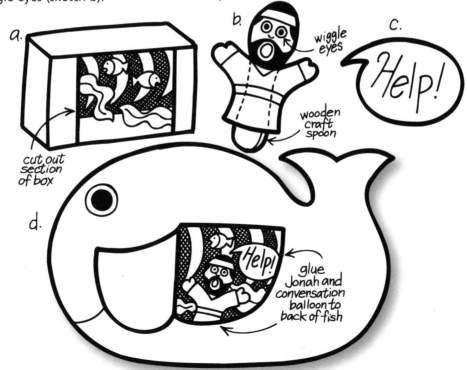

a. cut out section of box

b. wiggle eyes / wooden craft spoon

c. Help!

d. glue Jonah and conversation balloon to back of fish / Help!

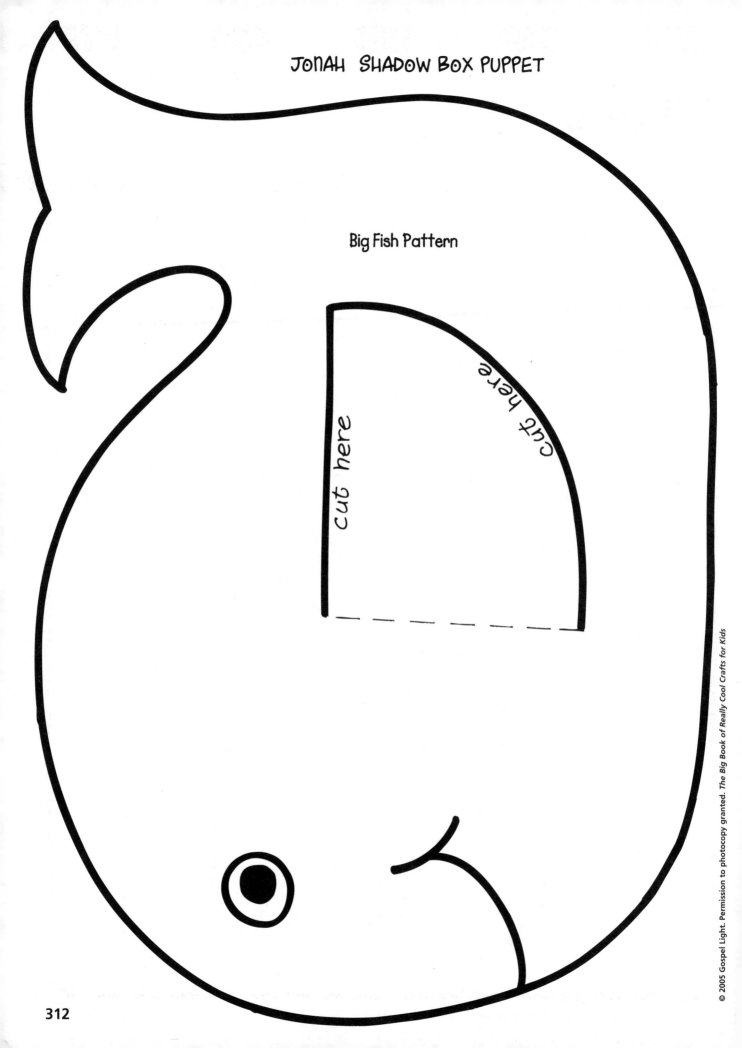

JONAH SHADOW BOX PUPPET

Big Fish Pattern

cut here

cut here

Puppets

Materials: Paper Bag Lady Puppet Patterns, lunch-size paper bag, white card stock, photocopier, felt pens or crayons, glue, scissors.

Preparation: Photocopy Head, Arm and Leg Patterns onto card stock—two copies.

Instruct each child in the following procedures:

★ Cut out one head, two arms and two legs.

★ Use felt pens or crayons to color cutouts.

★ Glue head to flap of paper bag as shown in sketch on next page.

★ To form feet and knees, fold legs on broken lines indicated on pattern.

★ Glue top of arms to sides of bag.

★ Glue top of legs onto lower edge.

★ Draw clothing details.

Conversation:

What will you name your puppet? What are words your puppet could say about God's love?

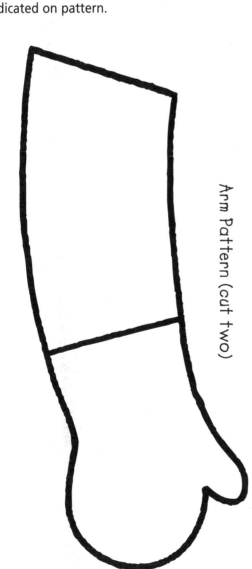

Arm Pattern (cut two)

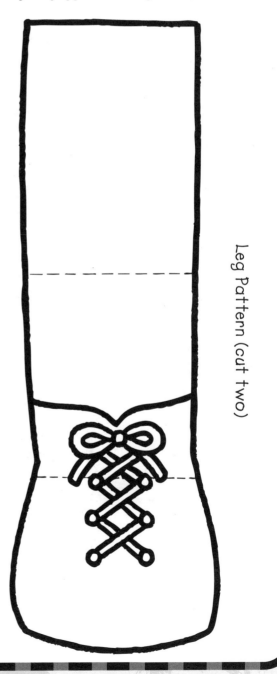

Leg Pattern (cut two)

PAPER BAG LADY PUPPET PATTERN

Head Pattern

Puppets

Materials: Bible, solid-colored fabric, wood-grained Con-Tact paper, small twigs, fake fur, string, permanent fine-tip felt pens, chenille wire, pencil, glue, fabric scissors, hole punch, measuring stick. For each child—one large, empty sliding matchbox, one Tootsie Pop, two wiggle eyes.

Preparation: Cut fake fur into very small pieces to be used as hair and beards. Cut string into 17-inch (42.5-cm) lengths—one for each child. Cut fabric into 8-inch (20-cm) squares—one for each child. Cut chenille wires into 8-inch (20-cm) lengths—one for each child. Break small twigs into approximately 1-inch (2.5-cm) lengths—one for each child. Cut Con-Tact paper into 4¾x3-inch (11.9x7.5-cm) rectangles—one for each child. Remove matchbox from matchbox cover and punch holes in sides of matchbox cover (sketch a).

Instruct each child in the following procedures:

★ Pull backing off Con-Tact paper and apply to front of matchbox cover.

★ Glue twig piece to front of matchbox cover to make a door handle (sketch a).

★ With matchbox cover removed, thread string through both holes. Tie ends of string in a knot and trim ends (sketch a).

★ Wrap fabric square around top of Tootsie Pop to make Peter's head (sketch b). Secure fabric in place by wrapping center of chenille wire twice under the head. Bend ends of wire to make arms.

★ Glue fake fur on fabric for hair and beard. Glue on wiggle eyes. Use felt pen to draw nose and mouth.

★ Lay Peter puppet inside matchbox. Slide box into matchbox cover and set upright on flat surface. Pull on both sides of string to make Peter pop up (sketch c).

Enrichment Idea: Glue brown craft sticks across the top of matchbox cover to make a door. Line the inside of matchbox with dark blue construction paper and stick gummed stars on paper for background.

Conversation:

Open Bible to Acts 12. **We can do a puppet show with your Peter Pop-Up Puppet. Let's act out the story of when Peter knocked on the door of his friends' house while they were praying for him.** Knock on matchbox door. **A girl named Rhoda answered the door and was so surprised to see Peter, she forgot to open the door! Peter knocked on the door again, and this time Peter's friends invited him in.** Open matchbox and take puppet out

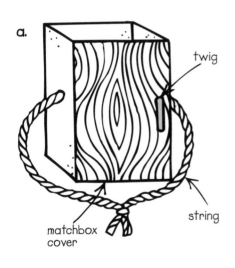

a.

twig

matchbox cover

string

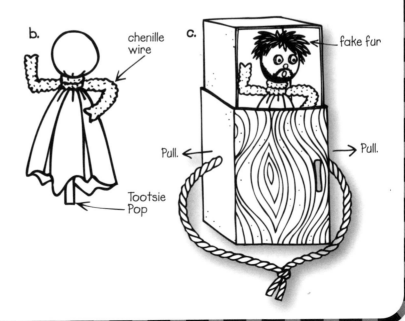

b.

chenille wire

Tootsie Pop

c.

fake fur

Pull.

Pull.

Puppets

Materials: Royal Puppet Patterns, collage materials (sequins, metallic doilies, acrylic jewels, thin ribbon, yarn, etc.), felt pens in a variety of colors, scissors, stapler and staples, craft glue, shallow containers, pencil. For each child—two paper plates, self-adhesive Velcro fastener.

Preparation: Trace King/Queen Pattern onto paper plates as shown in sketch a—one for each child. Extend cutting lines at the top. Trace Castleworker Pattern on the center of remaining paper plates. Cut out finger holes in all puppets. Put collage materials in shallow containers.

Instruct each child in the following procedures:

FOR KING OR QUEEN PUPPET:

★ Cut out king/queen puppet from paper plate (sketch b).

★ Draw and color puppet to look like a king or queen (sketch c).

★ Glue on collage materials to decorate puppet.

★ Bend paper plate and overlap ends in back to make a cone shape. Staple together (sketch c).

★ Put your thumb and index finger through the holes to be your puppet's arms.

FOR CASTLEWORKER PUPPET:

★ Cut out castleworker puppet from paper plate.

★ Draw and color one side of puppet to look like a castleworker. Clothing ideas for different occupations: an apron for a cook or baker; a collar for a jester; fancy clothes for a herald, musician or steward; simple clothes for carpenters, maids or stableboys (sketch d).

★ Turn puppet over and color the back of puppet.

★ Use paper plate scraps to make hats or other accessories for your puppet.

★ Attach Velcro to fronts of hands (sketch e). You may put the servant's hands together or apart.

★ Put your index and middle fingers through the holes to be your puppet's legs.

Conversation:

What are some things you like to do that entertain people? (Dance, play music, sing, perform tricks, play sports, tell jokes, etc.) **You can use your puppets to entertain your friends or a younger brother or sister.**

a. extend lines / paper plate

b.

c. staple

d. cook / jester

e. Velcro / Velcro / steward

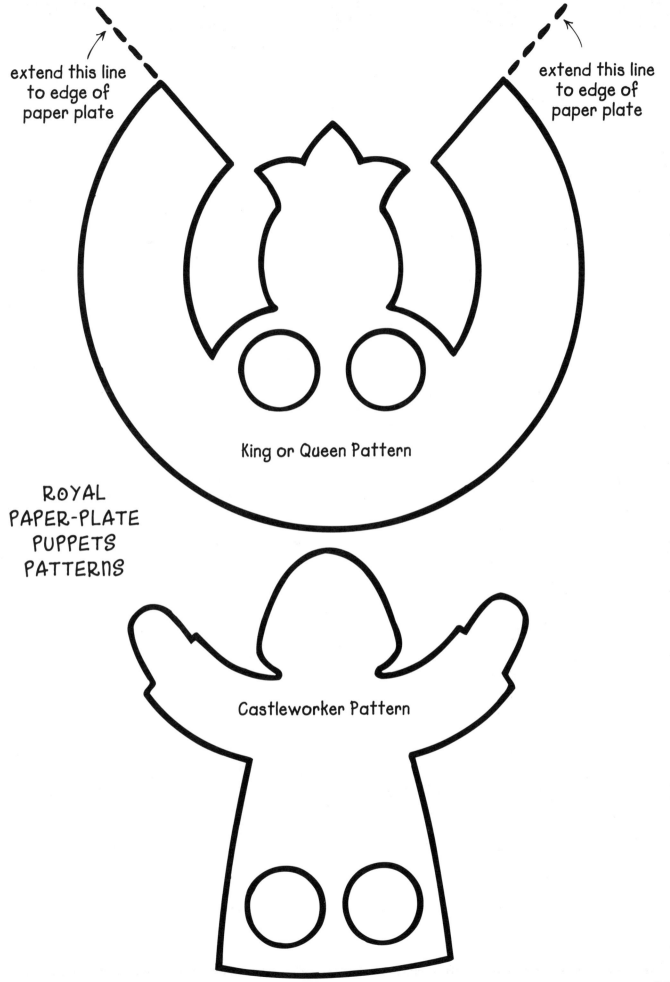

extend this line
to edge of
paper plate

extend this line
to edge of
paper plate

King or Queen Pattern

ROYAL
PAPER-PLATE
PUPPETS
PATTERNS

Castleworker Pattern

Puppets

Materials: Tube sock, 3-inch (7.5-cm) Styrofoam ball, toilet paper tube, plastic sandwich bag, rubber band, felt pen, glue, scissors, pencil. For facial features—medium-sized pom-pom, large wiggle eyes, black yarn, felt and fabric scraps, ribbon.

Instruct each child in the following procedures:

★ Cut toilet paper tube into a 2-inch (5-cm) length.

★ Spread glue around top edge of tube and gently insert into Styrofoam ball (sketch a). This forms the neck of puppet.

★ Place ball and tube in plastic bag and insert into sock. Slide ball to the end of sock. Secure rubber band around neck of puppet (sketch b).

★ Insert hand into sock and place index finger in tube. Make a pencil mark on the outside of sock at location of thumb and middle finger (sketch c).

★ Remove hand from sock and cut small finger holes at pencil marks on each side of puppet (sketch c). If edges of hole begin to unravel, spread glue along raw edges.

★ For nose: Glue pom-pom onto front of head. For eyes: Glue wiggle eyes onto front of head. For mouth: Cut felt into shape of mouth and cheeks. Glue onto front of head (sketch d).

★ For hair: Cut yarn into 24-inch (60-cm) lengths (approximately 50 strands). Tie yarn in the middle of the length (sketch e). Spread yarn so wig covers sides and back of head and glue in place. Once glue has dried, braid hair and use ribbon to secure braid (sketch f).

★ For clothes: Glue scrap of fabric around shoulders to make a shawl (sketch g).

Conversation:

What's your puppet's name? What does your puppet like to do on Saturdays? Let's tell a story about a Saturday ball game. What position does your puppet play?

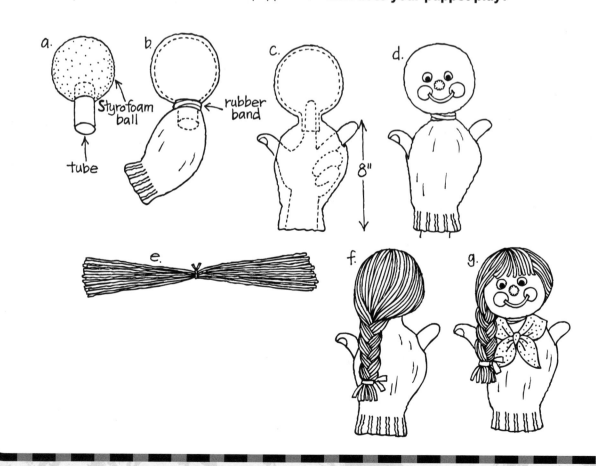

Indices

Craft Index

Bible Verse Index

Bible Story Index

Honor Your
Sunday School Teachers

SUNDAY SCHOOL
TEACHER
APPRECIATION DAY
Third Sunday in October

On Sunday School Teacher Appreciation Day the Third Sunday in October

Churches across America are invited to set aside the third Sunday in October as a day to honor Sunday School teachers for their dedication, hard work and life-changing impact on their students. That's why Gospel Light launched **Sunday School Teacher Appreciation Day** in 1993, with the goal of honoring the 15 million Sunday School teachers nationwide who dedicate themselves to teaching the Word of God to children, youth and adults.

Visit **www.mysundayschoolteacher.com** to learn great ways to honor your teachers on Sunday School Teacher Appreciation Day and throughout the year.

NOMINATE YOUR TEACHERS FOR SUNDAY SCHOOL TEACHER OF THE YEAR!
Winner Receives a Dream Vacation to Hawaii!

An integral part of Sunday School Teacher Appreciation Day is the national search for the **Sunday School Teacher of the Year.** This award was established in honor of Dr. Henrietta Mears—a famous Christian educator who influenced the lives of such well-known and respected Christian leaders as Dr. Billy Graham, Bill and Vonette Bright, Dr. Richard Halverson and many more.

You can honor your Sunday School teachers by nominating them for this award.
If one of your teachers is selected, he or she will receive **a dream vacation for two to Hawaii,** plus free curriculum, resources and more for your church!

Nominate your teachers online at **www.mysundayschoolteacher.com** or call the Sunday School Teacher Appreciation Day hotline—**1-800-354-4224**—to receive more information.

Sponsored by

Gospel Light

Helping you honor Sunday School teachers, the unsung heroes of the faith.

Partners

More Great Resources from Gospel Light

The Big Book of Bible Story Art Activities for Ages 3 to 6
Young children will love hearing favorite Bible stories as they enjoy creative art activities. Instructions for making puppets, collages, chalk art, friendship bracelets and more are provided to help children create Bible story art. Reproducible, perforated pages.
ISBN 08307.33086

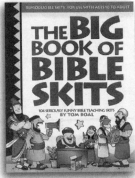

The Big Book of Bible Skits
Tom Boal

104 seriously funny Bible-teaching skits. Each skit comes with Bible background, performance tips, prop suggestions, discussion questions and more. Ages 10 to adult. Reproducible.
ISBN 08307.19164

The Really Big Book of Kids' Sermons and Object Talks with CD-ROM
This reproducible resource for children's pastors is packed with 156 sermons (one a week for three years) that are organized by topics such as friendship, prayer, salvation and more. Each sermon includes an object talk using a household object, discussion questions, prayer and optional information for older children. Reproducible.
ISBN 08307.36573

The Big Book of Volunteer Appreciation Ideas
Joyce Tepfer

This reproducible book is packed with 100 great thank-you ideas for teachers, volunteers and helpers in any children's ministry program. An invaluable resource for showing your gratitude!
ISBN 08307.33094

The Big Book of Christian Growth
Discipling made easy! 306 discussion cards based on Bible passages, and 75 games and activities for preteens. Reproducible.
ISBN 08307.25865

The Big Book of Bible Skills
Active games that teach a variety of Bible skills (book order, major divisions of the Bible, location references, key themes). Ages 8 to 12. Reproducible.
ISBN 08307.23463

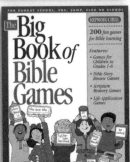

The Big Book of Bible Games
200 fun, active games to review Bible stories and verses and to apply Bible truths to everyday life. For ages 6 to 12. Reproducible.
ISBN 08307.18214

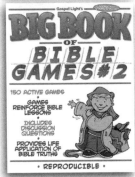

The Big Book of Bible Games #2
150 active games—balloon games, creative team relays, human bowling, and more—that combine physical activity with Bible learning. Games are arranged by Bible theme and include discussion questions. For grades 1 to 6. Reproducible.
ISBN 08307.30532

Gospel Light
God's Word for a Kid's World!™

To order, visit your local Christian bookstore or www.gospellight.com